THE INTERNET PUBLICITY GUIDE

HOW TO MAXIMIZE YOUR MARKETING AND PROMOTION IN CYBERSPACE

V.A. SHIVA

ALLWORTH PRESS
NEW YORK

Published by Allworth Press
An imprint of Allworth Communications
10 East 23rd Street, New York, NY 10010

Cover design by Douglas Designs, New York, NY

Book design by Sharp Designs, Holt, MI

ISBN: 1-880559-60-9

Library of Congress Cataloging-in-Publication Data
V. A. Shiva Ayyadurai
The Internet Publicity Guide/V. A. Shiva Ayyadurai.—1st ed.

Includes index.

1. Publicity and Internet. 2. Technology and civilization.
3. Computer networks - Social aspects 4. Interactive media - Social Aspects. I. Title.

96-84658

Manufactured in the United States of America

Dedicated to My Past and My Future

To my Aachi, Pati (Chinnathai) and Patia (Vellayappa)
my grandparents

To Zoe
my partner in life and exploration

Contents

Preface

FOLLOWING THE WRITING OF *ARTS AND THE INTERNET,* TAD CRAWFORD, the publisher of Allworth Press, and I spoke about a growing need of those who were developing Websites on the Internet—the need for publicity. A Website is only as good as the number of people who visit it. Over the past three years, our team at Information Cybernetics, Inc. and at Millennium Productions, Inc.—the interactive solutions and strategies firm I started in 1993—were also getting many requests from our clients for strategies to promote their sites to increase traffic.

Based on our recent activities in helping our clients develop creative methods of increasing traffic to their sites and the needs of the market, Tad and I decided that I would write a book called *The Internet Publicity Guide*. The book was to be a guide to not only shed light on the possibilities of the Internet, but also to prescribe real strategies for increasing traffic to one's Website. As in the case of the first book, *Arts and the Internet,* we wanted to create a book that would educate the reader about the Internet and also inspire readers to pursue their own creative activities to learn more about the *communications* revolution taking place, a revolution that is fostering mass individualism and global one-on-one communications as never before.

I would like to thank all of the customers and clients of General Interactive, Inc., Information Cybernetics, Inc., Millennium Productions, Inc., and Millennium Communities, Inc. who have provided me with valuable experiences to formulate the contents in this book. In particular, special thanks to AT&T Business Marketing Division; JC Penney; Modem Media Advertising; Lotus Development Corporation; Walt Disney World Epcot Center; Very Special Arts National; Very Special Arts Massachusetts; Orion Capital Corporation; Alvin Ailey American Dance Theater; American Repertory Theater; General Interactive, Inc.; Harvard-Square.Com; Arts-Online.Com; and Shibuya.Org.

I would like to thank Tad Crawford, the publisher of Allworth Press, for encouraging me to write this book and being patient during the various phases of the project. His incisive comments and criticisms were key in developing and reformulating various chapters.

Special thanks to those individuals whose association created the experiences I needed to write this book. Those include Zoe Helene, Bruce Padmore, Brant Wojack, Jean Chen, Pilar Boutté, Nathanael Pine, Neil Devine, Roland Westgate, Brad Dupee, Ed Latham, Phil Hendrickson, Kazushito Yoshida, Luanne Witowski, Akintayo Adewole, Rick Fredkin and Jeremy Teres. Many thanks to those whose contact and discussions served to formulate my ideas and thoughts, including Tom Zawacki, Dana Welch and Craig Lambert of Modem Media, Bob Vignec of Epcot Center, and Paul Rickett and Kyle Gjersvold of Very Special Arts.

A very special thanks to John Bradley for his continued support and invaluable wisdom and advice. Also a very special thanks to my sister Dr. Uma Dhanabalan and my nephew Sivaji Dhanabalan for their great encouragement and support.

I also cannot forget Dr. V. Siva Davamani, Marty Feuerman, Melvin Roth, Dr. Les Michelson, Dr. James H. Williams, Jr., and Dr. Swamy Laxminaraynan, who were mentors to me during various phases of my educational process. Without them, I would never have written this book. Finally, my deepest love and thanks to my parents, Meena and Ayyadurai, who continue to be the source of the flame that leads me forward.

V. A. SHIVA AYYADURAI
Cambridge, Massachusetts

Introduction

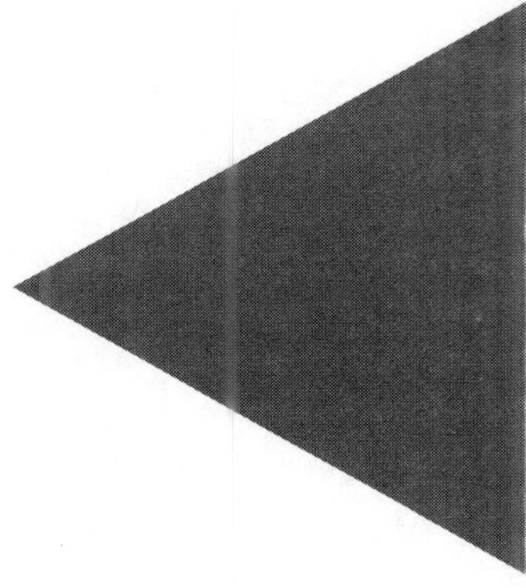

Vision

MOVING TO THE UNITED STATES IN 1970 WAS BOTH CHALLENGING AND frightening, and, in the end, quite rewarding. Looking back, my family's coming to the U.S. and establishing ourselves in a new land went through three distinct phases. First, we had to establish our base in this new place. This included finding a home, setting up bank accounts, registering for school, finding new jobs, and making new friends. Second, we had to learn the rules of the land and the strategies for success. This included learning the customs, incorporating the local slang, understanding the laws, and learning the tricks of the trade. Third, we had to find our particular niche in the society and how we could best serve ourselves and the society at large through our day-to-day activities. Fundamentally, this third phase involved establishing relationships and building a community of influence with others as well as fostering those relationships for both personal and financial gain.

Looking back, our three phases of emigration to the U.S. and looking forward to being your guide to emigrating you to the world of the Internet, I believe that these three similar phases can be applied. As your guide, I will to take you through a similar three-phased approach to using the Internet as a vehicle for publicity and for helping, over the long term, to build your community of influence.

First, you must establish residence on the Internet and learn what the Internet really is before Internet publicity is of any value. In the first part of this book, entitled "Internet," I will teach you what the Internet is and how to establish residence on this new cyber-land. For those of you who have Websites, you have taken the first steps in setting up our residence. Second, just as I had to learn the rules of the land and the strategies for success when I came to the U.S., you will need to learn the rules of Internet "netiquette," and the powerful strategies that will help you reach others and have others visit you at your Website on the Internet. This is covered in part two of the book, entitled "Publicity." Third, we will explore ways for you to establish relationships with those visiting you at your Website, and how to create a niche for you and your organization in a Web community. This is covered in part three of the book, entitled "Community." Establishing yourself as part of a Web community will help develop your circle of influence and will further support your publicity goals.

The title of this book is *The Internet Publicity Guide.* If you review the definition of "publicity" and the definition of "communication" in any standard dictionary, you will find that the terms are almost synonymous. This book could have been entitled *The Internet Communication Guide.* The goal of Internet publicity is to communicate your Web presence to others on the Internet and have qualified traffic visit your Website. To be successful at Internet publicity, you must first understand the Internet, then understand the customs and tricks of the trade to be able to draw people to your Website; finally, you must realize that the goal of publicity and communication is to build relationships with your Web visitors so that they will go back and tell others to visit your site. This is the real challenge of Internet publicity: building online relationships and a community of influence.

I believe that the only revolution is the communications revolution. And, publicity and communication are two sides of the same coin. This book is fundamentally about communications and how you can use the Internet to communicate your ideas, products, etc., to people outside of your organization as well as to enhance communication within your organization. The goal of communication, in my opinion, is to build relationships. It is these relationships that serve to profit us either emotionally or financially. The Internet can be used to build such relationships.

So the real question should be how is this book going to help you to use the Internet to build relationships? I am not really interested in writing a book to teach you how to use the Internet, but my goal here is to inspire you to create a vision and formulate your own thoughts of what is possible. If you want to read a book on simply how to publicize your site on the Internet, there are other books with cookbook recipes.

The goal of this book is to provoke your own imagination and ideas and engage you so that you start to look seriously at what is possible with the Internet. I will give you my knowledge and experience and guide you through what is possible today. But keep your imagination open, and explore.

Back in 1978, after nearly seven years in the U.S., while a student in junior high school, I developed one of the world's first electronic mail (e-mail) systems on a computer network connecting three major medical colleges. I was recognized by the prestigious Westinghouse Science Talent Search Award Committee for the development of that e-mail system. Looking back, I understand why I was given an award. The scientists and technologists on the awards committee knew, back in 1979, more about what e-mail meant for humanity than I had ever conceived.

Today, e-mail is a household word. E-mail, very much like the one I developed in 1978, is used on the Internet for communication among millions of people around the world. The Internet is not a computer network connecting just three medical colleges, like the computer network on which I developed my e-mail system. It is a computer network connecting millions of businesses, homes, universities, government agencies, individuals, and organizations in more than one hundred countries. The Internet offers a host of tools for communicating and sharing digital information. E-mail is just one of them. There are many other tools that the Internet offers, as this book will describe.

The Internet, developed by the U.S. government on advice from the Rand Corporation in the mid 1960s, has existed for more than three decades. Why then has the Internet become a household word today? There are two key reasons for the Internet's current popularity.

First is the pervasive use of e-mail, with e-mail addresses appearing on many business cards alongside phone and fax numbers.

Second is the development of the World Wide Web (WWW), an Internet tool developed in the 1990s by Swiss scientists to access and present multimedia information in a convenient and user-friendly manner.

The WWW is to the Internet what the first Macintosh was to computers. The WWW enables access to information on the Internet at the click of a mouse, without sophisticated computer hardware and the need to know a lot of techno-babble. The WWW has created the foundation for users of the Internet to build their own "homes" or Websites on the Internet. A Website has a front entrance, known as a *home page*, and can have various rooms, Web pages, containing pictures, text, video, and sound. Each Website has its own address, or Universal Resource Locator (URL), very much like a street address. By simply supplying a URL, a user can jump to any site on the WWW in the world.

I can browse millions of Websites with the click of a mouse button. I can get as much information from the Website as the owner has made available. Many diverse groups and individuals have built Websites on the Internet. Religions, government agencies, political groups, artists, galleries, schools, and countless others (including dogs) have Websites.

The cost of creating a Website and making that Website address accessible to the nearly twenty million people on the WWW is pennies compared to traditional means of advertising and communication. Thus, as many are saying, the WWW is "leveling the playing field." This means that a local recording artist in Arkansas has equal access to a Website as a major multibillion-dollar corporation. That same local artist can forget about having a show on a major television network.

The WWW allows you and me to browse the Internet very much like browsing a bazaar, hopping from one storefront to another, only a lot faster, since distance is now collapsed. From my home computer in Cambridge, Massachusetts, I now have access to as wide a diversity of views as I had from my family's apartment in Bombay. I can peer into multibillion-dollar corporations such as Disney, Sony, and Paramount. And, at the click of a mouse, I can, with equal ease, listen to the works of a country singer in a small town in Billings, Montana.

There are unwritten laws in the bazaar of the Internet. There are do's and don'ts. And such laws do not come from a centralized authority, but are organically developed by communities of ordinary people like you and me. While there are governing organizations, the Internet is fundamentally untamed, decentralized, and free. This is what makes the Internet so revolutionary.

The Internet is experiencing massive population growth. The number of people on the Internet and the number of people getting computers are growing exponentially. More than 40 percent of American families and more than 50 percent of American teenagers own a personal computer. In 1994, more computers than TVs were sold to U.S. households. Today, it is estimated that more than forty million people are on the Internet; of this forty million people, nearly twenty million people are on the WWW, the graphical multimedia version of the vanilla Internet; 65 percent of new computers sold worldwide in 1994 were for the home; and 90 percent of those to be sold this year are expected to have modems and CD-ROMs. The population of the Internet is growing at a rate of ten percent per month.

The Internet is spearheading a communications revolution where space and time are collapsed. Unlike the information revolution, which was about broadcasting information to as many people as possible, the communications revolution offers individuals the ability to have one-on-one interactive multimedia communications across thousands of miles and many international time zones. This communications revolution is making it possible for disparate groups to connect and share knowledge and information as never before in history.

So, why did I write this book? First, to awaken you to the possibilities of what this communications revolution has to offer. Second, this book is written to teach, in a step-by-step manner, how to participate in the new global community and how to use this new technology to become more self-reliant in promoting and publicizing yourself. This book will teach the basics as well as more advanced techniques for using the Internet. Third, I wrote this book to inform you that the Internet is a viable vehicle for building relationships and online communities. This is, in my opinion, the real power of the Internet.

Remember that the Internet is simply a vehicle for communication and publicity. And, publicity is the vehicle for establishing relationships, relationships which help to build a circle of influence within an online community for furthering that publicity.

▼

Internet

1 The Vehicle

LEAPS IN EVOLUTION AND SIGNIFICANT CHANGE ONLY TAKE PLACE WITH the development of new and powerful tools. The mass media has done a great job in making "Internet" a household word. Yet few really know what the Internet is and why it is so important. In my experience, I have discovered that when someone understands what the Internet is and, in particular, where it came from, they immediately realize it is a powerful instrument of change.

The Urge to Communicate

In 1981, I entered MIT as a freshman. In addition to overloading myself with courses, I also participated in a research project on Tadoma at the MIT Speech Recognition Laboratory. Tadoma is a fascinating method that deaf-blind people can use to communicate. In Tadoma, deaf-blind people "listen" to speech signals using their hands. The palms and fingertips of the human hand have more sensors per square inch than the retina of the human eye. The hands, in this sense, can "see" better than the eyes. One deaf-blind person places their entire hand on the other person's face and "listens" to the air flow, upper and lower lip movements, vibration, and tongue position as the other person speaks. Incredibly, the deaf-blind individual is able to make sense of what is being said. I learned a great deal from this research. The most important research result was more philosophical than scientific: Human beings have a deep urge to communicate and will use any resource and faculty for such communication.

In spite of our history, our laws, great walls, and barriers, the urge to communicate dominates our desires. Many experts said that the Berlin Wall would never fall. Many felt that Russia and the U.S. would always be at odds. They were all proven wrong. In spite of our many problems, I am optimistic that this desire to communicate will be the saving grace of humanity. I also believe that this urge to communicate globally has manifested itself through the creation of the Internet.

History

Where did the Internet come from? And what is it? The answers to these two questions are central to understanding the real nature of the Internet and its significance in modern communications.

In the early 1960s, the U.S. government was moving forward in its cold war activities. Communism was the enemy: Russia was bad, anyone who collaborated with Russia was evil, and only America stood for democracy. Mass media served to broadcast thirty-second sound bites and images to support this policy of antagonism and distrust. American citizens who communicated with Russia or sympathized with communism were alienated and called un-American. The cold war was a time of discouraging communication and putting up barriers between East and West, North and South. The U.S. Department of Defense worked day and night to prepare for war. They set up an elaborate system of command and control for the generals and the politicians to hide in mountains, and to communicate and survive in the midst of a major war or nuclear holocaust.

In early 1964, someone in the U.S. Department of Defense came to an eye-opening realization that a single bomb could effectively eliminate any form of command and control between the Pentagon and military installations around the world. The Rand Corporation, a major consulting company and think tank for government and industry, was called in to solve this problem.

In August 1964, the Rand Corporation, after an in-depth study of the command and control setup of the U.S. Department of Defense, published a series of eleven papers called *Distributed Systems*. In these papers, the Rand Corporation recommended the creation of peer-to- peer communications, and a message-passing system code named "hot potato." They said that with peer-to-peer communications and message passing, the command and control of the U.S. would survive in the event a massive thermonuclear blast destroyed the Pentagon.

Peer-to-peer communications? Before we can understand this, we need to understand the boss-to-peer communications system. The Pentagon, at the time, had a boss-to-peer communications system. Boss-to-peer communications can best be described by the illustration in Fig. 1.

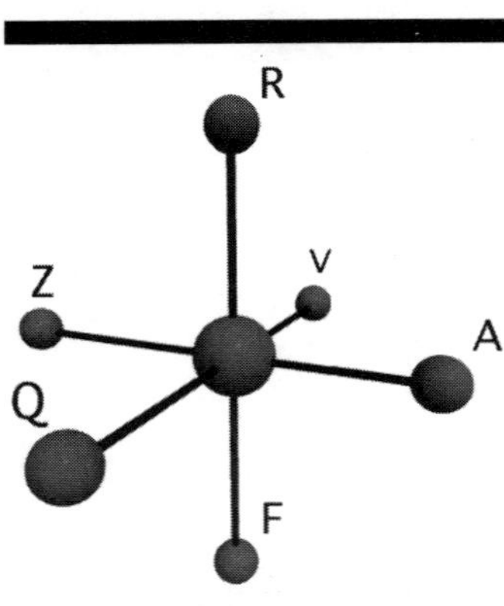

Fig. 1. Boss-to-Peer Communications

In the structure shown in Fig. 1, the Pentagon, in the middle circle, was the boss and at the center of all command and control communications. The middle circle was connected to a set of nodes or peers represented by the circles on the outside. This boss-to-peer system was analogous to a hub-and-spoke system of a wheel. If you take out the hub, the whole wheel falls apart. If the Pentagon, the hub, is destroyed, then no communications are possible between any of the nodes at the end of each spoke. For example, a message from Site A, such as "Are you alive?"

destined for Site Z, would never be communicated once the Pentagon was destroyed.

Peer-to-Peer

Rand suggested peer-to-peer communications or distributed communications in which there was no boss. The new system would be composed of peer-to-peer interconnections that put no single system in charge. If the old system was wheel-like, the new system was sphere-like, in which every node was connected to every other node and to the Pentagon center through multiple links. Peer-to-peer communications is best illustrated by the diagram in Fig. 2.

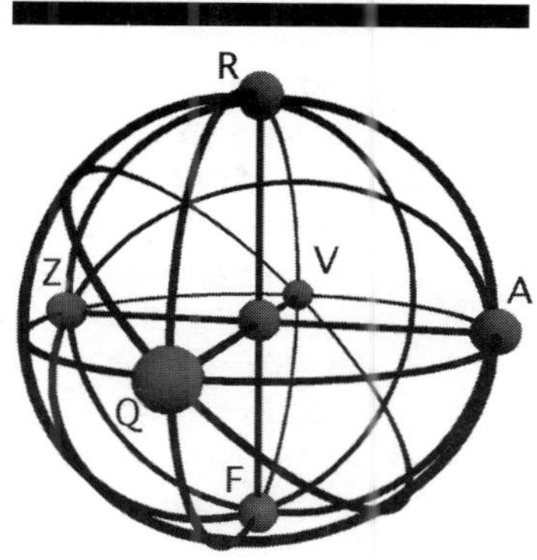

Fig. 2. Peer-to-Peer Communications

Under this new system, the system of communication cannot be destroyed by bombing its hub, the Pentagon. In this system, even if the Pentagon were bombed, a message from Site A can still be relayed to Site Z by several alternate routes. Consider again the message, "Are you alive?" Peer-to-peer communications offers several routes for this message to be passed through, including from Site A directly to Site Z, from Site A to Site Q to Site Z, or from Site A to Site F to Site Q to Site Z. There many other combinations. Thus, in a war scenario, it becomes virtually impossible to stop this message from reaching its destination.

Message Passing: Packet Switching

The Rand Corporation made recommendations not only for peer-to-peer communications, but also for the implementation of message passing. Message passing was developed to ensure speed in the communication of a message from one site to another.

Message passing takes advantage of peer-to-peer communications by offering a protocol or set of rules for breaking up the message into pieces and then reconstructing it. In this case, the message "Are you alive?" could be broken into the words, "Are," "you," and "alive." (We ignore the question mark.) Now using a message-passing protocol: the word "Are" may be sent along the direct route Site A to Site Z; the word "you" may be sent along the route from Site A to Site Q to Site Z; and the word "alive" may be sent along the route from Site A to Site F to Site Q to Site Z. The message-passing protocol ensures that when "Are," "you," and "alive" appear at Site Z, they are magically reconstructed to form the original message "Are you alive."

Why all the trouble? The reason for message passing is to ensure speed regardless of the traffic along any one route. Using message passing, packets of the message are broken up, routed, and switched along different routes in the most expeditious manner. This message-passing protocol came to be formally known as packet switching.

In 1969, packet switching was fully designed and implemented by Bolt, Beranek, and Newman (BBN) under a contract from the U.S. Defense Department's Advanced Research Projects Agency (ARPA). Also in 1969, an experimental network was created that incorporated both peer-to-peer communications and packet switching. This network was called ARPANET. ARPANET was the beginning of the Internet. It was conceived by Bob Taylor, the director of computer research at ARPA. In addition, many other people, including Charlie Herzfeld, Larry Roberts, Vinton Cerf, Jon Postel, Steve Crocker, Bill Naylor, Doug Englebart, and Roland Bryan were key contributors to the building of the ARPANET. These people were at ARPA and were the heads of the early node sites (e.g., Site A, Site B, etc.) such as Stanford, SRI International, and University of California at Santa Barbara.

ARPANET was a government-funded research project. The original networked sites were military bases, universities, and companies with Defense Department contracts. As the size of this experimental network grew, so did concerns for security. The same networks used by companies and universities for military contractors were becoming more and more accessible to the public. As a result, in 1984, ARPANET split into two separate but interconnected networks: one for military use and one for educational use. The military side of the network was called MILNET. The education side was still technically called ARPANET, but became more commonly known as the Internet.

The Internet became a high-speed electronic transportation mechanism, linking key sites at government agencies, defense contractors, colleges, and universities. But other independent networks were also under development. Soon, many of these independent networks began seeking permission to connect themselves to the high-speed lines, or *backbone,* of the Internet. Thus, the Internet grew to become a *network of networks.*

In 1990, ARPANET was formally dismantled, but hardly anyone noticed because by then the Internet had become independent of ARPA. The Internet, with peer-to-peer communications and packet switching, stood on its own two feet and became an organism that was more than the sum of its parts.

In 1991, the Internet, which had already become a network of networks, became available to ordinary citizens. More colleges, companies, individuals, artists, and government agencies hooked up to the Internet. The Internet ceased to be a network dedicated to the purpose of defense. It became a global communications medium open to the general public.

Thus, the Internet, a network accessible to the general public for global communications, developed from the need to protect and insulate the U.S. from attack by foreign powers. Ironically, engineers and scientists who had used their talents to create weapons, created an instrument for global communication. Professor Melvin Kranzberg, one of the world's pioneers in the history of science and technology, commenting on such ironies, once wrote, "Engineers, in general, live in the suburbs, vote Republican, and mouth the clichés of conservatism. Actually, if unwittingly, they are greater social revolutionaries than many wild-eyed political radicals. Without necessarily meaning to, they invent new products, processes, systems, and devices that produce profound sociocultural transformations." His statement epitomizes the irony in the creation of the Internet.

TCP/IP, SLIP, and PPP: What Are They?

In the context of the previous discussion, you are now well equipped to understand the terms TCP/IP, SLIP, and PPP. As you recall, the Internet is composed of peer-to-peer communications and packet switching. Recall, as well, that packet switching is a set of rules, or protocol, for passing messages on the Internet. TCP/IP, SLIP, and PPP are the names of the actual protocols for passing messages. That is all they are. So when you hear someone throwing around these terms, don't be afraid. They are just a bunch of rules that have been translated to computer format (software). When you get an Internet connection, you will be using the software that makes use of TCP/IP, SLIP, and PPP. The difference between the three protocols is the kind of network they run on.

TCP/IP stands for Transmission Control Protocol/Internet Protocol. It is the protocol used for packet switching on high-speed lines and networks. SLIP and PPP stand for Serial Line Interface Protocol and Point-to-Point Protocol, respectively. SLIP and PPP were developed for use on modems so that a home computer could *slip* into the Internet.

Internet Protocol Addresses and Domain Names

TCP/IP offers the services of Internet Protocol addresses and domain names to keep track of every computer on the Internet. Every machine that is connected to the Internet via TCP/IP has to be uniquely identified. Without a unique identifier, the network doesn't know how to get messages to your machine. If there is more than one machine with the same identifier, the network doesn't know where to send the message.

The Internet identifies computers on networks by assigning an Internet Protocol address or IP address. IP addresses are often four numbers separated by three periods. For example 212.186.4.4 is the IP address of a machine on the Internet. In one sense, every computer on the Internet is "just a number." Whenever a message is transmitted between two computers anywhere on the Internet, one IP address refers to the computer sending the message and the other IP address refers to the computer receiving the message. Without IP addresses, communication on the Internet would be impossible.

Fortunately, for end users like ourselves, we do not have to know and keep track of IP addresses in order to send and receive messages. The domain name system of the Internet resolves this problem by assigning an English-like name called the domain name to the IP address. All Internet sites, therefore, are identified by a unique domain name. The domain names are made up of two pieces of information separated by a period. The first piece of information is an identifier unique to the organization or company. The second part, called the domain identifier, comes after the period. There are seven domain identifiers established by the Internet Network Information Center (InterNIC). They are:

DOMAIN IDENTIFIER	MEANING
.arpa	ARPANET identification
.com	Commercial company
.edu	Educational institution
.gov	Any government body
.mil	Military
.net	Internet access provider
.org	Nonprofit agency

All domain names have one of these seven domain identifiers unless they are based outside the U.S.

Some examples of domain names are *cbs.com, mit.edu, nasa.gov*; these domain names are for the broadcasting company CBS, the educational institution MIT and the government agency NASA, respectively. When an institution connects to the Internet, it must register its domain name with InterNIC. Domain names, like IP addresses, must be unique to avoid confusion.

Seven Internet Concepts

The Internet is the fastest growing communications medium. Those who choose to use it need to be aware of the nature and conditions of this new cyber-landscape. Now that you have learned the history of the Internet, what peer-to-peer communications is, how packet switching works, and what domain names and IP addresses are, you are ready to appreciate the seven key concepts of the Internet.

The first concept is that the Internet is not an end. It is a means. Physically, it is like a highway, the transport mechanism, not the destination. The Internet links millions of computer sites together, so you can travel on it to send and receive information from one site to another.

The second concept is that the Internet creates a "oneness" of each site or location in both time and space. Every node or site is equal because of peer-to-peer communications. Space and time give way to a communications medium that equalizes distance and spans time zones. Sitting at a computer in an artist's loft in the south end of Boston, one can pull information from a computer located in a studio in Chile one second, and then switch to view other information on a computer located in a gallery in Finland the next.

The third concept is that the Internet is under no one's control. It is true that until now, in the U.S., our tax dollars provided the bulk of funding for the backbone links. But now the Internet has taken on a life of its own. If the U.S. government were to withdraw completely its support tomorrow, the effect on the Internet might be the equivalent of a nuclear blast. The Internet would still survive! And that's precisely what it was designed to do.

The fourth concept is that the Internet has community standards. These standards are organically developed without the dictates of a central authority. This feature of the Internet will help to solve many of the more ambiguous issues of copyright, censorship, and security as opposed to some top-down mandated government regulation. Just like in the "Wild West," there are unwritten laws. Those who violate the unwritten laws are "flamed," or subject to harsh criticism via e-mail and public forums. Marketing and promoting yourself on the Internet requires an intimate understanding of this concept of community standards.

The fifth concept is that the Internet is people-based, not government-based. No government committee in Washington, D.C., sat down, for example, to create and implement the concept of newsgroups; someone on the Internet came up with the idea of sharing ideas on a particular topic via a system where all messages are saved one after the other for others to view. Today, there are ten thousand newsgroups with participants worldwide.

The sixth concept is that the Internet is blind to race, color, caste, creed, and the like. In one issue of the *New Yorker,* there is a cartoon that shows a dog sitting in front of a computer screen with its paws on the keyboard, saying to another dog nearby, "On the Internet, nobody knows you're a dog." Well, on the Internet, nobody knows your name, age, gender, or nationality. All they know is what you say and what digital work you choose to show. The ingrained prejudices that many bring to any human encounter are greatly reduced in this medium.

The seventh concept is that the Internet is its own culture. Some call it a cyberculture. Just as someone traveling from the U.S. to France would respect and regard the ways of the French, so should those traveling in cyberspace.

The World Wide Web

The Internet, remember, is not the end but the means. There are various tools that help you take advantage of the Internet. Among them are e-mail, newsgroups, mailing lists, file transfer protocol (FTP), Archie, Telnet, Internet Relay Chat (IRC), Gopher, WWW browsers, WWW search engines, and WWW directories. These are the various tools that allow you to communicate, find information, and share information with other computers and sites. In the next chapter, "Tools," we will explore each of these tools in detail.

For now, the important thing to understand is that the reason you are reading this book today is because of the development of the World Wide Web. The WWW made the Internet accessible to the masses. Remember that the Internet has been around for nearly thirty years, but the reason for its explosive growth is because of the WWW.

What is the WWW? Is it another network like the Internet? Or is it a piece of the Internet? Neither. The WWW is, above all, a method. Yes, a method. It is not a network; it is not a piece of the Internet.

The WWW is a method or way of organizing information and files on the Internet. In the 1990s, a group at CERN, the European Particle Physics Laboratory in Geneva, Switzerland, developed this method. They said that the WWW "was developed to be a pool of human knowledge, which would allow collaborators in remote sites to share their ideas and all aspects of a common project."

Using the WWW, a music lover in New Zealand, for example, can access a multimedia WWW document, or Website, of a French recording artist. This Website may contain information such as a picture of the recording artist, a text of the artist's biography, an audio clip from one of the artist's CDs, and a video clip from one of the artist's live performances.

The key to understanding the power of the WWW is this: the picture could be on the artist's home computer, which is physically located in France; the text could be on the artist's manager's computer, which is physically located in the U.S.; the sound clip could be on the recording label's computer, which is physically located in London; and the video clip may be on the promotional company's computer located in Germany.

The WWW helps to manage and fuse distributed pieces of information seamlessly into one document or Website. This ability to fuse diverse information from distributed sources, potentially all over the globe, is the key to the power of the WWW. The information (text, graphics, sound, video, etc.) that comprises a WWW document, or Website, can be viewed literally worldwide. With the WWW, the Internet comes to life for the ordinary person, offering multimedia information at the click of a mouse. Before the WWW, the Internet was keyboard driven. To interact with the Internet, you had to use the keyboard to enter esoteric commands.

Who Is on the WWW?

The Internet is becoming a meeting place for artists, engineers, retailers, educators, and many others. The Internet is quickly sweeping into more and more households and pulling people from every profession into it. Its uses are unlimited for anyone who knows how to tap its potential. By the year 2003, conservative estimates predict that more than one billion people will be on the Internet.

I have collected various demographic statistics and graphs that will help you assess who is on the Internet today and what the trends are. If you review these graphs, you will notice that the Internet offers an attractive marketplace not only to market and promote yourself, but also to sell products and services directly online.

The current demographics reveal that there are nearly forty million on the Internet. Of the forty million on the Internet, the statistics reveal that nearly twenty million have access to the WWW. Most of those on the Internet are educated and middle to upper income. Women are the fastest-growing group. The demographics are presented in Figs. 3 through 6, on the following page.

In reviewing the above graphs, it is apparent that nearly 50 percent of Internet users are between the ages of twenty-five and forty-four. The average income is between \$50,000 and \$75,000. These users surf the Internet daily. Studies also reveal Internet users watch 25 percent less television. Based on current usage statistics, many experts predict that by the year 2005, more people will use the Internet than watch network TV.

Those on the Internet are educated and have well-defined tastes. They enjoy discussions, have fun exploring, and are willing to spend money on art and entertainment. For those who want to create an audience for their wares, these demographics are excellent. Furthermore, this group of Internet users will also purchase products online. By the year 2000, more than $1 trillion of commerce will be conducted using the Internet each year.

Coopers and Lybrand, one of the world's most respected management consulting agencies for major corporations, has said that "businesses should act now to seize the new opportunity that electronic distribution channels represent. Merchants who consider this as an either/or option are making a big mistake." The Internet

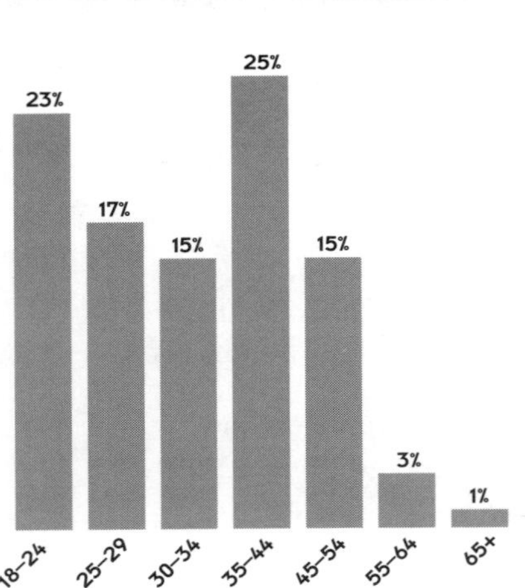

Fig. 3. Age Distribution of U.S. Internet Users

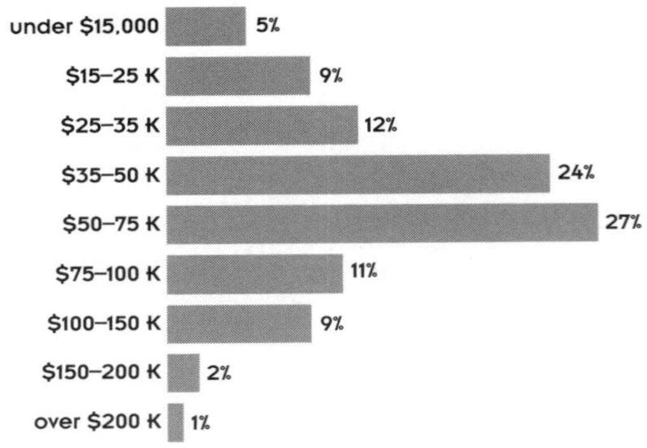

under $15,000 5%
$15–25 K 9%
$25–35 K 12%
$35–50 K 24%
$50–75 K 27%
$75–100 K 11%
$100–150 K 9%
$150–200 K 2%
over $200 K 1%

Fig. 4. Household Income of U.S. Internet Users

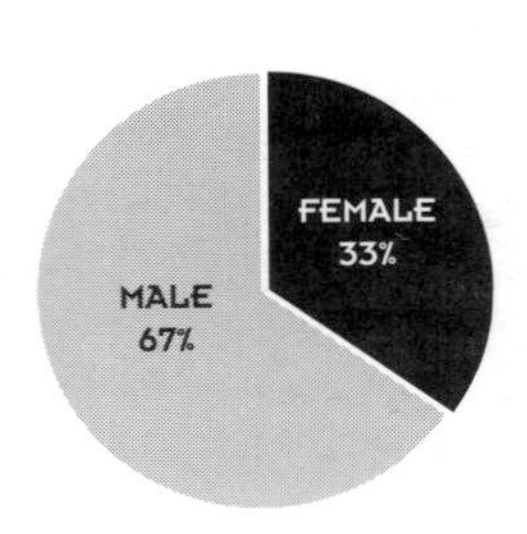

Fig. 5. Gender of U.S. Internet Users

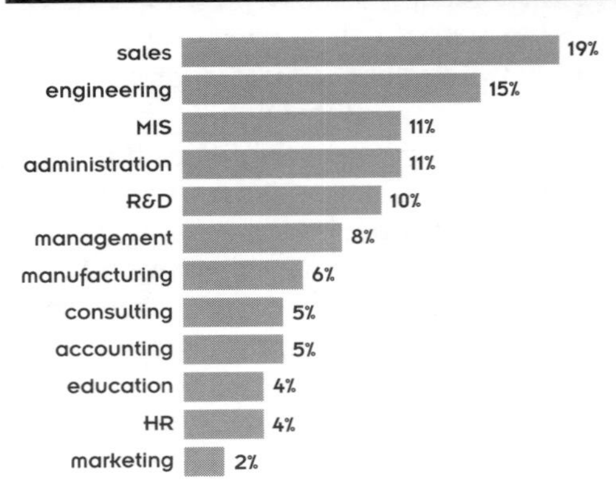

Fig. 6. Job Functions of U.S. Internet Users

offers cost-effective and far-reaching promotional and marketing benefits for building those businesses.

Today, many organizations suffer from the inability to reach and to engage their potential audience. From my research in neuroscience, I learned that in human beings the speech communication centers of the brain are juxtaposed with the motor cortex. This means that those who have serious speech communication impairments typically have movement problems or are disabled. Organizations today are disabled by their lack of tools to reach and to communicate with their potential audience. Businesses with great products struggle to make the right connections, while their growth remains paralyzed. The Internet is a powerful vehicle for communication that empowers businesses and individuals to go directly to their audiences. It is an instrument of change. Learning how to use this instrument and the various tools it offers, will make you an active participant in using this medium for publicity.

2 Tools of the Trade

THERE ARE VARIOUS TOOLS THAT YOU CAN TAKE ADVANTAGE OF WHEN executing a publicity plan using the Internet. Among them are electronic mail (e-mail), UseNet newsgroups, mailing lists, file transfer protocol (FTP), Archie, Telnet, Internet Relay Chat (IRC), Gopher, WWW browsers, WWW search engines, and WWW directories. By understanding what these tools are and by learning how to use them, you can take advantage of the Internet. Do not be scared by the technical-sounding terms used to refer to these tools. These tools are software programs for communicating and navigating on the Internet. They are analogous to other tools such as a pager, telephone, car, or bus you may use to communicate and travel in the physical world.

E-Mail: Electronic Mail

All of us have sent letters, postcards, packages to our friends and family. Electronic mail, or e-mail, is a way of sending electronic messages using the Internet. E-mail has been in use since the beginning of the Internet. With access to the Internet, you can send and receive e-mail to and from any one of the forty million people who are on the Internet today. To use e-mail, you first need an Internet account from an Internet access provider. An Internet access provider is a company that will literally give you connection to the Internet from your computer at your home or office via an Internet account. In chapter 3, "Getting On," you will learn how to get in touch with an Internet access provider and obtain your own Internet account.

Before you can send and receive e-mail, however, you need an Internet account. Once you obtain an Internet account, you will automatically be given an e-mail address. The e-mail address comprises three parts: an account name, the @ symbol, and the domain name of the Internet access provider.

Brant Wojack, a musician and student at the Berklee College of Music, recently obtained an Internet account. He wanted to use e-mail to communicate with other musicians and industry representatives on the Internet. He needed first to obtain his e-mail address. Internet access providers have their own domain name. The Internet access provider that Brant used had the domain name of *arts-online.com*. Brant also had the opportunity to choose his own personal account name. He chose, for obvious reasons, "brant." Fortunately, no one else had taken the name brant. Thus, his e-mail address became *brant@arts-online.com*. This e-mail address is verbally read, brant at arts-online dot com. The @ symbol is used to separate the user account name from the Internet access provider's domain name. Brant immediately placed his e-mail address on all of his stationery, promotional kits, and business cards. It is quite common now to see e-mail addresses alongside phone and fax numbers on business cards. The e-mail address allows anyone on the Internet to contact Brant directly.

The actual sending and receiving of e-mail is done through a software program called an e-mail reader. There are many popular e-mail readers on the market. These e-mail reader software programs are available through the Internet access provider. E-mail readers present e-mail in an easy-to-read format and usually allow you to save and search messages. E-mail readers provide convenient ways of responding to e-mail. You can, for instance, read an e-mail and then forward that e-mail to a friend using these programs. This forwarding feature is particularly useful in passing on valuable information to colleagues. When you forward or send e-mail you send it to another person's e-mail address.

For those beginning on the Internet, I encourage you to learn how to use e-mail. E-mail is the most widely used tool on the Internet. More people use e-mail than they do the WWW. All of the nearly forty million on the Internet use e-mail. Only twenty million use the WWW. Thus, it is imperative that you learn how to use e-mail to reach the widest possible audience on the Internet. As you use the Internet, you will find that e-mail becomes second nature. You will begin to ask others for e-mail addresses just the way you ask for telephone numbers. Mastering e-mail will prepare you for other activities on the Internet, such as using UseNet newsgroups.

UseNet Newsgroups

To many users on the Internet, UseNet becomes their sole vehicle for participating on the Internet. Next to e-mail, UseNet is the most widely used feature of the Internet. No special hardware is required to access UseNet, only software. This software, known as a news reader, is often made available by the Internet access provider.

The UseNet was originally developed for the exchange of technical information; however, the UseNet soon became more because of the development of newsgroups. Newsgroups were developed for nontechnical subjects, such as hobbies, social interests, politics, and other news items. Today there are more than ten thousand newsgroups from both technical and nontechnical topics. If you can think of a topic, more than likely there is already a newsgroup for that topic on UseNet. Newsgroups can get very specific. There is one newsgroup, for example, on audio equipment; and there is another newsgroup for high-end audio equipment.

Understanding the use of newsgroups also requires a better understanding of what the UseNet is. First, the UseNet is not a network, but rather a feature or service offered by the Internet. One way to think of UseNet is as an organized e-mail system, except that there is no single person receiving the e-mail. Messages that you or anyone else using UseNet sends are sent to a newsgroup section. The UseNet is not managed or controlled by anyone specifically, but is more a matter of communal control. There are no written rules about the kind of language that can used in submitting an article to a newsgroup or about behavior on UseNet. There are however generally accepted community standards, or "netiquette," for communicating in newsgroups.

Newsgroups are essentially ongoing conferences devoted to specific topics and are conducted by public e-mail. The first newsgroup ever created was used to convey and discuss the latest news about the Internet itself. To participate in a newsgroup, you first have to subscribe to the newsgroup. Subscribers to newsgroups participate in newsgroup discussions by posting their messages to the newsgroup. The posting of a message makes that message publicly available to everyone accessing that newsgroup. Posting a message is as simple as sending e-mail to that newsgroup. There are no membership requirements for newsgroups. Anyone who can read a newsgroup's message is free to add comments to a given message thread. A message thread is a list of messages and replies that constitute the newsgroup's discussion.

Once inside a newsgroup discussion, you may respond by either replying to the originator of the message privately or by sending a response to the newsgroup for everyone to read. Because newsgroups are composed of so many people all expressing their opinions, arguments can ensue. When this happens, it is termed "flaming" and it can often lead to "flame wars," in which more heated dialogs occur. There is sometimes a fine line between a respectful, reserved argument and flaming.

As mentioned before, there are more than ten thousand newsgroups on UseNet today. The UseNet user community has tried to create newsgroups that are tightly focused on a subject. To help differentiate newsgroups, conventions have been developed to name newsgroups. There are various levels of naming that help to specify and categorize a newsgroup. The first level of identification of a newsgroup is a generic identifier that lets you know immediately whether the newsgroup is technical, social, recreational, or some other general category. Here is a list of the generic identifiers and their associated categories:

GENERIC IDENTIFIER	CATEGORY
biz	Business
comp	Computers
news	General news items
rec	Recreational (hobbies and arts)
sci	Scientific
soc	Social
talk	Debate-oriented
misc	Newsgroups not in the above categories

In addition to the above types of newsgroups, there is also the UseNet "underground." There is a smaller set of newsgroups with the generic identifier "alt" where stronger language and behavior are tolerated. Some have compared these newsgroups to underground newspapers.

Following the generic identifier, there is usually a second level of identification using the primary subject area identifier. The primary subject area identifier identifies the general topic of the newsgroup. For example, birds is the primary subject area for the newsgroup *rec.birds,* which is dedicated to discussing the fine pleasures of bird watching; biology is the primary subject area for the newsgroup *sci.biology* which is dedicated to biology-oriented topics; and tasteless is the primary subject area for the newsgroup *alt.tasteless* which is dedicated to discussing weird and bizarre material.

In many cases the newsgroup is broken down beyond the primary subject area to a second level. The second level of identification occurs when a newsgroup becomes too broad for the subscribers to gain value from it. For example, the newsgroup *rec.arts.books* and *rec.arts.movies* are dedicated to different aspects of the arts. The newsgroup *rec.arts.books* serves to discuss authors, books, and the publishing industry in general. The newsgroup *rec.arts.movies* is a group to discuss all aspects of movies and moviemaking. Finally, there are newsgroups that can have even a third level to get even more specific about the topic of discussion.

Once you subscribe to a newsgroup, you will at some point want to post your own comment or message. UseNet newsgroups were designed to inspire and support such communications between users in an open forum. I encourage you to join several newsgroups that you find interesting. Learn to use newsgroups. They will be central to your success in promoting yourself on the Internet. (The next part of the book, "Publicity," will give you more details on how to use newsgroups to reach targeted audiences. The more specific issues of netiquette and signatures will also be covered in that part.)

Mailing Lists

Once you have an e-mail account, you can subscribe to Internet mailing lists. Mailing lists are similar to newsgroups, but they are far less interactive. You put your e-mail address on a mailing list of a particular topic. The items sent to those on a mailing list are more likely to be articles and longer pieces of information, rather than the short comments that typify newsgroups. Also, while it is necessary to key in a command or two to read the latest newsgroup messages, the material sent to mailing list members automatically arrives via their e-mail address. In most cases, getting your name added to a mailing list is as simple as sending an e-mail message to a given e-mail address.

You can subscribe to various mailing lists. There are mailing lists on such topics as archaeology, arts, comics, and politics. My friend John R. Howe, a writer, is currently completing his first book. As a writer, John belongs to various mailing lists for writers. A mailing list for members of the National Writers Union, for example, first alerted John to the potential value of the electronic rights to his book, a biography of an Alaskan naturalist. As John recalls, "I was in the middle of negotiating a contract with a university press, and one of the threads on the mailing list gave me most of the information I needed to talk intelligently with my publisher about this cutting-edge issue." Mailing lists, therefore, can become a practical resource to stay current with issues related to a particular field.

Telnet

Telnet is a basic Internet service that allows you to access remote computers as if they were local to you. To use Telnet, you must have the Internet domain name of the remote computer. The domain name could be *acme.com*. Upon Telnetting to the remote computer, you are presented with a login message. By entering a valid user name and password, you can log into the remote computer as if it were your local machine.

Telnettable sites include libraries, universities, government agencies, and private systems. In libraries, you can call up the card files. In universities, you can look into campus directories and library files, access databases, and see what's new on campus. Most public service sites let you use the login name "guest" or "demo" and any letters for the password. If this is not successful, the site probably does not want you Telnetting in.

FTP: File Transfer Protocol

File Transfer Protocol or FTP is the standard protocol for copying files from computer to computer on the Internet and was one of the first tools developed on the Internet. This tool enables you to connect from your local computer to a remote computer on the Internet. Once you are connected to the remote computer, you can view and browse lists of files on the remote computer. With FTP you can retrieve or download a file from the remote computer to your local computer. Similarly, you can place or upload a file from your local computer to the remote computer. FTP allows files to be transmitted in either ASCII or binary mode. The binary mode should be used on all files that are not plain text ASCII documents. Graphic images, sound files, video files, and word processing files should all be transferred using binary mode.

Like Telnet, FTP allows you to access remote machines. However, where Telnet allows you access to the power of the remote machine, FTP limits you to sending and receiving files. When you connect to a remote computer using FTP, you will receive a login prompt. Logging in using the login name "anonymous" often allows you to proceed by entering your e-mail address as the password. You are then allowed to see a directory of files that you may download. Recently, I found a site in Chile that had some great free software or "freeware." I was able to download the software and have it running on my machine in a few minutes. If I had to write the same piece of software, it would have taken me weeks.

In the above case, I knew exactly the name of the file that I wanted to get from the computer in Chile, and I also knew the domain name of the computer where the file was located. This may not always be the case. For example, suppose you are a musician and you want to retrieve a piece of software that allows you to play MIDI audio files on your computer. Before you can use FTP, you need to know the file name of that piece of software and the domain name of the remote computer having that file. The Internet tool Archie can help.

Archie

Archie can help in finding the domain name of the remote computer that has the file that you are interested in. Archie was the first information retrieval system developed on the Internet. Archie consists of two components: a central database and a search program for finding items in that database. The database contains the names of files available on FTP sites throughout the Internet with the associated domain name of the computer containing that file. The Archie search program allows you to type a file name and find the domain name of the remote computer containing that file. To build its database, Archie periodically connects to FTP sites and downloads lists of all files that are on those sites. These lists of files are merged into a database that can then be searched.

To use Archie's searching features, you connect to a site that has an Archie database. Once you are connected, you can search the database for a file. Because the database only knows the names of the files, you must know at least part of the file name for which you are looking. For example, if you are the musician looking for the software program that will play MIDI file, you would search the database for the word "midi." The Archie program will return the domain names of all remote computers having a file starting with the word "midi." You can then use FTP to go to one of the remote computers and retrieve the file.

One of the limitations of Archie is that not all sites on the Internet are part of the Archie database. There may be files that fit your specification but because they are not in the Archie database you may never find them. Despite such limitations, however, Archie is still a very useful tool for locating files to download through FTP.

Gopher

Gopher is another tool for distributing information on the Internet. Those sites on the Internet that distribute information using the

Gopher system have Gopher servers. Users accessing Gopher servers are provided with a menu-based interface for accessing information. The function of Gopher is similar to FTP. Displaying or downloading a file using Gopher, however, is as easy as selecting an item from a menu. This ease of use, plus the ability to put descriptive titles on the menu items, makes Gopher a much easier method of browsing files than simply using FTP.

Gopher is a text-based browser. A browser is a program that allows users to view lists of files and the contents of files. Browsers also contain features for moving between files with varying levels of ease. Gopher falls short of other browsers, such as WWW browsers, in that it does not have the ability to integrate images, sound, and video nearly as well as WWW browsers do. However, Gopher+ (a Gopher extension run by many sites) does have support for basic WWW pages and can handle some of the formatting commands.

Internet Relay Chat

Internet Relay Chat, or IRC, is a service that was developed in the late 1980s that enables multiple people to "talk" simultaneously by typing words on the keyboard. Like many other tools on the Internet, IRC is a client/server application. People who want to talk with each other must be running the IRC client software on their local computer and they must connect to a remote computer that is running the IRC server software. Once on the server, they select the channel on which they want to talk. Channels are often named for the topic they discuss, if they restrict themselves to a particular topic.

When you are involved in an IRC channel, you can write to the other participants from your terminal while you see what others are writing on theirs. This is an interesting way of having a real-time conference, but speed of communication is rather slow since typing is much slower than speaking. It does, however, allow everyone to participate equally and prevents one person from taking over the conversation by "shouting " or "talking" continuously. IRC differs from UseNet in that messages posted to IRC are displayed instantaneously in real time.

IRC is composed of groups or channels. Just as UseNet offers access to thousands of newsgroups, IRC offers access to thousands of channels. Many UseNet newsgroups have corresponding IRC channels. If you have a question, you can simply join a related IRC group and ask any of the members of that group the question. Anyone who knows the answer will give it to you immediately in real time.

An IRC channel is always prefixed by the character #. Since IRC came into being, there are certain channels that have earned a reputation. The two that I have found to be quite fun and interesting are #hottub and #hamlet. The #hottub channel started as an attempt to simulate the atmosphere in a spa-type hot tub. This was one of the first theme channels to be created on IRC. The #hamlet channel gives you a front row seat to the most popular computerized theater. On #hamlet, individuals assume different parts in various Shakespeare plays and perform them at certain times during the day.

Because of IRC's real-time nature, it is extremely addictive. People enjoy spending hours talking back and forth with other people around the world. Many deep friendships are created on IRC channels, and IRC has even spawned many romances (though the lovers rarely meet face to face). IRC keeps people's identities private by allowing you to pick a nickname. Some have called IRC the CB radio of the Internet. Business owners, for example, can use IRC with a WWW browser to have real-time discussions about entrepreneurialism, a recent trade show, or legal rights issues.

WWW Browsers

All the tools that were mentioned so far have one major distinction compared to the WWW and WWW browsers. These tools can all be run without using a mouse; they are keyboard-driven tools. The WWW and WWW browsers were designed to be used with a mouse.

WWW browsers are software programs that enable you to read and navigate WWW documents or Websites. Using a WWW browser and a mouse, you can literally point and click at elements called "hyperlinks" and an action will take place. The action may involve taking you to another page, downloading a sound file, or transporting you halfway around the world to another document on another computer. WWW browsers can only be used to navigate and read documents that are encoded in a language called HyperText Markup Language (HTML). HTML allows a single document to contain text, color, images, sounds, and movies. Any item, such as a sound file, can be hyperlinked to another document, image, or sound. As the user views a document, portions of the document may be selected by the user to cause other related documents or items to be retrieved. HTML documents are always text documents that have special commands in them that indicate pictures, sounds, movies, hyperlinks, and formatting.

There are many WWW browsers on the market today. The first browser was developed at the National Center for Supercomputing Applications (NCSA) in Urbana-Champaign, Illinois. This browser, called Mosaic, was developed by Marc Andreessen and Eric Bina. Marc Andreessen left NCSA to start Netscape Communications, Inc. Netscape is the developer of perhaps the most famous WWW browser, called Netscape Navigator. Cello, another browser, is also popular on the WWW. Many other companies are building WWW browsers.

Online services, such as America Online (AOL), Prodigy, GEnie, CompuServe, Microsoft Internet, and Delphi, have been forced to develop WWW browsers. Why do I say forced? These online services have their own private "pay-per-view" computer networks, which are not a part of the Internet. For years, these online services have had several millions of customers using their private networks. When the Internet WWW took off in 1994, many of these customers demanded that they be given access to the Internet WWW or they would leave these private networks and get accounts on the Internet through an Internet access provider. To satisfy their customer base, these online services quickly developed WWW browsers to enable their customers to access and view WWW Websites.

Unfortunately, the early WWW browsers developed by these online services were slow and lagged behind in technology compared to Netscape's Navigator. Many are now playing catch-up with Netscape in terms of WWW browser development. Microsoft Corporation has made major leaps in developing its browser, Explorer, which, next to Navigator, is fast becoming a popular browser.

WWW Directories

Internet WWW directories can be used to find Websites on the Internet. WWW directories are like the Yellow Pages. They are organized by categories such as arts, computers, and travel. Within each category are subcategories, and sub-subcategories. At the deepest level of these directories are listings of Websites on the Internet that correspond to the category or categories. Since everything is mouse driven, a user simply points and clicks to navigate to a Website of interest.

Today there are more than three hundred Internet WWW directories. The oldest and most famous is called Yahoo, which began as a project for two Stanford graduate students. Millions of people visit Yahoo every day and find interesting Websites to explore. Yahoo does not charge for a Website to place a listing in its directory. Yahoo makes money by selling advertising banner space at various locations on its Website to companies such as Honda, Coca Cola, AT&T, and others.

For those of you who have a Website, it is vital that you post your Website address on the right Internet WWW directories to attract the right kind of clients. In the chapters ahead, we will explore methods of using WWW directories to market yourself on the Internet.

WWW Search Engines

WWW search engines are powerful tools for finding Websites based on user-defined criteria. The criteria for most search engines is a word or set of words. Different search engines use these words in different ways to locate Websites. There are three major ways in which search engines use these words to locate a desired Website.

The first is to look for the words in the actual text of the document. For example, the search engine Alta Vista, by Digital Equipment Corporation, literally searches millions of WWW documents on the entire Internet and locates all Websites that have the set of words prescribed by the user. If you type in the word "music," this search engine will display a list of all Websites that have the word "music" in the text of the Website. You can also combine words. For instance, entering "landscape AND photography" will return all Websites that have both the words "landscape" and "photography" in the text body of the Website.

The second way search engines use words to locate a Website is to look for those words in specific parts of the Website, such as the heading or the title. Thus, the person registering a Website with these search engines must make sure that the header or title has the significant words. Otherwise, the Website may be hard to find.

The third way search engines use words to locate a Website is by comparing the words given by the user to descriptive keywords attached to that Website. When a person registers a Website with some search engines, they can associate keywords describing their Website. These keywords may or may not appear in the textual body of the Website. The keywords, therefore, could be more conceptual descriptors of the Website. For example, a Website for Boston Ballet might have the keywords "theatrical production" associated with it, even though the words "theatrical" and "production" may never appear in the textual body of the Website.

There are many search engines on the Internet WWW. The two earliest search engines were Yahoo and WebCrawler. America Online, seeing the expanding use of WebCrawler, bought it in mid 1995. Yahoo, started by two Stanford graduate students, is a full-fledged company, backed by major venture capital. These and other search engines do not cost anything to use. Similar to WWW directories, these search engines make money through corporate and business advertising.

The tools presented above are the basic ones you will need to know to make effective use of the Internet. New software tools are being written to navigate, access, and distribute information on the Internet every day. In the third part of this book, "Community," some of the latest and most powerful tools in development will be discussed.

While these more sophisticated tools will no doubt revolutionize our activities on the Internet, e-mail and the WWW will still be the mainstays of Internet communication. By learning how to use these and the other tools described above, you will create the basis for continuing to level the playing field of the Internet.

3 Getting On

THERE IS A BIG DIFFERENCE BETWEEN "GETTING ON" THE INTERNET AND "being on" the Internet. Getting on the Internet is the process of gaining physical access to the Internet by using computer hardware and an Internet access provider. Being on the Internet means building your own storefront or Website on the WWW. The next chapter will discuss being on the Internet.

If this distinction is not clear, some analogies may help. Getting on the Internet is similar to buying a TV and watching programs. Being on the Internet is similar to building your own TV station and putting on your own programs. Getting on the Internet will allow you to access information on the Internet using the various tools described above. For example, getting on offers you access to forty million people via e-mail. Getting on lets you "tune in" and interact with the thousands of Websites. Getting on lets you participate in chat sessions, order books and CDs online, send messages to the White House, and participate in news surveys.

What Hardware Do I Need?

The first step to getting on the Internet is to make sure you have the right hardware. To get on, you can use just about any old machine. Even extremely slow machines with 300-baud modems allow access to the Internet. However, to use the WWW and to run WWW browsers, you will need more than an old machine and a 300-baud modem. There are five basic pieces of equipment you will need to get on the Internet and to use the WWW. They are: computer, keyboard, monitor, mouse, and modem.

In terms of the computer, you can use an IBM PC compatible, an Apple Macintosh, or a larger workstation such as a SUN machine. If you are using an IBM PC compatible, you will require at least Windows 3.1 running in 32-bit extended mode. You will need a hard disk that leaves at least 20 megabytes (MB) (preferably 60MB) free, 4 to 8MB random access memory (RAM) (preferably 8 to 32MB), and a speed of 33MHz 486 (preferably 100 MHz 486). If you are using an Apple, you will want one of the faster Macintoshes or Power PCs. For workstations, both SUN and Silicon Graphics offer inexpensive powerful machines.

Keyboards for all computers are standard. Buy a keyboard that you like and feels good. If you are planning to use your computer often, buy a wrist pad along with the keyboard. Wrist pads can help prevent certain injuries caused by strain and overuse.

A good monitor is also extremely important. Since you will be spending a lot of time looking at it, make sure that it is color. A good monitor will produce a black that is very black with no hints of gray, and a white that is solid, even, and very white. Get a VGA-compatible monitor or a Super VGA, which is even better. VGA stands for Video Graphic Array. Images on the WWW are either in GIF format or JPEG format. GIF images are limited to 256 colors. JPEG images may have up to 16.2 million colors. VGA can handle up to 256 colors. Super VGA can handle all 16.2 million colors for a stunning display of graphics, JPEG images, or movies.

You will also need a pointing device, such as a mouse. A mouse is critical to using the WWW. Go to a store and test those available. You can purchase a good mouse for approximately $20. More expensive ergonomic mice are also available. Choose a mouse that you feel comfortable with.

Finally, you will need a modem. "Modem" stands for modulator-demodulator. You will need at least a 14.4K modem. However, a 28.8K modem is becoming a standard. Make sure that your Internet access provider can support 28.8K. You can also buy an ISDN modem. ISDN stands for Integrated Services Digital Network. These modems are available for a little more than the cost of a regular modem but require ISDN phone lines. ISDN phone lines are now available in many large cities. The line charge rates vary, but seem to average approximately $30 per month. ISDN gives you multiple 56K lines and enables you to transfer data and voice simultaneously. Of course, provider fees are higher for ISDN connections as well. Whatever modem you buy, it should be Hayes compatible. Hayes is the company that pioneered much of commercial modem technology. Nearly every modem conforms to Hayes standard.

How Do I Get the Hardware?

Before you lay out your money for hardware, you need to shop around. There are many choices. Large cities have computer superstores with warehouse-type layouts and huge savings, but even the smallest communities have computer stores. Magazines also offer an abundance of computer ads, and you can buy them direct from some companies. The question then is do you buy from a store or from a magazine via mail order?

Magazines, such as *Computer Shopper*, offer the primary advantage of both choice and price. Even computer superstores cannot compete with the sheer number of mail-order companies in a single magazine. Mail-order companies can keep their prices low because they do not need a well-staffed storefront. Magazines also offer the latest technology. Because computer stores tend to enter into agreements with certain manufacturers, they are tied to the release schedules of those companies. Magazines have no such limits, and new companies with new technologies appear in every issue.

The primary advantage of computer stores is that they are useful in emergencies. A computer store is essential when you do not have time to wait for shipment, even if it is the next day. Superstores also often offer prices that are close to the prices in magazine ads. If you are a smart superstore shopper, you can walk away with a purchase that closely matches the magazine's price, especially when considering shipping charges.

The final advantage of a store over a magazine is the security of knowing what you are buying and where you are buying it. With a magazine, you go on faith. I recommend combining the best of both worlds. Buy from a magazine as much as possible, since savings and choice outweigh the pros of buying locally. You may want to go to a local store to get an idea of price and features. You can use the store to play around with different systems and to get an idea of what works for you. Then turn to the magazine ads to make the purchase.

Another interesting way to purchase is online. Most of the major computer manufacturers now allow you to order computers directly from their Websites. This type of online ordering is similar to ordering from a magazine.

When buying computers, another important consideration is whether it is better to buy from a large company. The answer depends on whether you are buying the computer itself or some kind of peripheral device. If you are buying the computer itself, realize that the basic computer system is made up of components that are only made by only a small number of manufacturers. While there are differences in reliability, durability, design, and speed, all the components, regardless of manufacturer, should work well. This extends to PCs manufactured by famous names such as IBM and Compaq and to Macs (now available in clone models just like PCs), most of the important components of Apple computers are not made by Apple.

The fact that there are only a few manufacturers for each of the major components in a computer means that the prices for these components can be kept low. Price gouging is relatively unknown to component manufacturers. The quality of the equipment from the big old companies probably won't be any better than those of the small new ones. Big companies tend to produce lots of machines at once. Many times buyers must live with flawed designs until current stocks have been sold. Smaller companies, with smaller runs, can afford to make functional and ergonomic changes more quickly.

I have used both big-name systems and no-name systems. Except for rare instances, there are no differences in overall quality between machines purchased from big companies and small companies. The main difference, regardless of whether the computer was purchased from a big or a small company, is how the individual components of the computer were assembled. Most computer problems arise from the pieces not being put together correctly. Thus, the most important thing to remember when purchasing a machine from either a big or small company is to make sure the company offers a good return policy and a good warranty.

If you are buying peripherals (or components), you should always purchase a well-known brand. To choose the correct company, read product comparison reviews in popular computer magazines such as *Byte* and *Computer Shopper*. Components could be parts such as a disk drive, power supply, or memory chips.

What Software Do I Need?

Getting the right software is important. There are various pieces of software necessary to connect to the Internet. To save yourself time, I urge you to get all of the necessary software at one time rather than in a piecemeal fashion. Those people who obtain the software piecemeal often spend a lot of unnecessary time installing it and resolving various cross-integration issues.

To get on the Internet and to use the various Internet tools, you will need the following software:

- FTP: File Transfer Protocol is a program that lets you transfer files from remote computers. This is the primary way that you send and receive data when not using the WWW.
- Telnet: This program allows you to log onto to a remote computer as if it were attached to your computer. This is necessary to access your remote accounts on your provider's machine.

- Archie: An Archie program finds files on the Internet that fit a search word you provide. Once you locate a file, use FTP to transfer it.
- NetNews: NetNews is a news reader that allows you to peruse any of the thousands of special interest newsgroups on the Internet.
- E-Mail: An e-mail reader allows you to receive and send personal electronic mail to anyone on the Internet.
- SLIP/PPP: A Serial Line Interface Protocol or Point-to-Point Protocol program is needed for your computer at home to talk to the Internet. This program takes care of communicating between your modem and the Internet.
- WWW Browser: A browser such as Netscape helps you view information on the Internet in a graphical user interface (GUI) environment using a mouse.

Sounds like an awful lot of software? It would be if you had to obtain it individually. Fortunately, most Internet access providers will give you all this software when you sign up.

The Internet Access Provider

After you have the hardware and the proper software, the last thing you need to get onto the Internet is an Internet access provider. Today there are thousands of local providers. At first, I recommended using local providers closest to where you live. However, I no longer believe that many of these local providers will be able to stay in business. Furthermore, many of them provide poor customer service.

Today, I recommend NETCOM and their proprietary software, NetComplete, which provides all of the software mentioned above. More importantly, the software is easy to install, set up, and use to connect to the Internet. Once you are connected, you can use the Netscape browser Navigator to view the WWW. NETCOM is a national provider, meaning that you can get on the Internet through a local phone call from anywhere in the U.S.

▼

4 Being On

BEING ON THE INTERNET IS DIFFERENT FROM GETTING ON THE INTERNET. Getting on involves hardware, software, and an Internet access provider to gain the physical access to the Internet. Being on does not require that you even own a computer or have access to the Internet. Being on means having a Website on the Internet.

You Do Not Need a Computer

Being on the Internet does not require a computer. This is important to understand. You do not need to own a computer, or have Internet access, to take advantage of the World Wide Web. You do not need to own a car to have a billboard advertisement on Interstate Route 80. You do not need to own a TV to broadcast a TV commercial. Having a TV, however, would give you a better idea of how your commercial looks and how to develop your commercial more effectively. Likewise, having a computer with an Internet connection would enable you to understand the medium better, but it is not critical to the success of your being on the Internet.

What is a Website?

For starters, consider a Website as the digital version of your current print brochures or materials. In these materials you use graphics, text, and design elements to represent yourself or your company in the best way. A Website contains that same information, digitized and laid out in a format for viewing on a computer screen. That information is accessible to anyone who has your Website address on the Internet. A Website address, commonly referred to as the Universal Resource Locator (URL), lets anyone find you on the Internet. A user can visit your site on the WWW by simply typing the URL address into any standard WWW browser.

A URL address has three basic components: a service, a domain name with optional port, and a path with an optional file name. The first component, the service, tells the WWW browser how to retrieve the file. The service may be one of the following:

- file://
- http://
- gopher://
- telnet://
- news://

The second component of the URL is the name of the machine or domain name such as *iseei.com*. The third component of the URL is the path name and file name of the item you want to retrieve. The third component, if missing, will force the WWW browser to load a default file. Some examples of legitimate URLs are:

- http://www.arts-online.com
- http://www.arts-online.com/allworth/home.html
- http://www.cbs.com

At *http://www.arts-online.com,* you will find an online multi-arts community for artists and arts organizations, such as Boston Ballet, Alvin Ailey, and Very Special Arts. At *http://www.arts-online.com/allworth/home.html,* you will find the Website of my publisher, Allworth Press. Allworth's Website contains reviews of books for visual and performing artists and writers, along with legal advice. The Website at the URL *http://www.cbs.com* is owned and operated by CBS and offers a variety of information including David Letterman's Top Ten List.

A Website is obviously more powerful than a printed brochure. Unlike a brochure, a Website is interactive. Not only can users view your material, but they can also order a product immediately, request additional information, post their comments about your material or products, sign an electronic guest book, or let you know that they stopped by your Website using e-mail. A Website brings your information directly to your audience and brings your audience directly to you. The cost of preparing a Website compared to a traditional printed brochure is one reason why new Websites are appearing on the Internet every twenty minutes. The cost alone is a feature that can save you thousands of dollars a year.

Why Create a Website?

There are many reasons to create a Website. It can

- generate valuable new leads and mailing lists of prospective clients
- create awareness of your products and services
- provide detailed presales information on you and your organization
- increase your profits by attracting new customers from the Internet WWW's twenty million young, educated professionals with household incomes of more than $50,000
- create new sales channels you won't find anywhere else
- distribute your products and services faster and more flexibly
- position yourself and your organization strategically for the twenty-first century

- improve customer service
- enable you to update your information instantaneously
- collect prospective client demographics
- cut overhead costs
- find new partners and allies around the world

Creating a Professional Website

There are two main phases of being on the Internet. The first phase involves creating a professionally designed Website, one that is both aesthetically pleasing and technologically sound. Although it may seem obvious, many organizations often neglect this first phase. They simply take their printed brochures and "place" them on a Website. Using interns or "technical" experts, such as a local computer whiz, can make some Websites look amateurish. Most Websites are simply text with a smattering of bad clip-art graphics. Even multimillion-dollar companies have Websites that look like they were developed by a grade-school student.

Because of the increasing traffic on the Internet, many people are starting to realize that they need a professionally created Website. A successful Website should look as professional as a thirty-second TV commercial. It should contain the proper design elements and represent the image you have worked for years to build. There are potentially twenty million people on the WWW who will see your Website. You should make sure they see the best image possible. There are ways to cut corners to reduce your budget, but do not skimp here.

Web page design is becoming a real profession. There are many who are claiming to be Web page designers because they learned HTML and some software graphics program only a few months ago. You do not want someone using your company to experiment. When seeking a professional Web page designer, make sure that the company or the individual satisfies the following basic criteria:

- basic knowledge about the Internet
- professionally trained or equivalent experience in graphic design or other related design area
- has been in business for at least one year
- has an existing portfolio of clients
- has professional training or knowledge in marketing and how to merge traditional marketing with interactive marketing

By all means do not select an amateur to do your Website. It will cost you if you do. You may not realize your mistake immediately, but you will at some time in the near future. You are better off spending the time and money to have a professional create your Website.

The other major ingredient of a successful Website is useful technology. Once your Website is up, how are you going to receive feedback? How will you communicate with the Internet community? If you have a computer and Internet connection, there are a variety of ways. If you do not, there are certain services available so you can stay in touch with your customers.

With new technologies, Websites can have automatically changing content and other advanced features. These features and services can make your Website truly interactive so that it stands out among the thousands of sites already on the Internet. As more sites appear, you will want to distinguish yourself from your competition.

The Anatomy of a Website

There are several important characteristics of a successful Website:

- professional design
- fast display of graphics and text
- ease of navigation
- easy ways for viewers to communicate with you and to order information
- frequent updates or content changes
- an area for people to tell you their likes and dislikes
- the element of fun (people want to enjoy their visit)
- marketing enticements, such as coupons, online giveaways, etc.
- links to other interesting sites

If you plan to take your Website seriously for the long-term, integrate as many of the above elements into your design as possible. A thoughtful and calculated approach will yield a Website that will earn you positive feedback and comments from your site's visitors.

Finding a Home for Your Website

Once you have successfully developed a professional Website, the next step is finding a home for your Website. If you have a great-looking Website that is going to draw people in by the thousands, and one that is going to generate thousands of new leads, new opportunities, and increase your business, the last thing you want to do is place that site on an Internet server that is going to be so slow as to discourage potential clients. Finding the right home is critical to your success.

Finding a home for your Website means finding a company that has dedicated machines and an Internet connection that will allow your Website to be seen. You have to shop to find the best rates for placing this information online.

There are several factors to consider when thinking about where to place your Website. The most important are:

- What type of machine is the server, and how powerful is it?
- What type of connection to the Internet does the server have and how many people use that connection?
- How many people can access my material?
- what is the focus or theme of the server? To whom does it cater?
- How does the server or site promote itself, and how will people find this server among the thousands on the Internet?
- How good is the customer service, should you have a problem with your site?

The technology today is so new that most people do not consider these questions. They do not know what a server is, let alone which is the right one for their Website. Most of the new Websites popping up are the result of companies and organizations rushing to put something online without considering all the factors. Many do not have a clear goal of what they want their Website to accomplish. Most companies and organizations do not think past the creation of a Website. This will not work.

What type of machine is the server, and how powerful is it?

The first question to be answered is what type of server a company is running. A server is simply a very powerful computer that is connected to the Internet. The reason it needs to be powerful is because thousands of people are connecting to it daily, retrieving information, and asking the computer to perform certain tasks. Without a powerful computer, people trying to look at your information have to wait for long periods of time, which means lost customers.

What type of connection to the Internet does the server have and how many people use that connection?

The question can be rephrased as: How is the server connected to the Internet? This is a fundamental question that could have a great impact on your site. The type of Internet connection to the server "hosting" your Website is a major factor in determining how many people can visit your site.

Consider a public relations company that has phone lines coming in, and a finite number of operators to answer those phones. Obviously, the more phone lines coming into the company, and operators working at the company, the more customers a company can handle without giving a customer a busy signal. Assume that the number of phone lines coming into the company is the Internet connection and that the number of operators answering those calls is the server.

Now consider that you want a public relations company to take care of all your phone calls so you can get on with business. What would be the most important demand that you would make on this public relations company? Probably it would be to make sure that any prospective clients don't receive a busy signal. You cannot afford missed opportunities. You would want the company that had the most phone lines to answer calls, and the most efficient operators to process those calls.

When considering a company to place your promotional information online via your Website, you want a company that has a dedicated T1 Internet connection. This T1 connection is like having more than one hundred phone lines. In addition, you want a company with a server that is fast and efficient at answering requests.

How many people can use the lines? Internet access providers are in the business of selling you a phone line to the Internet. In other words, they have hundreds of phone lines to the Internet, and they will sell you the right to use one of those phone lines to access the Internet. The rub here is that the one phone line they sell to you is not exclusively yours. Up to ten others can share the same phone line.

Most Internet access providers have thousands of people tying up phone lines getting onto the Internet, while others, including your prospective clients, are trying to get to the information you may have placed on their server. This means that although an Internet access provider may have a T1 connection, your potential customers may still experience delays accessing your Website because they are competing with people who are using the same lines to get onto on the Internet. As a result, many people have moved their Websites away from the Internet access providers' generic servers.

How many people can get to my material?

The number of people who can access your site depends on many factors. The two most important are the type of server and the type of Internet connection. Picking the right company with the right Internet connection and server will determine the number of users who can access your site.

The other factor is the type of information they are retrieving from the server. If everyone visiting the server is downloading large amounts of text, graphics, audio, or video, there will be a bottleneck in accessing the server and your Website.

What is the focus or theme of the server? To whom does it cater?

The next question is one that few people have considered because the Internet is so new, but one that should be a fundamental concern to you. Internet access providers are not in the business of providing a new market for you or your company. Internet access providers do not cater to any individual or organization. Internet access providers make money by selling Internet access. If you want to get on the Internet yourself with your computer and "surf" the Internet, you would call on them. Remember, getting on the Internet, and being on the Internet are totally different. Many assume that once they get on the Internet using an Internet access provider, they should also put their Website on that Internet access provider's server. This can be a big mistake.

For example, imagine a magazine that has no focus, and prints whatever a company or individual pays them to. The same holds true for Internet access providers. You will be able to find software companies, automotive companies, artists, labels, airlines, all on the same server.

When thinking about placing your print advertisement in a magazine, your first step should be to identify a magazine that reaches your target market. If you are a record label, you wouldn't place your ad in a travel magazine. You would find a magazine that targets your audience. This analogy holds true for placing your Website.

How does the server or site promote itself or how will people find this server over the thousands on the Internet?

The server where you place your Website can be fundamental to the success of your Website. Using the magazine analogy, you now want to ask, "How does this magazine promote itself?" Or, in this case, "How does the server promote its URL address?" A site that caters to your target market is extremely important.

The server needs to be promoted constantly through traditional media, as well as on the Internet. The more a server advertises itself directly, the more people will come to that server—and to your site. It's just common sense. But the astonishing fact is that there are few Internet access providers who advertise the URL address of their server in traditional media. Again, Internet access providers do not target a particular audience to their server. They provide space on their server and leave advertising in your hands.

The Website activities of Young Concert Artists (YCA) of New York are an example of these principles. In mid 1995, YCA, working with Millennium Productions, Inc., developed a great-looking Website. However, their Website's home was a server in Hong Kong that was slow and did not directly relate to the arts. As a result, Young Concert Artists decided to move their site away from the server in Hong Kong to a more niche-oriented, arts-specific server with the domain name *arts-online.com*. The new server at *arts-online.com* had four important characteristics: it was connected to a dedicated T1 line; it was for arts-specific clients; the domain name of the server was advertised and promoted in more than thirty major arts magazines and journals worldwide; and the server was powered by one of the fastest computers on the market.

Young Concert Artists' decision to change their server had immediate results. As YCA pointed out, "We already had a great-looking Website, but hardly anyone was able to find it. Furthermore, when people came to our Website, the site came up really slowly. The *arts-online.com* server, on a high speed T1 line, displayed our Website ten times faster. We have been getting fifteen to twenty unique visitors at our Website every day since our change of servers. Furthermore, we get glowing reviews from our visitors on our design, as well as speed of access." Moreover, YCA's Web design, combined with the speed of access, encourages visitors to make frequent stops to their site.

Being on the Internet, therefore, requires a clear understanding of the principles outlined above. Before you decide to be on the Internet, plan your strategy carefully and make sure that you have covered all the important areas. A successfully planned presence on the WWW will position you for the next step—cyberpublicity and marketing your Website to potential visitors.

5 Setting Up Shop

ONCE YOU HAVE YOUR WEBSITE ON THE INTERNET AND HAVE PUBLICIZED it (see part two, "Publicity"), it may be valuable to use your cyberspace storefront to conduct commerce. The Internet provides mechanisms for online transactions. Businesses are using their Websites to sell appliances, tickets, and even dogs online. In addition, many are also realizing the use of the Website for customer service and support.

Success Stories

Some of you may be thinking that it is a wild idea to sell products and services and to service clients online. A few success stories will make you realize that it is not.

- "All Weather, Inc., spent about $3,000 to rent space in an online 'mall' to promote sales of a swimming pool alarm. In less than a year, it has received $500,000 in orders from around the world." —*Infoworld*
- "Federal Express and other firms have found a powerful model in using the WWW to service their customers. On the Internet, people can now check a FedEx shipment's status at any time, virtually anywhere, without the hassle of voice-mail menus, queues, and other delays." —*Internet World*
- "Digital Equipment Company sold over $15 million in product via its Internet site to customers in 1994." —*Internet World*
- "PC Gifts and Flowers—Stamford, Connecticut. Sold more than $4 million in 1994, selling through the online service Prodigy, with only two million members. Typical 'hits' per day are between 25,000 and 30,000. Now consider that the Internet has over thirty million members." —*PC Week*
- "PC Financial Network has accounts with assets totaling more than $2.8 billion (6/95) from 100,000 online consumers." —*PC Week*

The Handel and Haydn Society, the oldest continuously performing arts organization in the country, is another success story. The Handel and Haydn Society was one of the first classical music organizations to get a Website in early 1995. Deb MacKinnon, associate director of audience development, decided to continue the society's Web presence during the 1996–1997 season. Why? Because it was a huge success during the 1995–1996 season. As Ms. MacKinnon points out, "Our Website paid for itself several times over in the number of ticket sales and orders we transacted from online leads. In addition, our organization was viewed as contemporary and cutting-edge as we reached out to new audiences for classical music. Most exciting was receiving e-mail from all over the globe. It has been a wondrous PR tool and will continue to be an integral part of our marketing campaign."

Ordering on the Net

One of the main reasons that the Internet and the WWW are so popular is that they enable businesses to take electronic orders for products. The fastest-selling items on the Internet are music CDs.

This should be good news to musicians. Buying tickets and booking reservations also appear to be doing quite well on the WWW. Taking orders electronically can save money on printing costs, telephone time, and personnel.

There are two ways to take orders over the Internet and WWW: e-mail and WWW forms.

E-mail offers an effective means for taking orders on the Internet. Since e-mail is the most rudimentary service the Internet has to offer, all forty million users have it. When you publicize your product or service via UseNet newsgroups or your WWW site, ask those interested to send a check to your mailing address or to e-mail their credit card number and its expiration date to your e-mail account. As e-mails come in, check credit cards for validity, place the orders, and send the user back some form of e-mail for acknowledgment. Using listservers, as described in chapter 20, "Intelligent Agents," you can create automatic response systems for users requesting ordering information.

Using WWW forms is another way to take orders. These interactive forms can be designed for the user to input data and information directly into fields. One advantage of forms is that you can e-mail the contents of a form to an e-mail address. Another advantage is that you can change the look and feel of your form at any time, without having to notify anyone. The forms are created in HTML as part of your Website. Many books are available that can show you how to design forms using HTML.

Cash Collection

Once you have an order, the next step is to determine how the customer will pay for it. There are three ways to collect payment from the customer. The first way is via credit cards. Most people are shocked to learn that they can make credit card orders over the Internet. People do transactions by phone or mail, so why not by the Internet? Credit card transactions via the Internet are not only possible, but are done every day. Credit card processing represents the easiest, quickest, and surest way of collecting payment on the Internet. In processing credit cards, the important questions are how is the information being transmitted, is it safe, and who is clearing and validating the card?

Credit card information is transmitted by typing the credit card number into a form and then sending that information in an encrypted format over the lines to the server (you) where the number is decrypted and made available for you to process. Credit cards can be cleared and validated either by you or by a credit card bureau. If you already have the capability to clear cards, then you are all set. If not, a bureau will charge somewhere on the average of 4 to 5 percent for processing the card.

The second way to collect payment is to accept checks. While credit cards are more convenient, some people will refuse to use credit cards over the Internet. This method is very much like normal mail. If you accept checks worldwide, specify that on your e-mail or interactive order form.

The third way to collect payment is through purchase orders. This requires a bit more work, but essentially the customer enters their account number and a password. These two pieces of information are tied to a pre-established line of credit. You look up their account number and directly charge that account number.

Order Fulfillment and Customer Service

Once an order has been processed, it is vital that the order be sent out efficiently and quickly. However, fulfilling an order over the Internet should not be any harder than filling mail or phone orders. If customer service is important, you can also set up a form-based system for your clients to check the status of their orders. Federal Express, for example, now allows you to check the status of any package using their Website, which has saved the company millions of dollars by reducing customer support calls. If you are an organization receiving hundreds of calls requesting the same information, it may be worthwhile to design a customer service strategy for using your Website. Chamber Music America, according to Dean K. Stein, the executive director, receives more than four hundred calls a week from its nearly twelve-thousand-person membership. Most of the calls are requests for basic information. A Website with an FAQ (Frequently Asked Questions) section would help reduce those calls.

Setting up and running a shop on the Internet can actually be easier than maintaining an actual storefront. Understanding the basic mechanics of taking orders, processing orders, and fulfilling those orders is the key.

6 Security

ALL OVER THE WORLD, PEOPLE ARE TAKING MORE PRECAUTIONS TO safeguard themselves and their property. The Internet and the WWW are not exempt from these problems. As time goes on and the Internet becomes more complex and more populated, you can expect to see more and more people looking for ways to use the Internet dishonestly. As Nicholas Negroponte points out, "The next decade will see cases of intellectual property abuse and invasion of privacy. We will experience digital vandalism, software piracy, and data thievery."

Know Thy Enemy

The Internet is a huge place that hosts more than forty million people. Unfortunately, not all of them are honest. Statistics show that only 10 percent of computer crime is reported and that a mere 2 percent of computer crime results in convictions. Losses from computer crime rose to more than $60 billion in 1995. Given the growth rate of the Internet, these numbers will only get worse.

There are some fundamental issues, myths, and truths behind crime on the Internet. There are two basic types of criminals: soft criminals and hard criminals. Soft criminals are like kids who ring doorbells and run away; they do things to see how far they can go without being caught. They are not seeking to do damage or to steal, but are merely seeking knowledge of how things work and are going about it the wrong way. Hard criminals, on the other hand, use the Internet and the Web to profit illegally. Such criminals often know all sorts of ways to hide their activities and may even band together to share the fruits of their illegal endeavors.

Generally, you do not need to be concerned with the first type of criminal. These soft criminals typically get tired of their games and eventually leave. The second group, the hard criminals, are a threat. A system as large as the Internet is not completely secure and does have holes and crevices that a hard criminal can take advantage of.

Within the group of hard criminals, the worst criminals could be those within your organization. A friend of mine who owned a major telecommunications company contacted me to help him with a security issue. He had an employee who set up his entire computer network. One day, this employee demanded that my friend immediately fire someone else in the organization or he would leave. Obviously, my friend, the owner of this $100 million company, was not going to be bullied and refused to fire the other individual. A few days later, the employee who made demands left. He left with various secret passwords into the entire company's computer system without any documentation or logs. It took a lot of money and time from security experts to close "holes" and "backdoors" this individual had left in the computer system.

After further investigation, the individual who left was found to have a history of joining a company and then leaving if his demands were not met. He had a history of using his knowledge of his employers' computer systems to make demands for salary raises, increased stock options, etc. The lesson is that your worst enemy could be someone already within the organization. The solution is to do thorough background checks on the individuals you hire to maintain you computer systems. Are they ethical? What do their previous employers say about them? Questions like these could prevent major security breaches.

Before you can begin to appreciate the specific crimes, you need to be familiar with some terms from the criminals themselves. The media has used the term "hacker" and uses it inappropriately. Hackers prefer "cracker," "phreak," "phracker," and "pirate" as the proper terms for people who participate in illegal activities involving computers and telecommunications systems.

A cracker is someone who breaks into computer systems by bypassing or guessing logins. Such criminals are a severe threat, because if they can gain access as a privileged user, they have access to incredible amounts of billing information, credit card numbers, and other highly personal data.

Phreaks, sometimes called "phone phreaks," are people who hack phone systems. These people are specifically trying to scam long-distance time, break into voice mail systems, or other phone-related intrusions.

A phracker is a combination of a phreak and a cracker. A phracker breaks into both phone systems and computer systems. A phracker specializes in total network destruction. Generally, phrackers tend to be worse than phreaks because they have more knowledge of advanced systems. Phrackers can bypass not only phone systems, but also computer systems.

Finally, data pirates tend to be computer oriented. Their forte is stealing commercial software, modifying it to run without needing serial numbers or other startup keys, and posting their data in warez sites. A warez site contains stolen software set aside for the downloading pleasure of all the pirate's friends and clients. Pirates place most warez sites on an innocent company's computer. This makes it hard to catch the pirates. This is similar to real-world pirates stashing stolen treasure in someone else's house or land, and retrieving the treasure secretly when it is convenient.

Common Crimes

There are three general types of crimes: misrepresentation, theft, and illegal transactions. Misrepresentation and fraud are sure to grow on the Internet. One of the reasons that misrepresentation will become a problem is that on the Internet it is so easy to appear as anyone or anything you want. The Internet is a great vehicle for breaking down discriminatory behavior because users do not have to reveal skin color or handicaps. The Internet is also a way for local businesses to sell their goods and services to a global audience. This same feature of the Internet also enables criminals to hide themselves or to present themselves as someone they are not, or to sell something that isn't what they claim it is.

Creating a scam Website, for example, is possible. Fortunately, it is not as easy as it might seem because the scam artist has to place the Website at an Internet provider's computer. Most providers know whose content they are hosting, and frequently examine sites since they have direct access to the information. Thus, it is relatively easy with the URL to trace the criminal right to the provider's door.

Theft can take many forms on the Internet. Phrackers or pirates can break into a system and take space on that system for themselves. Also, they can gain access to your system, steal credit card numbers, and use them to make illegal purchases. Another form of theft is to steal someone's access code in a private WWW site, log in as that person, and either steal, modify, or destroy data.

Intercepting communications between servers is yet another form of theft. This type of computer crime is perhaps the most feared, but is actually quite difficult to commit. The other forms of theft are more common.

Finally, plagiarism is also a form of theft on the Internet. Taking text, sound, images, or movies from a non–public domain source and using them without proper credit or permission is illegal. This type of theft is simple on the Internet, where copying a file is a matter of a click of the mouse and a few seconds of time. The WWW itself is especially vulnerable to plagiarism attacks. If plagiarists see a neat graphic or technique at a site, they can easily copy, or "borrow," it.

Illegal transactions are a totally different type of crime. There is a huge cry for servers that will make credit card transactions safe. But safe for whom? Although such servers might protect consumers from having their credit card information ripped off in midstream, they would do nothing to protect the store owner from criminals who use fraudulent credit card numbers or false identities. However, this exact same problem exists in the physical world.

Protection

Fraud and misrepresentation can be avoided in several ways. First, a company trying to commit fraud usually does not take time to create a proper cover. If you are shopping at a company, glancing at the URL can often be most revealing. Most large- and medium-size companies have their own domain names. Likewise, companies committing some type of fraud usually have little noncomputer access information, such as telephone numbers and addresses. Most legitimate companies advertise as much as possible and give e-mail, fax, phone, and address information. A toll-free phone number is a good sign. If you are unsure of the stability of a particular business, simply call the company's area code and check whether the business is listed in directory assistance. A call to the company itself can tell you a lot.

Everyone seems to fear having their credit card information stolen when they type it into a form requesting the card number on the Internet. Often, users type into a field and then continue their sessions. If the user then leaves the computer turned on and unattended, anyone who walks by that computer can go back to the Web page that required the credit card number and steal it. To avoid this problem, two solutions are available: do not leave your computer unattended in a public space, or request that the field for credit card entry is a password field, so that the number is never visible on the field when typed in.

To protect yourself from plagiarism, immediately register your material with the Register of Copyrights, Copyright Office, Washington, DC 20559. If your material has been plagiarized, document the theft's occurrence. So that you have solid proof, print out the Web page where the plagiarized material is hosted. Also document the originality of your work by showing the dates and times are earlier. With the proper documentation, simply call the offending party and inform them that you have ownership and that they should immediately cease using your material. If this does not work, simply take it to the offender's lawyer. With the proof, you should be able to obtain a settlement.

One of the simplest ways to safeguard against illegal transactions is to have your order-entry system checking credit card numbers against the credit card checksum standard. You can run this algorithm on any credit card number to determine whether it belongs to the valid sequence of numbers. Although the algorithms do not tell you whether the credit card is really a credit card, at least it prevents people from typing 11111111 as a credit card number and having it work.

Perhaps the best way to ensure that transactions over the Internet are protected is to make sure that there is a secure server. The most secure system is one that transmits information in an encrypted format.

Encryption

Encryption is a technique for hiding data so that it can be seen only by those for whom it is intended. Simple encryption schemes exchange one character for another. For example, the word "dcnngv" is an encrypted form of the word "ballet," where each letter in the word "ballet" has been incremented by two to create the encrypted form. Obviously, this type of encryption can be broken, and is not very secure.

Today there are much more complex encryption schemes that are virtually impossible to break. Thus, keeping data encrypted is a great way to secure that data. The encryption of digital documents ensures that sensitive information cannot be decoded even if messages are intercepted. This encryption is now available for the transmission of credit card information, etc. The technology can be used in the same way for the transmission of sensitive environmental information. The Internet's de facto standard for encryption is PGP, which stands for "Pretty Good Privacy." PGP lets you encrypt a message so that only the intended recipients can read it. There are also protocols that allow a message to be signed so that recipients can verify that it came from the supposed sender.

PGP is available for a range of platforms, including DOS, Macintosh, and UNIX. Encryption works by using coding and decoding keys, copies of which are (securely) sent to people whom you want to allow to read your encrypted messages. There is some doubt about the legality of using public domain versions of PGP outside the U.S., however, commercial versions are available. Encryption is increasingly being used on the Internet for banking transactions. First Virtual Bank, an Internet bank, uses this technology.

There are a variety of other technological solutions available that can give WWW users a measure of security that had been lacking earlier. Several WWW graphical interface providers, such as Netscape, are developing secure transmissions on the World Wide Web. Secure HTTP is an interoperable extension of the WWW's existing HyperText Transfer Protocol that provides communication and transaction security for WWW clients and servers. Secure HTTP works by a user clicking a "secure submit" button that causes a client program to generate encryption for the information on the form using the client's public key. The Netscape Web browser provides an encryption system called Secure Sockets Layer (SSL), based on the RSA Data Security's public-key algorithm, to scramble sensitive data. Basically, the SSL is a protocol layer that sits between the TCP/IP and HTTP protocols.

There are several other similar protocols available, and a committee of the W3C Consortium is looking at developing standards for the incorporation of authentication, message integrity, and privacy.

Break-in?

The best way to know if someone has broken into your system is to see if your information has been damaged. If you notice that there are garbage characters or missing pictures or elements, it is likely that either security has been breached or your provider has had a major problem.

You should insist that your provider or service bureau routinely check disk space usage, communications lines, login files, network statistics and logs, and, most importantly, that your provider have firewalls and wrappers.

Firewalls and Wrappers

When shopping for a service provider or a service bureau to host your Website, you should always ask them if they have either firewalls or wrappers. Firewalls are either software or hardware that protects ports and keeps pirates from penetrating security. Ports are access points to your computer. The function of a firewall is to allow only certain trusted domain names to access your system. Other domains simply get a "connection refused" message. By restricting the millions of domain names so that only one or two get in, you are instantly restricting access to your system from the outside.

Firewalls are not good for a Website because you want people to visit your Website. Firewalls are good on FTP and Telnet ports because these are the ways in which intruders can cause serious damage, by getting direct access to the data on your Website. Firewalls do little, however, to keep pirates internal to your system at bay or to keep out pirates sophisticated enough to fake a trusted domain name.

The second line of defense, wrappers, helps address this problem. Wrappers are available from the CERT site. CERT was created in 1988 by DARPA to address computer security incidents. CERT is currently run out of Carnegie-Mellon University in Pittsburgh, Pennsylvania, at *cert@cert.org*. Wrappers run as a layer of software around other software. In other words, a user FTPing to you would first get the wrapper, which would then engage the real FTP process. The user does not know that the wrapper exists and cannot detect any difference in the system. In other words, wrappers can act as firewalls and actually refuse users based on their login names. Wrappers can be used to keep out the known criminals. Set up correctly, a wrapper can be a pirate's worst nightmare.

New laws to regulate the Internet are in the works. We are entering a period of major confusion and infighting within the legislative branches and courts in the U.S. and abroad as the new freedoms of the Internet are ironed out. The most critical issues facing the courts today with regard to the Internet are: What does privacy mean? What does copyright mean? How can we handle the fact that there are no national boundaries? What differentiates obscenity from art?

Many court battles have already begun. As they continue, laws will come and go. The issue will be who really creates the new laws: will it be a few politicians or the citizens of the Internet? I favor the latter. The Internet has a social etiquette that has developed without government intervention. Perhaps this organic force will be the basis of the new laws.

▼

7 Copyright

THE PROTECTION OF COPYRIGHT AND INTELLECTUAL PROPERTY ON THE Internet will be one of the most important and hotly contested issues of the new millennium. This strikes at the core of our entire current economic system, which is based on the ownership of property and remuneration for the use of that property.

► One Step at a Time

Every time I have given a talk to creative people who produce intellectual property, the question "How will my stuff be protected on the Internet?" invariably pops up. The simplest way to protect intellectual property and copyright on the Internet is to attach a copyright infringement notice with the data, similar to that done with books. This notice could be of the form:

> This data is copyrighted—for holders of copyright, see individual records. The data is made available for the purposes of research, environmental information, and educational activities. Any use of the data for other purposes, including for all commercially related activities, must have permission of the individual data custodians. Any

use of the data must acknowledge the holder of copyright as data custodian.

This notice obviously won't prohibit someone from infringing the copyright; however it does provide a recourse through the courts if necessary, and makes users aware that the data is copyrighted. Generally these methods won't dissuade the dishonest user.

So is there a way to protect the artist and the creator and producer of information and intellectual property? Ever since I have been on the Internet, I have been perplexed by the conundrum of digitized property. The problem is this: if digitized property can be reproduced and distributed all over the planet without cost, without our knowledge, without its even leaving our possession, how can we protect it? How are we going to be paid for the work we do with our minds? And, if we can't get paid, what will assure the continued creation and distribution of such work?

As John Barlow states, "Since we don't have a solution to what is a profoundly new kind of challenge, and are apparently unable to delay the galloping digitization of everything not obstinately physical, we are sailing into the future on a sinking ship. This vessel, the accumulated canon of copyright and patent law, was developed to convey forms and methods of expression entirely different from the vaporous cargo it is now being asked to carry. It is leaking as much from within as from without."

The Real Issue

The creation of multimedia content and digital libraries raises profound issues with regard to notions of copyright and intellectual property. John Perry Barlow remarks that "notions of property, value, ownership, and the nature of wealth itself are changing more fundamentally than at any time since the Sumerians first poked cuneiform into wet clay and called it stored grain. Only a very few people are aware of the enormity of this shift, and fewer of them are lawyers or public officials. Those who do see these changes must prepare responses for the legal and social confusion that will erupt as efforts to protect new forms of property with old methods become more obviously futile, and, as a consequence, more adamant."

The real issue at stake is, can property ownership and freedom of communication commingle in a medium as vast and as fluid as Internet? This is the real issue. Many antiproperterians take the position that since shared information still resides with its creator long after it has been passed along, trying to treat information as an object is a flawed approach. Creativity, they argue, does not depend on a government-granted monopoly. "Consulting, support, performance, and service—these are all ways in which creators can make money of their abilities without appealing to intellectual property rights," reads one private citizen's recent posting on a UseNet newsgroup. "Removing such rights would not deny creators the right to profit from their labors; it would, however, allow all of society to share in the benefits of their work."

The other issue is that information is, by nature, intangible and hard to define. Like other such deep phenomena as light or matter, it is a natural host to paradox. Attorney and copyright expert Pamela Samuelson tells of having attended a conference convened around the fact that Western countries may legally appropriate the music, designs, and biomedical lore of aboriginal people without compensation to their tribes of origin, since those tribes are not an "author" or "inventor."

"But soon most information will be generated collaboratively by the cyber-tribal hunter-gatherers of cyberspace," as John Barlow says, "and perhaps our arrogant legal dismissal of the rights of 'primitives' will soon return to haunt us."

Four Views

Before we can develop any new methods to resolve the core issue, it is important to understand the landscape of cyberspace and how Internet users deal with this issue today. First, cyberspace has no national or local boundaries to contain the scene of a crime and to determine the method of its prosecution; worse, no clear cultural agreements define what a crime might be. Basic unresolved differences between Western and Asian cultural assumptions about intellectual property can only be exacerbated when many transactions are taking place in both hemispheres, yet, somehow, in neither. There appear to be four groups of views by the users of the Internet on this issue:

- *Information Wants to be Free.* These people believe there should be no copyrights or other protections of intellectual property; everything made publicly available should be public domain.
- *Right of Attribution.* These people believe that the only rights owed to authors and creators is the right of attribution; otherwise, all information is free.
- *Limited Use Rights.* These people believe that copyright has validity, but minor infringing behavior, whether "fair use" or not, should be legal.
- *Strong IP Regimes.* These people adhere strictly to intellectual property protections.

As Lance Rose has pointed out, no one segment dominates the

other; rather, we can expect that each segment will continue to attract adherents well into the future. The issue then becomes whether copyright laws should be extended to override the beliefs of people in categories A and B, or if we want to conform primarily to the behavior of people in categories C and D.

How to Protect Your Property

There are five ways of protecting property in cyberspace to varying degrees.

The first way is what I call full protection. Full protection is simple. Just don't put your property on the Internet.

The second way to protect property is using the copyright statement shown above. This will serve as a deterrent but is not 100 percent guaranteed.

The third way to protect property is by using the power of the Internet community. Until the West was fully settled and "civilized" in this century, order was established according to an unwritten code, which had the fluidity of common law rather than the rigidity of statutes. Ethics were more important than laws. Understandings were preferred over laws, which were, in any event, largely unenforceable. There is a strong tradition on the Internet to develop user norms and practices in an almost ad hoc, yet slightly anarchistic, fashion. Fair use norms on the Internet include forwarding e-mail messages, or a portion thereof; quoting portions of UseNet and mailing list postings; and making private noncommercial copies of texts downloaded from FTP, Gopher, or Websites. In most instances, Internet denizens adhere to rules of netiquette and commonsense practices that do not violate acceptable net practices. Flagrant disregard for net rules can result in net "community policing" and admonishments by fellow "netters" to follow ethical practices.

Internet culture abides by netiquette, which may itself serve to keep a violator of copyright in check. If someone submits an infringing posting to a newsgroup, for example, the Internet's response is egalitarian and swift: the poster may be publicly flamed, privately chastised, or even added to the user's "bozo filter," and henceforth blocked from that UseNet. These norms of netiquette can also be used to deter intellectual property violations. Stealing someone's artwork or image from a Website, for example, may also be subject to the Internet's rebuke. If a conscientious citizen on the Internet sees a piece of stolen property appearing on another Website, that citizen can either notify the offender, or the victim, or both. Note that as the Internet population has exploded, this trait of self-policing and netiquette has not yet abated. Rather, it appears to have remained an integral part of the socialization process of the Internet.

The fourth way to protect property is through advanced technological solutions. One method uses strong cryptographic algorithms. This method gives an electronic publisher even stronger control than that exercised by most traditional publishers. The use of encryption technology will allow for copyright statements to be encrypted into the document and thus be transferred with the document wherever it goes. The prodigious Ted Nelson, who coined the term "hypertext" in 1964 and conceived of Project Xanadu (a virtual repository for the textual, visual, and auditory artifacts of civilization), has formulated a novel approach to the copyright problem. In his Public Access Xanadu (PAX) system, documents are encoded with accounting software, which tally royalty payments and bill patrons' accounts accordingly. Royalty fees will buy fair use privileges for the documents or portions thereof, and the patrons' monthly bill include connect time, storage and transmission charges, and publication fees, crediting royalties from others for work read online—basically, a pay-by-the-byte system. Systems like this one are now online.

The fifth way of protecting property on the Internet is either to craft new laws or bolster existing ones. This was the approach taken in the Green Paper on "Intellectual Property and the National Information Infrastructure," which was released by the Working Group on Intellectual Property Rights in July 1994. The paper recommended that the Copyright Act of 1976 be amended slightly to accommodate the advent of digital information. Specifically, the paper recommended that digital transmission of a copy of a copyrighted work be considered an act of copyright infringement; "first sale" rules for works transmitted digitally be abolished; and copyright infringement could be construed if technological devices are used to circumvent copy-protection schemes that copyright owners have created. Legislation is now being developed based on the Green Paper.

For those interested in learning other ways of protection, Tad Crawford, attorney and publisher, has co-authored *The Writer's Legal Guide* (Allworth Press). This guide offers both historical and practical information on dealing with the issue of copyright. The guide also addresses how to protect all types of multimedia objects, including text, graphics, and audio.

Copyright of Hyperlinks?

How will copyright be adjudicated and managed for hypertext links? The explosion of WWW servers and the increase in WWW traffic (now the fastest growing part of the Internet, with an exponential increase in registered servers over the last eighteen months), poses new intellectual property questions. Some say that these hypertext links create a value-added service to the main document containing the links. The question is: will the author of the link document want compensation when someone traverses his or her own links? Does the author of a link document infringe copyrights in the works to which links have been created as unauthorized derivative works? Does a user of someone else's links infringe any copyright interest of the link author?

Authors of hypertext links would, of course, like to be free from claims of infringement for linking portions of other authors' documents, yet be able to assert copyright control over traversals of their links by other users. Obviously, an issue such as this one can become quite tricky. The issue, moreover, exemplifies the kinds of complexities that the WWW introduces in terms of copyright law.

Using Copyrighted Material

If you are going to use material on the Internet for which you do not own a copyright, then you must obtain permission from the copyright holder. This usually means contacting the copyright holder and obtaining permission in writing to use the material. This may sometimes incur a charge. For material subject to U.S. copyright law, the Online Copyright Clearance Center has been set up to help with obtaining permissions, "ease permissions burdens, and consolidate payments for rights holders."

Other Problems

The copyright scheme is not especially well suited to assigning ownership interests when there is collective development. We have already seen this problem in multimedia, to which the copyright clearance process could provide some relief, but there remains the difficult issues arising from "message bases," digital sampling, and product produced by groupware.

The creation of multimedia works will, in many instances, depend upon securing copyright in an economically feasible manner, while guaranteeing that creators are justly compensated for their works and that the moral integrity of their work is kept intact. The concept of copyright in the electronic environment is therefore legally challenging and socially provocative.

Publicity

8 The Basics

A WEBSITE IS ONLY AS GOOD AS THE NUMBER AND KIND OF PEOPLE WHO come to it. If you have spent a great deal of time getting on the Internet and building your Website, you cannot afford to ignore the importance of cyberpublicity. Cyberpublicity is the art and science of promoting your presence in cyberspace and getting the kind of exposure you need. Cyberpublicity will also serve to give you statistics on the number of people who visit your site. Thus you can gain useful demographic information on the people visiting your Website.

Who Am I?

The first step in cyberpublicity is to determine who you are. You should take some time to think about it. I normally recommend that clients take some paper and a pen, or word processor and keyboard, and jot down the words or phrases that describe them. Most people or businesses know who they are, but they have never tried to categorize themselves using words and concepts. The end product of this exercise should be one paragraph, at most fifty words, describing who you are; up to twenty keywords that characterize your organization; and up to ten words that describe the broad categories that are related to your organization.

Recently, I helped to cyberpublicize a small business owner who owns and operates an independent record label. He wrote a fifty-word statement describing who he was, the mission of the label, and the kinds of musicians it serviced. Next, he gave me twenty keywords. These twenty words were: "new age, music, soft, easy listening, contemporary, New York, haunting, award-winning, Celtic, musician, guitar, flute, vocal, piano, sitar, Indian, bamboo, Grammy." These keywords reflected the traits of the organization. Finally, he gave me a list of ten words describing the categories under which his organization could be indexed: "weddings, concerts, labels, distributors, retailer, music, awards, entertainment, Celtic, Indian."

This type of information is central to starting a cyberpublicity campaign. Take time to get the keywords and categories right before proceeding.

Netiquette

Once you have taken the time to figure out who you are, you are ready to start your cyberpublicity campaign. But before taking any direct action, you need to understand the nature of your medium and the rules of the game. As mentioned earlier, users of the Internet, including the WWW and UseNet, are expected to follow a set of guidelines for their behavior called netiquette. The complete guide to netiquette is available through another newsgroup called *news.announce.newusers,* which has articles on the latest guidelines. Before you begin to communicate your information using e-mail, newsgroups, or the WWW, I encourage you to read the articles at that newsgroup thoroughly.

One netiquette rule is that insulting, degrading, or racist comments are intolerable, unless you are in one of the underground "alt" newsgroups. It is also important to keep your communications succinct. If you are excerpting or quoting someone else's article in your communication, keep the excerpt short and relevant to your communication. Despite what newspapers and some PR companies say, newsgroups are really not for promoting business items, advertisements, get-rich-quick schemes, or other similar postings. Blatant postings to solicit customers are unequivocally condemned. It is acceptable, however, to mention a service, Website, local store, or company in the context of the rest of the articles posted in a newsgroup. Direct soliciting is considered forbidden. Multilevel marketing schemes, form letters, and other such methods are a major breach of netiquette. While the users of the Internet may not have direct control of what you communicate, the Internet is very quick to condemn that kind of behavior.

Cross Links

Linking your Website to other related sites and directories is the first step in your cyberpublicity campaign. The maximum of ten words you chose earlier to describe your Website helps identify which WWW directories and indexes to which your site should be linked. You should post your site address to as many relevant directories and indexes as possible. I always encourage clients to post their Website address to the top-five WWW search engines: Yahoo, WebCrawler, Lycos, InfoSeek, and Excite. It costs you nothing to post on these directories.

Surf the Internet to find other Websites similar to yours. There are many other sites that can serve as perfect jump sites to your own. Once you find a site that attracts a similar audience to yours, find the e-mail account of the Webmaster, or the person in charge of running the Website. Send an e-mail to this person asking for a reciprocal hyperlink. A reciprocal hyperlink is like saying, "You scratch my back, I'll scratch yours." Tell them that you will provide a hyperlink to their site if they provide one to yours. This is a great way to become known within your audience and narrowcast on the Internet. Having your Website posted at other popular sites similar to yours can make your site popular overnight.

Newsgroups

The next major area to post your Website address is at UseNet newsgroups on the Internet. These are, as previously mentioned, very specific groups that are easy to subscribe to and post messages on. There is a discussion group for almost any topic imaginable. By analyzing the words and categories you use to describe yourself, you should be able to find the newsgroups that are relevant to you. Some of these newsgroups reach hundreds of thousands of users every day, so make sure your postings are well thought out.

If you have experimented with newsgroups, which is a prerequisite, you will notice that the most effective postings are well-reasoned, logical, properly laid out, have good grammar and spelling, and don't ramble. Try to follow the same pattern. Remember, some users coming to the Internet via one of the other online services, such as America Online or Microsoft Network, are paying by the hour to receive their newsgroup information. Nothing will annoy them more than receiving long and pointless postings. Keep this in mind when you write. Some subjects need many lines of explanation, but do not use up valuable space to say nothing.

Good grammar and spelling are sometimes difficult to maintain when typing quickly, but do try. Your presentation reflects the image and credibility you have worked hard to create. Construct sentences properly. An odd spelling mistake is easily tolerated; a message full of them will invite disdain. Make sure that you post informative messages to the group. Any message directly promoting your Website is not considered proper netiquette.

In terms of netiquette, the best method of promoting your Website is to participate in an ongoing newsgroup discussion. At the bottom of each article you post, make sure your signature has your Website address. A signature is a several-line block of text that can be added to any article that you post on a newsgroup. Using signatures, as described above, is an accepted form of advertisement that will bring many people to your site. Do not just join a newsgroup and leave a message like, "Hi! My name is _____, come visit my Website at _____" You will suffer the wrath of that newsgroup. Become an active participant in the group's discussion and offer information to the newsgroup. Find ways of talking about your Website in the context of the newsgroup's discussion. You will get what you give. It is true that this kind of interaction may take more time than simply posting your Website address on a directory or search engine, but it will be well worth it.

Cross-Publicize

As long as there is a physical world, do not ignore traditional means of marketing your Website address. Publicity should not exist in a vacuum, and cyberpublicity is no exception. If you spend money to set up your online presence, then protect that investment by promoting your online Website address in brochures, at performances, shows, in press releases, etc. Start using your new Website address in your current advertising and on your business cards.

Mention your Website address in your radio spots and magazines or newspaper ads. If you do it right, you will actually be adding value to your traditional publicity by enabling people to go to cyberspace to get more information about you. Such cross-publicity increases the value of your traditional advertising. Think about it; it would cost you a fortune to place all the information on your Website in print or on TV or radio ads. The promotion of your Website address on traditional publicity materials is like providing a physical hyperlink to your cyberspace billboard.

Hold Promotional Offers

Hold promotional offers on your site. Offer discounts on products or tickets for customers who visit your Website. Promotional offers are a way to continue the cycle of cyberpublicity on a regular basis. It will not be sufficient to cyberpublicize only once. By creating promotional offers or new features, you can have reason to continue the cycle of cyberpublicity.

Guest Book and E-Mail

Internet publicity is based on feedback from your audience. This is a key difference from traditional publicity. Guest book and e-mail forwarding can give you feedback from your Website visitors.

A guest book can be a simple form containing fields such as name, address, phone, e-mail address, and zip code that you can ask Website visitors to fill out when they visit your site. Most visitors will not fill out such a form unless you either offer them something (a promotional offer) or ask them a question that requires their input. You need to be clever and creative to get people to fill out your guest book. You could, for example, give a visitor 5 to 10 percent off the price of tickets, CDs, purchases, etc., for filling out the guest book. Guest book entries become a valuable resource. The entries become a mailing list of future clients.

Adding an e-mail forwarding link to your Website is a must. An e-mail forwarding link will allow visitors to contact you directly. Visitors can give their comments on your Website, as well as feedback on the service or product you provide.

Acquiring Demographics

Unlike traditional publicity and advertising, the Internet lets you know, numerically, how effective your publicity efforts are. The Internet maintains log files. These log files can be used to determine the number of unique visitors coming to your site. Each entry in the log file is stamped with the date, time, and IP address of a remote visitor. One big mistake many people make is to count each entry in the log file as a unique visitor to the Website. Each entry in the log file records everything from the user accessing text to images; therefore, a single user requesting a single document might actually result in several entries in the log file as the document and images associated with the document are being received.

Suppose, for example, you run an art gallery on the WWW. You may have done all your cyberpublicity on WWW directories, newsgroups, etc., and are now interested in knowing how many unique users are coming to your site. You should ask your provider for the log file. When you receive the log file, you can either get an expert to help you analyze it or you can make estimates. Teaching you to analyze log files is beyond the scope of this book; however, there is one quick method to estimate the number of unique users.

First, determine how many images, on average, you have per page on your Website. Suppose, for example, you have an average of ten images per Web page. If you have ten thousand entries in the log file, simply divide the number of entries by the number of images. This will give you a total of one thousand unique users to your Website. This is an approximation. If you do learn to read log files, you can ascertain which parts of your Website are heavily trafficked and which are not.

The most accurate way to find out the number of hits you receive per page on your Website is with a page counter. A page counter simply increases the number each time the page is viewed by the user. Because each page on the Website can have its own counter, you can easily see how many times each page has been accessed. You probably have seen counters throughout the WWW. Page counters have another advantage. They tell users how many people have visited your site. You can, therefore, build perceived value in displaying such information. Implementing page counters involves some special programming. You should ask an expert to assist you in implementing a page counter on your Website.

In addition to using log files and page counters, forms, such as guest books, are great for generating demographic information. How do you get someone to fill out a form? The most obvious way is to ask questions in a form that a user fills out and submits to you via e-mail. You can then collate the information and use it in any way you like. There are many types of demographics that you can solicit in this manner. You can ask questions about improving your site—whether it is too slow, whether it provides enough graphics, too many graphics, or whether it is easy to use. Internet users, in general, like to give their opinion. Once you get demographic information, you can use the standard methods of market analysis to understand your audience. A good database system can help in collating the information you receive from your forms.

Cyberpublicity is both an art and a science. The preceding discussion has laid the foundations for cyberpublicity and should serve as a guide for your Internet and marketing promotions effort. There is, however, a lot more to discuss in terms of the intricacies of effective marketing planning.

Plan Your Publicity

Online and offline publicity helps your business rise above the noise level on the Internet, but it takes planning and preparation. Publicity is an ongoing part of your marketing program, not a one-shot effort you make when you launch your business. With a proper publicity plan, you have goals for how you want your company portrayed in the media over the long term, and some tactics, weapons, and targets that will help you achieve those goals. With a good plan, you'll generate important coverage of your business at exactly the right time and in exactly the right places.

Key Elements of a Good Publicity Plan

Here are the key elements of a good publicity plan.

- *A competitive analysis.* The art of publicity is creating published articles or TV and radio coverage that casts your company in a favorable light. To begin, you'll want to know how your company and its competition are perceived by and presented in the media now. Study newspapers, magazines, and online publications related to your business for news of your competition and your own company to find out how each of you are being presented in the press. List every company that has been covered in one article or another (along with the name of each article's author), and then list some key messages that are being conveyed by the publicity that's been done so far. This analysis will give you a good sense of the current publicity climate, so you'll know what has to be done to change it.

- *Key messages.* List some of the main qualities or advantages you want reflected in media stories about your company. Think in terms of competing with other firms. Cast your key messages in terms of your adversaries, such as "Higher quality than Acme Widget." Your goal is to have these key messages reported or implied in any news story that's done about your company.
- *Press materials.* Make a list of materials you'll distribute to members of the press, and then prepare them. You will probably send out a press kit, which includes some background about your company, products, and key personnel, one or more press releases about the specific events you're publicizing, and perhaps some product photos or slides. Use black-and-white four-by-five-inch photos of people, and color slides of products.
- *Publicity targets.* List all the magazines, newsletters, newspapers, and TV or radio stations you want to target as outlets for publicity about your company. Don't limit yourself to the obvious targets or major national publications. Go to a large library and research all the magazines that might cover your area of business. Phone or write each publication and obtain a copy of their editorial calendar, which tells you the deadlines for each section of the magazine or newspaper and also alerts you if there's a special editorial focus for an upcoming issue. And don't just target a publication—target a specific department and editor at each publication.
- *Story ideas.* For each one of your publicity targets, create a specific story idea or pitch. Your publicity plan should list story ideas that fit the editorial focus of each publication or department you target. Use the editorial calendars to tailor your pitches for specific issues of specific publications.
- *A media calendar.* This is your timetable for preparing publicity pitches and directing them to specific targets. You'll use the media calendar to make sure you have prepared press materials and story ideas for any particular media target and have sent them off in time to have an article actually written before the publication's deadline.

A proper publicity plan lets you map out a strategy for your publicity efforts several months or even a year in advance. Once you've identified your goals and targets, you can use the plan as a set of marching orders for carrying out your attack. A good and steady stream of publicity is a powerful advantage for your company in cyberspace, and a good plan is the key.

In this chapter we have covered some of the fundamentals of Internet publicity. Before proceeding further, it is important to understand the unique nature of the Internet medium itself.

▼

9 New Media

MANY MAJOR CORPORATIONS HAVE STARTED A NEW GROUP WITHIN THEIR own organization to solve problems in advertising on the Internet. This new group typically is called the New Media group. Such groups are grappling with the problems of how to build effective Websites and how to promote them. For these organizations, the challenge is to shift from the traditional advertising paradigms, to which they have become accustomed for more than ten decades, to the new paradigm of the Internet and interactive communication.

In the preceding chapters I have used the phrase "level playing field" to describe the egalitarian features of the Internet. On the level playing field of the Internet, an individual and a major multibillion-dollar corporation stand shoulder to shoulder. Each has the same constraints as well as ease of access to the Internet. For small businesses and organizations that have limited budgets for marketing and promotion, this level playing field offers a unique opportunity to give the majors in the industry some serious competition.

In some ways, individuals and small businesses may have a distinct advantage. Major companies and advertising agencies are used to traditional advertising. They are not used to the features of the interactive communication that the Internet offers; however, many major corporations, such as AT&T, JC Penney, Hasbro, John Hancock, and others, are investing millions to take advantage of interactive communication. Those who can learn the elements of interactive communication on the Internet will have a significant advantage over the established mass media forces.

Traditional Advertising

Not too long ago, I gave a talk at J. Walter Thompson (JWT), the second largest advertising agency in the world. I discussed the differences between traditional advertising and interactive communication. JWT, even today, has not made full use of the Internet or the WWW for its multibillion-dollar clientele. Why not? There are two reasons. One is that traditional advertising agencies, such as JWT, are already making billions of dollars in traditional media, such as TV, print, and radio, and don't see why they should become interactive. The second is that they are still not clear, with all due respect to JWT and other traditional advertising agencies, about how to create interactive communication. Thinking interactive requires effort and unlearning old ways. Learning new ways requires even more effort.

Traditional advertising is based on the reduction of information. Lots of information about a product or service is funneled through a narrow bandwidth of extremely costly TV, print, and radio advertising to create a thirty-second sound bite, a sexy photograph, a jingle, or a saying like "Let go my Butterfinger." The viewer never really knows the product, but neurons in the viewer's brain have been indelibly stamped with the short sound bite or image.

Traditional advertising is unidirectional. The advertiser finds a market for a product or service, creates a message, and splatters that message as far and wide as possible. The receiver of that message can either listen to it or not. There are few other choices. The advertiser is in the driver's seat. The viewer can go for the ride or get off. There is no room for audience response. There is no way to track accurately who heard the message.

Traditional advertising is costly. It is for the few and the rich. There is a finite number of TV stations, radio stations, and major magazines. Getting prime-time access to traditional means of advertising is cost-prohibitive for most businesses and organizations. When it comes to reaching a global audience, there is no level playing field in the world of traditional advertising.

Interactive Communication

I have used the word "communication" rather than "advertising" in conjunction with the word "interactive." Interactive communication is getting closer to real communication. Real communication is not just one person listening and the other person spouting out information, as in traditional advertising. True communication involves the mutual exchange of information and ideas.

Interactive communication is bidirectional. In an interactive situation, I am offered the chance to respond and make choices as to what I do or do not want to hear. I can ask questions and explore what interests me. On the Internet, for example, a user can communicate interactively by leaving e-mail messages, filling out forms, and even leaving notes in guest books to indicate likes and dislikes.

Interactive communication is personalized. On an Internet Website, if I don't like the look of the Web page, I can leave. If I like something, I can follow certain hyperlinks and probe deeper. Someone else coming to the same Website may have a very different experience than I did, based on what each of us chose to explore.

Interactive communication costs pennies compared to traditional advertising. On the Internet, a Website can be developed and maintained for pennies relative to the cost of developing a traditional marketing campaign. A Website can also be updated as frequently as desired.

In interactive communication the customer is in control, not the advertiser. This is a major paradigm shift from the world of traditional advertising. In interactive communication, the deliverer of a message must be a communicator of relevant, appealing, and up-to-date information. If not, the customer will come to a Website and hop to one of a million sites (or channels) that are available in a fraction of a second. This feature has made some people call the Internet "clickatron" because at the click of a mouse button, a user could be halfway around the world.

Interactive communication is about "infotainment" or "edutainment." Unlike traditional advertising, which is the reduction of information, the paradigm for interactive communication is to inform and educate. The best Websites make informing and educating the audience fun and entertaining. A Website should be organized for the user to explore information as deeply as they want to go.

Everyone Is a Publisher

As mentioned above, interactive communication demands that the provider of the information makes it relevant, appealing, and current. If one simply views their presence on the Internet, such as a Website, as a form of advertising in its traditional sense, success on the Internet will be slim. When building an Internet presence, you should view yourself as a publisher not an advertiser. This means that you have to provide relevant content, make changes to that content, and find ways to build a circulation (or increase traffic to the Website). If the content of an Internet Website has not changed for some time, for example, the audience for that site will steadily decline. The model of traditional advertising does not make all of these demands. Imagine that an advertiser had to change its TV ad every week? That advertiser would soon be out of business.

Advances in hardware technology are also further supporting the paradigm of publisher versus advertiser. The Internet, and the latest advances in low-cost computer hardware and equipment (scanners, CD-ROM readers and writers, video digitizing boards, and sound boards), are enabling many individuals and small businesses to become literally one-person publishers and "broadcasting" stations. Anyone with the right talent and hardware can become a publisher or create a radio station or TV station producing interactive communications that are current, appealing, and personal. This is what is meant by a level playing field.

Many journalists who understand this feature of the Internet and the low-cost desktop publishing technologies are concerned. As one journalist commented:

> Talking about journalism in this world is a whole other matter. Part of the reality is that we're funded by advertising, and you don't pay the full cost of all those wonderful stories we send out to you. In fact, you pay about 20 percent of the cost of them, and advertisers pay the other 80 percent. But, suddenly, if all of you become broadcasters—and it's very cheap for you to do it—all you need is a personal computer that you can buy for $1,000, a modem, a phone line. What's left for us? And where do we get the funding to have all of our talented journalists out gathering news and delivering it to you? To me, that's the big question. There's an economic question here of how traditional journalism continues. . . . So, the world is changing in a very rapid and dramatic way. I believe it's going to be good for democracy and good for the country. I'm not sure if it's going to be good for journalism.

Michael Hawley, a professor at the media laboratory at the Massachusetts Institute of Technology, looks forward to the democratization of communication. In a recent interview with the *New York Times*, he said, "In the past, producing information for broadcast media has required so many resources to become a George Lucas, that there can only be a few each century. The Internet is turning that upside down. In the future everyone will be able to contribute their useful bit."

Others, such as John Barlow, lyricist for the Grateful Dead, point out the current problems with broadcasting and traditional media in terms of tracking audience response. He says:

> All of the broadcast-support models are flawed. Support from either advertisers or government has almost invariably tainted the purity of the goods delivered. Besides, direct marketing is gradually killing the advertiser-support model anyway. Broadcast media gave us

another payment method for a virtual product: the royalties that broadcasters pay songwriters through such organizations as ASCAP and BMI. But, as a member of ASCAP, I can assure you this is not a model that we should emulate. The monitoring methods are wildly approximate. It doesn't really work. Honest.

Unlike traditional advertising and broadcasting, the Internet enables its users to receive exact numbers, or hit counts, on the number of people visiting a Website. Broadcast media guesses at best. The Internet can offer more accurate and reliable statistics for both advertisers and users without guesswork. For commerce and business, this capability will have significant impact.

Broadcasting vs. Narrowcasting

Many of you have heard the term "broadcasting." How many have heard the term "narrowcasting"? J. C. R. Licklider coined the term in his 1960 report to the Carnegie Commission on the future of television. It is a term that is being resurrected to describe another feature of the Internet's leveling of the playing field. Broadcasting refers to the method of reaching as many people as possible using traditional advertising. Narrowcasting refers to the method of making one's communication available to a niche-targeted audience. The Internet is to narrowcasting as today's TV is to broadcasting.

I'll give you a simple example. An emerging national poet, Richard Cambridge, recently finished a series of poems he wrote during his experience of nicotine withdrawal. His poems, the *Cigarette Papers*, were used by some medical therapy groups to help in healing others from nicotine withdrawal and breaking addictions. He wanted a way to reach as many of the other medical therapy groups as possible with his poems. In early 1996, he developed a Website on the WWW and narrowcasted his WWW address to other addiction and medical therapy groups. Poetry for use by medical therapists? Anyone will admit that is a niche market. Such niche marketing, or narrowcasting, would have been impossible with traditional media. On the Internet, using publicity, such narrowcasting becomes not only possible but also cost-effective.

Thus, the elements of narrowcasting, the features of interactive communication, and the ability for each of us to become publishers are democratizing communication. There are two factors that will determine the future leveling of the playing field and the continued democratization of communication. One is the price of hardware. Based on recent history, it appears that hardware prices will continue to fall. This can only benefit the consumer. The second factor is accessibility to the Internet.

Most organizations, which struggle to raise money for their marketing budgets, can make those marketing dollars go a long way if they become participants, creators, and producers, rather than just consumers of information. This is what the Internet and interactive communication are all about.

10 Designing the Website

AS I MENTIONED BEFORE, THERE ARE A FEW ADVERTISING AGENCIES THAT are going interactive. One of them, Bollinger + Bonsels in Berne, Switzerland, recently published their "Ten Commandments of Internet Advertising." I would like to share them with you. They point out some of the important aspects of a Website.

The "Ten Commandments" are:

1. Become a publisher and provide valuable information.
2. If you don't have valuable information to provide, you are just not being creative.
3. If you don't have money for advertising, the Web is the medium to choose.
4. All business is global, but culture is local.
5. Don't worry about the target audience, but do care about them.
6. Don't waste your audience's time and money.
7. Lay tracks, and you'll be found.
8. Advertising on the Internet is a relationship, not a one-night stand.
9. Do it right the first time.
10. The future is not waiting for you, nor is the competition.

The design of a Web page is key to inviting visitors to return to your Website. In this chapter, we discuss twelve Web page design decisions your business or organization will need to make. As a business owner or organization director trying to design a system of Web pages, you have unique needs. I'll try to guide you through the process. When you're finished, you'll know a lot more about what goes into Web page design. You'll also have a set of design decisions to guide your own HTML adventures and to give to your local Web-page designer.

The Twelve Decisions

Together we'll examine together these twelve decisions:

1. Purpose
2. Main page and site organization
3. Site and domain names
4. Main graphic to highlight your site
5. Background color or texture
6. Basic page elements
7. Finishing touches
8. Photos and graphics
9. Forms to get customer response
10. Uploading and testing your pages
11. Registering and advertising your site
12. Maintaining your site

1. Purpose: Why Do You Want to Do This?

You'll save a lot of time and money by being honest with yourself right at the beginning. Just why are you doing this? What do you hope to achieve? What is your purpose? The checklist below may help you identify your purpose:

- "The World Wide Web is hot. Everybody is getting a Web presence. I'd better do it, too, or be left behind." This may represent your thinking, but you need more focus.
- We want potential customers to learn about our company, and gain a favorable impression of us.
- We want to develop a qualified list of prospects for our goods and services.
- We want to sell products directly from our Web pages.

Begin with patience and the long-term view. Your business results from the WWW may be immediate and spectacular. Then again, you may not make much of an impact right away. Be ready to be successful, but realize that some products and services don't lend themselves to this medium. Talk to your Web designer about how similar types of businesses are using the Web. Identify and state your purpose for developing your Website in one simple sentence.

2. Main Page and Site Organization

Some people call this a "home page." I like to think of it as your "storefront" on the World Wide Web marketplace. The main page provides an index to the set of pages that describe your business or organization. Your Web-page system on your Website will have several main sections, such as:

- *About Your Organization.* This section may include a vision or mission statement, history of your business, a philosophy of how you do business, etc. Sell the customer on why he or she should do business with you rather than with your competitor.

- *Product Lines.* With photos and text, describe the benefits of your goods and services to your customers. You can also show features, applications, or examples. Use a major branch for each major product line. You can also use your Web pages as a catalog, which you can update easily, inexpensively, and frequently.
- *Technical Support.* Some businesses find it useful to provide technical information, specifications, frequently asked questions, parts lists and diagrams, troubleshooting decision trees, etc.
- *How to Order.* This will include a form that e-mail's your customer's information to you.
- *Service Section.* This is free information of interest to your potential customers that will keep them coming back to your site for updates. It might be news of your industry, of a related field, or something unique or interesting. Give some thought to what service or services your Website will provide to draw customers to your storefront again and again.
- *What's New.* This section is where you put updates or new editions of a newsletter.

One of the first things your Web designer will do is ask you what you want to display on your site. Thinking about the points listed above will help you be prepared to explain your concept. This process of creating your site map and storyboard will be critical in getting your concept and vision across to your Web designer.

3. Site and Domain Name

Now you need to determine a tentative name for your Website. You may just want to use your existing business name, but your Website focus may be broader or narrower than your organization name implies. In that case, look for a name that is descriptive, unique, short, and memorable.

Now give thought to your domain name. You may currently be using your Internet service provider's (ISP) chosen domain name. You may be able to select a domain name that is related to your site name if the best names are not already taken. You can find out which names are still available by trying your proposed domain name at the InterNIC (*http://www.internic.net*) "whois" interface. Try the name that you'd like to use and see if it has been taken. You may have to try several variations until you find the right domain name.

You don't have to change the domain name, but it gives your site its own identity. Currently, the fee your Internet service provider pays for a new domain name is $100 to cover the first two years, and then $50 per year thereafter. The provider also may charge you a bit more for his trouble.

Another advantage of selecting a unique domain name for your organization is that you aren't so dependent upon your Internet service provider. Suppose your ISP raises prices too high or goes out of business? If you have a domain name you just have another ISP send notification that they are now assuming the address from their server. Your viewer base and links are protected.

You need to plan on two weeks' lead time to register a domain name, so get started with that right away if you're going to do it.

4. Main Graphic to Highlight Your Site

Your main page, or home page, needs a graphic to look inviting. Think about it as the sign over a storefront that beckons customers inside. A list of options to consider follows.

- No graphic. Just use headline text. This is the easiest way to go, but dull. If this is a do-it-yourself project, begin but don't end here.
- Clip-art graphic. Perhaps you have access to black-and-white or color clip art from a program such as Corel Draw®, or Word for Windows®, or Microsoft Publisher®. Make sure your image is copyright-free; you don't want your company to be sued. Always check first! Then convert the clip art to a GIF image. For clip art, JPEG image files are often larger than GIF image files.
- Scanned-in graphic. You may already have a company logo or an artist's drawing. You can scan this and convert it to a GIF image. Use your own scanner, or have a local computer service bureau (or Kinko's®) do this for you.
- Customized type fonts can be developed from programs such as Paint Shop Pro®, L View Pro®, or PhotoShop®, to save as a GIF or JPEG image.
- Scanned-in photograph with type superimposed. You can, for example, find some background pattern collections on the Internet. Download one of these patterns and superimpose your company's name over it. You can do this using Paint Shop Pro® or Adobe Photoshop®. Or you can let your Web designer do it for you.
- Customized computer art by a computer artist. This may cost you a few bucks, but the right graphic sets the tone for your site. Computer artists I work with can, for modest rates, produce beautiful work tailored for a company's needs.
- Image map combined with customized computer art. The image map lets a customer click on the subject in the graphic

that interests him or her. Image maps are cool but start to get expensive since they take more programming skill and require a special interface with your host computer. This is best left to a professional Web-page designer.

A few pointers:

- Try to keep your images under 40K, or your customer may lose interest. It takes time for images to download. The larger the image file the longer it takes. I've found that at least 75 percent of my site's visitors come with "autoload images" on; that is, they're automatically waiting for the pictures to download. You don't want to frustrate them before they have even had a chance to evaluate your site.
- Using interlaced GIF images helps keep your customer's interest as the graphic gradually displays over four "passes." The total time is about the same for interlaced or noninterlaced images.
- Not all your viewers have 256-color capability; many have only 16 colors. What does your graphic look like with 16 colors? Test!
- The best combination is a single sparkling graphic combined with text.
- The overall look of your home page needs to be graphically balanced, pleasing, informative.
- Your home page functions as your storefront. It needs to entice the customer to come in the door to look at the rest of what you have to offer. This is where a professional writer can help.

Okay, let's get back to the hard decisions you face.

5. Background Color or Texture

You want to set your Website off from all the rest. One way is with a well-designed graphic. The other is with a background texture and/ or color. Again, some options follow.

- Plain gray. This is your entry-level color scheme. All browsers can display it. The novice HTML writer can do this without even trying. I don't know why anyone uses gray when they can choose something brighter. Gray is ugly.
- Colored background and lettering. If you know the right codes, you can easily change the background color. Make the letters a contrasting color.
- Textured and colored backgrounds are proliferating on the Web. They are really pretty easy to create, like the tiled wallpaper used in your Windows® desktop. The addition of both texture and color will make your site special. But you have to be very careful that your text is easily readable when you're finished.

If they can't read it, visitors won't stay. Don't let the background overwhelm the text, but subtly complement it. Consider white.

6. Basic Page Elements

If you have lots of information you need to choose between using long or multiple pages. Long pages are good if you expect people to print out or download your pages for future reference. You can index these to internal "bookmarks" to help your customers find their way to needed information. The drawback is that long pages of 40K or more may be more than your customers will want to wait for. With multiple shorter pages, your index links jump to many shorter pages that treat just one subject each. These don't take as long to view, but if you think people will want to download or print out ten different pages, think again.

The following is a list of elements that you might want to include on every page.

- A page title that displays at the top line of your Web browser is very important because it often shows up in search engines, such as WebCrawler®, InfoSeek®, and Alta Vista®. Make this descriptive, using keywords that people might use to find your page.
- Top-of-page graphic. A small graphic at the top of each of your pages helps unify your Web pages. You can use a smaller version of your main page graphic, or perhaps a band at the top of the page with your company name and a small logo. I always call this file something like "page-top.gif." That way if I want to change it, I don't have to alter every page. Just upload a new image with that name. Do you want this top graphic to be centered, upper left, or upper right?
- Page background. Textured and colored backgrounds unify your pages. I call this file something like "page-bak.gif" so it can be changed easily. Alternatively, you can specify an RGB color for the background. Many Websites today use a simple white background for readability by many Web browser and monitor configurations.
- Headline type. Decide what size to use on the subpages and use it consistently.
- Text. Be sparing in the use of elaborate typefaces. More normal typefaces tend to look more modest and understated. There is such a thing as overkill.
- Last update. If your site features up-to-date information, let the visitor know when it was last updated. If you don't update frequently, leave the date off or the site will look untended.
- URL address. You don't have to include this, but consider it. That way it will be clear from the printed page how to return to your Website.

- Jump lines. If you have a complex site, you may want to have one- or two-word designations that will allow your customer to jump to another section of your Website. Most common is a "home" or "top of page" jump, sometimes using "clickable images" or "buttons."
- Links. The power of the Web is in its ability to link to any other page in the world. But be very careful. You've just got the customer in your store. Don't quickly send him away. Resist your impulse to show off your knowledge of cool sites until you have got your customer's name, address, and, hopefully, order. This is business.
- Signature. Sign your pages so the author is apparent (e.g., Designed by Rick Fredkin). Alternatively, you may want to include an e-mail address, which when clicked takes your customer to a "mail to" form to send you e-mail.

7. Finishing Touches

Here is a list of less essential but helpful elements you might want to include where appropriate.

- Horizontal rules. These don't take any extra time to download. They can be varied in length and width if you know the codes.
- Colored lines. These take a few seconds, but can spice up your page, especially if they are coordinated with the color scheme you have designed. Don't overdo it.
- Bullets are available as an HTML option to set off lists.
- Colored balls, arrows, and pointers are also available. But be careful. A little color goes a long way. Don't just add these to show off.
- Colorful "new" or "updated" markers draw your customers' attention to items you may have added recently. How about "sale" or "special"? Again, don't overdo it; only use one or two per page. More than that defeats the purpose.

8. Photos and Graphics

You'll want to illustrate your products or services to help tell your story. Or you may want to put your whole catalog online. Remember to use the <IMG ALT= > tag so customers who don't have graphics will know what the image shows.

It can be very effective to tell your story through a few pictures. Black-and-white images may be a bit less expensive, and are within the range of most hand scanners using a gray scale. Black-and-white images can easily be tinted slightly blue or brown to give an antique flavor. Color grabs people. Color images are best. Obtain professional-quality photos of your products locally, then send your Web designer the photos. You can also obtain stock photography from inexpensive

CD-ROMs from Expert and Softkey, or professional stock photography online from PhotoDisc (*http://www.photodisc.com*).

Remember to keep the size of the images small so that your customer doesn't have to wait all day to be able to see them. He or she may just click to another site and be gone; 20K to 40K is the acceptable range for people with 14.4K modems. You need to resize or crop the photos as needed so they fit appropriately on the page and don't take too long to download.

Clickable thumbnail images are one useful compromise. You can show the picture in a thumbnail-size image. If interested, the customer can click on it to display the larger photo. You can also give the image size, such as 57K, so the customer has an idea of whether or not to choose this option.

Type of image is important, too. GIF images can be viewed by all Web browsers, though as of April 1996, nearly all common browsers can see both GIF and JPEG images. JPEG images compress better and thus load faster, so are especially helpful for color photos. Usually, you'll find that a JPEG image is smaller than a GIF, but not always. Clickable images that offer a choice of JPEG or GIF are another way to go.

Other considerations include how the images appear on the Web pages. For example, do you want rectangular images with color to the edges or transparent areas around your graphics? Your Web designer will know how to make transparent backgrounds that make images appear to "float" over the page. Do-it-yourselfers can accomplish this using L View Pro® or Adobe Photoshop®.

Multimedia is getting more common and more Web browsers and computers support it, so you might want to include sound, animation, or video clips. For now, however, the "bandwidth" or modem speed of 14.4K or 28.8 bps is really too slow for much except perhaps Real Audio, which lets a user listen to audio without the need to download the audio file.

9. Forms to Get Orders or Customer Response

You need to connect with your customer. These options return information from your customer to you by e-mail.

- Guest books. You can entice potential customers to sign your guestbook and perhaps receive a free gift. Their answers to key questions help you qualify them as prospects to pursue by telephone or direct mail (or e-mail, for that matter). If you work this right, you might even be able to sell the information to mailing list companies. Just don't make your potential customers mad at you.
- Requests for information. Have a place for name, address, phone number, and other useful information, as well as check boxes to request information on certain products or services.

- Order forms. Ideally, you will take the order right online. Since people are still concerned with the security of their credit card information on the Internet, consider using a combination of an order form and a toll-free number. Former customers could order on the basis of credit information they have previously supplied. Or you might have a page that contains an order form your customer can print out, fill out manually, and mail in with a check.
- Shopping cart program. If you are selling a number of products directly over the Internet, you probably ought to invest in "shopping cart" software, so customers can put multiple items in their cart from any number of product pages. Upon checkout, they are given a total of their items, as well as tax (if any) and shipping charges.
- Secure server. If you're serious about selling directly on the Internet, invest in the extra cost of putting your pages on a SSL-compatible server, such as the Netscape Secure Commerce Server, which encrypts the information quite well. Perception is the real issue, not theft of information. The blue key at the bottom left of the user's screen will provide that perception, and it's worth the extra money you'll pay.

You will also have to decide how you will get the information from the Website sent to you by e-mail. This requires Common Gateway Interface (CGI) programming, and that is the really tricky part. To accomplish this, you can:

- Adapt CGI scripts that you find on the Internet. This takes a bit of programming savvy. You also need to befriend your host computer's system operator to let you have your own CGI-bin file.
- Write your own CGI scripts. This takes a lot of programming savvy.
- Hire a computer-science grad student to write your CGI script for you.

In most cases, the best solution is to employ your Web designer to take care of this for you. Some Web designers have highly tuned programming skills. Others develop partnerships with programmers to get your job done the way you want it. Your designer will also work with your host computer system operator to set up the program in a CGI-bin directory.

10. Uploading and Testing Your Pages

Once you have finished designing your pages, you need to upload them to your Internet service provider's server. You can:

- Upload the pages yourself. You'll need to do this repeatedly as you test and adjust your pages. This isn't too difficult if you already have a communications program such as ProComm Plus®. An even more helpful tool is CuteFTP, available in both Windows 3.1 and Windows 95. You can use this software to upload files to your Website.
- Send the pages to your Internet service provider on a diskette to upload for you. The provider may do this for you once or twice, but when you find the need for repeated changes to correct errors, the provider won't be happy.
- Have your Web designer upload and test the pages for you. If the designer is worth his or her salt, the designer will ask for your approval at key stages so you are fully satisfied with the final product.

11. Registering and Advertising Your Site

If you build it, will they come? Only if they can find you. There are several ways to register your Website. You will want to use all of these approaches, or pay your Web designer to do it for you.

- Signature. Subscribe to mailing lists and newsgroups likely to include potential customers. Actively involve yourself in the discussions, but don't overtly "push" your product. Let the signature at the end of your e-mail message do that for you. Use something like:

```
==============================================
MYCOMPANY, INC.                 John Doe, Owner
Your choice for general products and hardware.
========== http://www.mycompany.com ==========
```

Participation takes some time and work, but it's worth it, since you are targeting your marketing efforts toward those most likely to purchase your product. This is your job, though your Web designer can help you find the right mailing lists and newsgroups.

- Web search engines. There are a dozen or so search engines for the World Wide Web, such as Lycos®, Web Crawler®, AltaVista®, and Yahoo®. Resister your index page with each of these, or have your Web designer do it for you.
- Links from related pages. You may find some people in a complementary business who will agree to reciprocal links with your page, or one-way links for a modest fee. You know your industry better than your Web designer. To find these link sites, you need to explore the Internet for yourself.
- Links from industry index pages. There may be an advertising page that links all related pages at no cost. Tell them about yours. Again, this is your job.

- Send brief "press release" announcements to services that announce "what's new" on the Internet. You just might hit it lucky and have hundreds of people see the announcement and flock to your site—if you're selected for the weekly "scout report." You can send these announcements or have your Web designer do it for you.
- Print your Website address or URL on all your display ads, literature, stationery, and business cards. This will attract customers to your site to learn more about your business and your products.

12. Maintaining Your Site

Once you're up and running, after testing all your links and correcting the inevitable errors, you need to keep your Website current. You'll need to think of how to handle price changes, product changes, adding pages to describe other parts of your business, updating links that have become obsolete, updating images, and redoing the look of your pages.

You have choices here, too.

- Do it yourself. If you have developed your pages thus far by yourself, it'll be a snap.
- Have your Web designer train you or a staff member to update files. You might want to write this into your agreement with your Web designer ahead of time, especially if you have some computer talent within your company. With this option, you'll need to use the Web designer in the future only for major changes.
- Keep your Web designer on a retainer to maintain your pages monthly or as needed. This saves you or your people from having to become experts on HTML. Your Web designer becomes part of your team without being on your payroll; hire the designer as an outside contractor.

▼

11 Getting Visitors to Your Site

TOO MANY WEB MARKETERS WORK ON THE IF-YOU-BUILD-IT-THEY-WILL-come model. They won't. Once you build a Website you must give people a reason to come. A Website is a passive form of marketing, providing a signboard that points visitors to your products and services. To be most effective, a Website should be used in conjunction with the eight active forms of marketing that we will examine briefly in this chapter. Just how do small businesses on limited budgets entice visitors to their Websites?

Advertise Your Website to Web Search Engines that Index the Web

Search engines such as Yahoo, Lycos, WebCrawler, and InfoSeek index the Web. The actual registration process can be deceptively simple. A service called SubmitIt! (*http://www.submit- it.com*) provides a way to submit information to approximately fifteen of the most used indexes. If you do this late at night, when Internet traffic is at its lowest, you can transmit your business's online address and description to all of these within three-quarters of an hour. Done right, a person who is seeking, for example, a Web designer in southern New Jersey with experience in creating databases can quickly locate the right names. Customers will be able to pick you out from the increasing crowd of online vendors.

The danger is that the untutored can construct a carelessly written twenty-five-word or two-hundred-character marketing description that blows their opportunity to be seen by vast blocks of potential customers. These twenty-five words must be written to include the chief keywords by which customers will locate you. If you want to change your description in a month or two, it takes much longer than an hour to contact each of the services separately, and then convince or nag them into making changes.

You can pay modest amounts to several services to perform this important task for you. For example, my company Millennium Productions, Inc. (*http://www.mproductions.com*), offers, as part of all Website packages, to register each Website with the most important indexes. Similar services are available for a fee at PromoteIt! (*http://www.cam.org/~psarena/promote-it.html*) and WebPromote™ (*http://www.stpt.com/shc/wp.hmtl*).

Give People a Good Reason to Visit

A tried-and-true marketing approach is to offer something of value for free. A number of well-financed corporate Websites offer entertaining fare that changes constantly. While most small business Web marketers can't afford to compete, you *can* afford to offer valuable information. If you take the time to provide up-to-date information about your industry, for example, you'll find people returning again and again to your site, each time increasing the chance of their doing business with you.

Find Industry-Wide Linking Pages

Find industry-wide linking and negotiate reciprocal links to and from their Web pages. A trade association related to your field probably lists members. Several online craft centers, for example, offer free links to other crafters. If you are a hotel, be sure to get a link with "All the Hotels on the Web" (*http://www.stpt.com/shc/wp.html*). Consultants will seek links with the Expert Marketplace (*http://www.crimson.com/em/*) or try for a listing in the Virtual Trade Show (*http://www.vts.com*). Lists can seem endless. Surf the net enough to find which are the key sites for your field, and then seek links there. But remember, be judicious in your use of outgoing links. You've just got those people in your door; don't quickly send them away again.

Purchase Web Advertising

You can also purchase Web advertising on other sites, usually through a clickable ad with a link to your Website. If you place your ad on a carefully selected, high-volume Website, a certain percentage of their thousands of visitors will explore your Website, and hopefully like what they find. A whole industry has sprung up in the past year to act as brokers for such ads. One is WebConnect (*http://www.worldata.com/Webcon.htm*). Small businesses will need to find ways to test the effect of specific ads on the bottom line, perhaps by sending people from each ad to a different home page at their site, so they can monitor traffic from each ad.

Newsgroups and Mailing Lists

Become active in several of the thousands of Internet newsgroups and mailing lists. Find the groups that are most likely to be frequented by your potential customers—groups can be *very* narrowly targeted—and join in the discussion. You might find groups that relate to your industry by doing a bit of research with the Stanford Information Filtering Tool (SIFT) at *http://hotpage.stanford.edu/*, which searches messages about particular topics or companies voiced in thousands of newsgroups and mailing lists.

"Lurk" for a few weeks so you understand the particular culture of the group you are targeting, then find ways to add constructive comments to the discussion. At the bottom of each message include a "signature," a four- to eight-line mini-advertisement with your product, phone number, and Web address. Every time you contribute to the discussion, your mini-ad will be seen by hundreds. You'll find this approach can be fruitful, but like anything, success comes in response to hard work and persistence. Resist the temptation to send bulk e-mail messages to dozens of newsgroups—"spamming," in Internet parlance. People do it, but while it may bring customers, it doesn't offer the solid reputation and respect that will build your business in the long run.

Online Malls

Businesses in physical shopping malls benefit from the traffic flow of multitudes window-shopping in a single location. The same can be true online if you make your Website part of one or more of the many "malls" on the World Wide Web.

Some malls only include businesses that subscribe to a particular Internet service provider or pay a fee or percentage of their gross revenues. Others take any business that fits their particular criteria. Dave Taylor, for example, developed The Internet Mall (*http://www.iw.com/imall/*), a collection of more than three thousand businesses that meet under one "roof." The mall is illusory, however, since businesses in the mall are hosted on separate ISP sites all over the world. This, the largest mall, charges no fee to its businesses; instead it sells advertising to companies that pay for an ad in the high-volume entryway to this mall.

Cross-Publicize on Print Materials

As mentioned before, always include your e-mail and Web addresses on all your company's print literature, stationery, and display advertising. If people believe they can find out more about your products or services by looking online, many will do so.

Develop a Guest Book

Build a guest book on your Website to collect information about your customers, including vital statistics such as their e-mail addresses.

Be open on the guest book and tell the customer that you will use the e-mail address to get back in touch with them in the future. Through this method, you can begin to develop your own e-mailing list for future publicity. While it is wrong to conduct "spamming" via e-mail to a list of unknown e-mail addresses, it is perfectly okay to publicize your activities to those who have voluntarily given you their e-mail addresses.

These eight important ways to increase traffic to your company's Website can make all the difference. If you use most or all of these forms of marketing, chances are that two years from now you'll be bragging about your foresight in developing a Website when you did, rather than trashing Web marketing as just another fad where you threw good money after bad.

12 Anatomy of Search Engines

AS MENTIONED IN PREVIOUS CHAPTERS, THE USE OF SEARCH ENGINES IS critical in Internet publicity. There are many, many search engines on the market today. There are certain important things to consider in using search engines, including URLs cataloged, content, meta tag support, search levels, and others. An understanding of the criteria will help you assess the efficacy of the various search engines. An intimate understanding of the criteria will also help to accelerate your use of search engines for Internet publicity.

- *URLs Cataloged.* The more URLs cataloged, the more likely pages from your Website will be found through a search engine. Figures are reported by each site or other sources, and debate rages about who's biggest. Excite has a nice explanation of issues involved in the size debate at *http://www.excite.com/ice/counting/html.* No doubt the other search engines have their own opinions, of course.
- *Content.* Shows whether the engine catalogs the full text of a page or, instead, creates a description or abstract based on a page's text. Full text may be better because it ensures that every word from your Website will be available to match keywords entered by those consulting search engines.
- *Meta Tag Support.* Many believe that all search engines

acknowledge keywords and descriptions placed in meta tags. In reality, only a few do. The sites that support the tag explain how to use it in their online help files. Keep in mind that using the tag doesn't guarantee your page will become more relevant than other sites, but it does allow you to control the description that appears.

- *Search Levels.* Some search engines catalog everything on a home page but go no farther than this first level. Others go to all the pages linked to the home page, the second level. The process continues if the search engine continues to follow links deeper and deeper into the site.
- *Catalog Date.* The search engines may go out nightly to find new Web pages, but that work means nothing if the search engine catalogs aren't updated with this new information. Kudos to the engines that tell you how old their catalogs are.
- *URL Status Check.* WebCrawler is the only engine that allows you to check when your site was visited by the engine, a very nice feature that other engines might consider adding
- *Keywords Sold.* Only Open Text (*http://www.opentext.com/omw/preferred_c.html*) sells keywords. It began selling preferred listings in June 1996. Pay the money (beginning at $2,000 for six months), and you can appear in the top ten, guaranteed. A link to an article about this service is on the resource page. More commonplace are search engines that let banner advertisers purchase keywords. If the keywords an advertiser has purchased are entered, the company's ad will appear at the top of the page. Keyword-linked ads do not change the order in which pages are listed.
- *Page Popularity.* Some search engines determine the popularity of a page by analyzing how many links there are to it from other pages. Pages that are more popular may turn up earlier in a search over less popular pages, or popularity may be used in other ways.
- *Catalog Update.* Better search engines will constantly update their catalogs, but since the majority don't date their catalogs, it can be hard to tell how old the catalogs are.
- *Repeat Penalty.* Two engines will penalize sites using words too often as an attempt to spam the results. InfoSeek penalizes if keywords are used more than seven times in a meta tag. Lycos began penalizing repetition in May 1996. Lycos should be applauded for trying to control spamming. Unfortunately, the engine doesn't define what constitutes excessive repetition. As a result, Webmasters might inadvertently have their Web pages fall lower in the rankings. This is because many relevant Web pages have keywords that repeat "naturally." For example, Lycos

used to top-rank the home pages of County of Orange and the Orange County Register when the keywords "Orange County" were entered. Few would challenge the relevancy of highly ranking the home pages of the county government and the area's major newspaper. Now, those pages are buried in the listings. In their place are lots of pages of arguably lower relevancy. Ironically, one of the best ways to avoid the spamming problem without overt penalties might be to give more weight to a page's popularity, as explained above. A page with lots of links to it is in effect ranked by those across the Web. Good pages get lots of links; bad pages don't.

Methods of Making Your Website Appear More Relevant

There don't seem to be any magic methods that will make a page appear at the top of every search engine's listings. There's too much fluctuation on the Web for any page to claim a foothold, and all the engines handle relevancy slightly differently. However, there are some general tips that do help a page appear more relevant.

- *Have text on your home page.* Search engine catalogs contain the text read from the various home pages the engines visit. If a page lacks descriptive text, then there is little chance that that page will come up in the results of a search engine query. It's not enough for that text to be in graphics. It must be HTML text. Some search engines will catalog ALT text and text in comment and meta tags. To be safe, a straight HTML description is recommended.
- *Pick your keywords.* Focus on the two or three keywords that you think are most crucial to your site, then ensure those words are both in your title and mentioned early on in your Web page. Generally, most people will already have those words present on their pages but may not also have them in page titles. Keep in mind that the keywords you consider crucial may not be exactly what users enter. The addition of just one extra word can suddenly make a site appear more relevant, and it can be impossible to anticipate what that word will be. The best bet is to focus on your chosen keywords but also to have a complete description.
- *Have links to inside pages.* If there are no links to inside pages from the home page, it seems that some search engines will not fully catalog a site. Unfortunately, the most descriptive, relevant pages are often inside pages rather than the home page. You can also try sending search engines directly to your lower levels if they don't ordinarily go there.
- *Forget Spamming.* For one thing, spamming doesn't seem to

work with every search engine. Ethically, the content of most Web pages ought to be enough for search engines to determine relevancy without Webmasters having to resort to repeating keywords for no reason other than to try and "beat" other Web pages. The stakes will simply keep rising, and users will also begin to hate sites that undertake these measures. Efforts would be better spent on networking and alternative forms of publicity described below.

- *Network.* If your site fails to make the top-ten lists, then get together with those that do. Perhaps some might be considered competitors, but others might be happy to link to your site in return for a link back. After all, your site may appear first when slightly different keywords are used. Links are what the Web was built on, and they remain one of the best ways for people to find your site.
- *Relax.* Search engines are a primary way people use to look for Websites, but they are not the *only* way. People also find sites through word-of-mouth, traditional advertising, the traditional media, newsgroup postings, Web directories, and links from other sites. Many times, these alternative forms are far more effective draws than search engines. The audience you want may be visiting a site that you can partner with or reading a magazine that you've never informed of your site. Do the simple things to make your site most relevant to search engines, then concentrate on the other areas.

Search Engines Alone Are Not the Best: An Example

While search engines are an effective way to promote your Website, integrating such promotion with other mechanisms will prove to be more valuable. Phaedra Hise (Hise, Phaedra, 8/96, Page 102, On-Line: Website Promotions, 0891024), points out an incident where an art gallery owner had little success promoting the gallery site using just search engines. While its true that the electronic way to promote a Website is to list it with one of the Web's search engines, Yahoo, for instance, it may not be the only way. Some people make the mistake of relying too heavily on search engines to bring people to their Website, neglecting more traditional methods of promotion. Alan Klotz of PhotoCollect, a small photography gallery in New York City, found that print promotion worked better.

The gallery owner's Website debuted last September, and he immediately listed it with the dozen or so search engines. From Klotz's point of view, "What you do is jam in as many words as you can that best describe your site," he says. With luck, some of those words will match keywords that users enter to locate different sites.

When a user types in the keyword "photo," the search engine turns up hundreds of matching sites. The ones at the top of the list are those with "photo" in their description the most times. It's a system that Klotz says doesn't work well to get his site's listing in front of potential customers.

"If you type in 'PhotoCollect' as a keyword, it takes you right to my site," he says. "So it's good for people who know me but have lost my business card. The problem is that I want to reach collectors whom I haven't met, and those who search by 'photo' have to wade through 1,600 gallery listings before they find mine." Klotz knows that because he tested the search engines himself, visiting and typing in keywords to see where on the list his gallery turned up. None of the keywords put him at the top, he says, and after spending about $7,000, not including in-house labor, on developing the site, he was anxious for results.

So Klotz applied more traditional promotional methods to the new medium. He took out a small ad in the Sunday *New York Times,* listing the site's address, or URL. He also wrote a press release and sent it to industry magazines, two of which later featured the site in major articles. Soon he was seeing results. "Traffic at the site increased, and people referred to the magazine articles." The $125 newspaper ad attracted attention too. "I've gotten eight calls saying, 'What are all those letters above your phone number?'" he says. "Good thing I ran the phone number."

Klotz makes his high-ticket sales over the phone or in person, not directly at the Website. When customers call the number listed at the site, Klotz asks where they first learned about the site. "About a third say through the *New York Times* ad," he says. "The other two-thirds are from the magazine articles. Nobody has ever said they found me on a search engine."

Search Engine Study

In mid January 1996, Wilson Internet Services (WIS) conducted a study of the major search engines to check what results appeared for the keywords "Orange County" when default settings were used. This was to see whether a site managed by WIS, the InfoPages guide to Orange County, California, Websites, appeared in the top-ten results. Given its large number of Orange County listings, it seemed that InfoPages should appear in the top-ten results, or at least pretty high among sites listed. If it didn't, WIS had a perfect site to test various theories about search engine operation.

By "default settings" WIS meant those if one went to each search engine and simply typed in the words "Orange County" without using any advanced functions, operators, or changing any of the options that may have been present. WIS wanted to mimic what they believed the majority of people do when they visit a site. That meant sticking to lowest common denominator settings and thinking.

InfoPages was nowhere to be found. Could anything be done to correct this? For clues, WIS examined the results from the various search engines side by side. WIS also examined the content of top-ranking pages. The study reached the following conclusions:

- Keywords in title and on page. In general, pages that appeared in the top-ten listings had the keywords listed in their titles, then again on the page itself.
- Keyword repetition. The use of keywords several times within a page made it more likely to appear in the top-ten lists, especially if the words appeared more frequently in relation to other words on the page.
- Search engine spamming. Inadvertent or overt repetition of keywords helped some pages make the top-ten lists of some search engines, yet on others, it had no effect.
- Meta tags of no use. The successful pages were not making use of hidden descriptions and keywords via meta tags, so this was not seen as a magic method to achieve search engine success.

In order to test the above conclusions, WIS made small changes to pages within the InfoPages site and conducted various tests and logged the results

- *Test #1: Keywords in title and on page.* The title of the InfoPages home page (*http://infopages.com*) simply said "InfoPages." It was changed to say "Orange County and Southern California's guide to what's on the Web: InfoPages." The introductory text on the page was also changed from "What's on the Web in Orange County and Southern California" to "Orange County and Southern California's guide to what's on the Web," in order to make the words "Orange County" appear higher on the page. Similar changes were made to the InfoPages listings page (*http://infopages.com/listings/*) in order to see how this inside page performed versus the home page. Then the search engines were prompted to return to the site in mid January and recatalog the pages.
- *Results of Test #1.* By the end of February, immediate improvements were seen on WebCrawler. InfoPages first made the top listings, then later dropped the second page of results shown (WebCrawler displays twenty-five pages at a time). Even better success occurred in Lycos, where InfoPages eventually became the number-three listing. Elsewhere, the small changes didn't seem to be enough to get InfoPages anywhere near the top listings.

- *Test #2: Search engine spamming.* WIS didn't believe in search engine spamming—the multiple use of keywords solely as a means to make pages appear more relevant. WIS believed that the content of most Web pages is enough to help users find them without having to resort to overt, unjustified means of trying to trick search engines. While many dislike spamming, it does occur, so its effectiveness needed to be tested. There were hints that it might work: a top-ranked page from Texas was successful because it listed information for every county in Texas, an example of inadvertent spamming. All those repetitions of "County," with one "Orange" thrown in, pushed the page to the top of WebCrawler's listings. Similarly, a travel guide uses repetition of the words "Orange County" and "California" apparently as a means to make it more likely to appear in listings. It was successful with several engines. To test spamming, the InfoPages home page was left untouched, but the listings pages had "orange county orange county orange county orange county orange county orange county orange county orange county orange county" added to hidden comments on the page in mid February. That's nine repetitions, for those who don't want to count; eleven references in all on the page.
- *Results of Test #2.* The InfoPages listing page quickly moved to the top of the Excite listings, testimony to how quickly Excite keeps up with the latest changes on the Web, yet a sad indication that the engine can easily be tricked. On other engines, there were no significant changes.
- *Test #3: Meta Tags.* Some search engines allow the use of meta tags within the header information to control keywords and descriptions that appear. These were added in late March to the InfoPages home page.
- *Results of Test #3.* Adding meta tags made no difference in causing the InfoPages home page to appear higher.

▼

13 Advanced Netiquette

BEFORE WE PROCEED TO ADVANCED NETIQUETTE, LET'S REVIEW BASIC netiquette. Here is a summary.

- Don't insult or flame people.
- Only make postings in good taste. No chain letters, derisive comments, or inflammatory remarks.
- Don't publish copyrighted material without the permission of the owner.
- Get explicit, written permission to reproduce copyrighted material. If you're going to be giving your content to someone else to maintain, make sure the permissions are handed over with the documents.
- Take care in using trademarks.
- Do not reproduce trademarks or trademarked logos if there is a possibility of someone attributing your product to the owner of the trademark or logo.
- Don't publish links to someone else's pages unless you know that they want that exposure.
- While many documents you will encounter are meant to be reused and linked to, some aren't. Unless it's very obvious that the author of the document in question is creating a public resource, ask for permission before creating a link.
- Give people constructive feedback on the documents you read.
- Give back to the Internet.
- Try to publish documents that provide value to a broader audience than just your immediate one. As a distribution medium, the Web can provide a channel for specialized content that would be an economic impossibility in other media. However, many sites that claim to cater to very specific audiences have information with a much broader appeal, or information that, if only slightly enhanced or re-organized, would be useful to a much larger constituency. Once you've defined your target audience and created the perfect site for its needs, try to find low-effort changes that might enlarge the group of readers who will find your information useful.
- Strive for elegance and clarity.
- Publish things that solve peoples' problems.

Netiquette Schmoozing

If "schmooze" is foreign to you, don't worry. It denotes a cozy kind of conversation that people of any ethnic background or nationality can enter into and enjoy. Unlike some cold-blooded versions of networking that became popular in the late 1980s, its object is not collecting as many business cards or e-mail addresses as you can. Nor is electronic schmoozing aimed at making distant friends (though that often comes about as a by-product). For this method to prove rewarding, you must in your heart and soul actually value personal business relationships. Phoniness eventually rings as hollow on a computer screen as it does in a used-car showroom. And you'll quickly get bored if you cynically go through the motions of schmoozing with your arm ready to stretch out and grab the golden ring. So I'm assuming that you want to meet people who share your business interests and that you are prepared to spend time at your computer participating in discussion. You have an idea of where you wish to fish and how you'd like to come across. You still need to understand how to avoid committing the grand transgression of soliciting, because it's very easy to step over barely visible, rarely pointed out lines without realizing it. Let's begin by looking at two clearly acceptable examples of schmoozing and two examples of soliciting that would be decidedly unacceptable in most online discussion areas.

- *Netiquette Schmooze #1*
  To: all
  From: Ron Tyler
  Re: Etiquette?
  Does anyone know the appropriate way to address a supreme court justice? Is it just "your honor" or something else? We got a reservation from one at my bed and breakfast, and I don't want to make a fool of myself! Thanks, Ron.
- *Netiquette Schmooze #2*
  To: Geri Burkhardt
  From: Bruce Han
  Re: ADA
  I disagree with what you wrote about the disabilities act being a terrible burden on small businesses. In my seventeen-person accounting firm, we installed a ramp before we ran public seminars in our conference room, and bought a TDD machine for an employee who lost his hearing suddenly. Total cost for both: $5,500. The former gives us community goodwill (and one or two extra registrations) when we write on our brochures and ads "Wheelchair accessible." And the latter saved us the cost of recruiting and training someone new. Bruce Han

- *Solicitation #1*
  To: all
  From: Ron Tyler
  Re: Vacation ideas
  With the incredibly frigid weather in many parts of the country these days, your thoughts may be turning south. If so, there's no friendlier, more interesting destination in Florida than Key West, and no friendlier, more interesting place to stay there than the Buccaneer Bed and Breakfast. E-mail me for complete details on a special weekend package deal in Key West!
- *Solicitation #2*
  To: Geri Burkhardt
  From: Bruce Han
  Re: ADA
  Geri: Did you know that the cost of compliance with the ADA is a legitimate business expense, and therefore fully deductible? Our full-service accounting firm specializes in helping small businesses like yours keep your hard-earned profits legally out of the hands of Uncle Sam. We're friendly, experienced, and affordable. Let me know if you'd like to set up a no-obligation appointment.

Did you notice significant differences? Schmoozing is purposeful chitchat likely to be of interest to others, while solicitation involves a blatant invitation to do business. Netiquette Schmooze #1 consists of one of the most common forms of appropriate discussion, a business-related question. Note, though, that Ron's question sets his business in a highly favorable light likely to make others curious to know more. If a curious someone does ask, "Where are you located?" and then, "Geez, Key West—I was thinking of going there in April. Tell me about your B&B," he's allowed to present the selling points of his business to his heart's content. Netiquette Schmooze #2 consists of another common form of participation—contributing views on an issue. Here Bruce responded substantively to a comment by Geri and subtly injected the description, "my seventeen-person accounting firm." Over time if Bruce continues to post reasoned, socially enlightened arguments and experiences linked to his name and a phrase like "my seventeen-person accounting firm," regulars needing accounting services are going to turn to him.

Solicitation #1, addressed to "all," has no purpose or context other than conveying Ron's marketing information. It also has no discussion value or informative content—you wouldn't learn anything by reading it. Note too that it ends, like any good advertisement or direct-mail piece, with a call to action. Although schmoozy in tone, it comes across unmistakably as a sales pitch. It would therefore be removed from or provoke criticism in every area that enforces a "no commercials" rule. Solicitation #2 reminds me of classic ambulance chasing—as in lawyers going to the funerals of accident victims and tucking their business cards in the suit pockets of the family members. Here Bruce joins an ongoing discussion but instead of furthering the interchange, he injects his selling agenda where it's beside the point. As in solicitation #1, Bruce recites his selling points and concludes with an invitation to call him. In addition, several phrases crop up in his note that one rarely encounters outside of marketing pieces, such as "small businesses like yours," "hard-earned profits," "the hands of Uncle Sam," "affordable," and "no-obligation appointment." Bruce does offer some helpful information about the deductibility of ADA compliance expenses, but he then switches unnecessarily to selling mode.

"People who haven't been working for themselves don't know that there's any other way to market besides advertising," says Alice Bredin, who has been a home business expert on Prodigy and writes a column on home business for *Newsday*. "Marketing means setting up a billboard somewhere by running big ads on radio, TV, or in a magazine, and if you can't afford that, well, at least on online services you can slap your message up in front of people's eyes and they are going to buy from you. Actually, the reverse is true. Being online is like being at a party, and the other people there aren't likely to buy from you if you just come up and tell them what you do. But after you talk awhile about where you're from, ask them about their businesses, you exchange information, maybe then you've made a business connection." It's foolish to think that one note you wrote in half an hour is going to perform magic for you," says Bredin. "Instead, when someone posts a note, take off your salesperson's hat, or at least tilt it to the side, and give that person some help. Get a little relationship going, and they'll get a trial run with you that might get them wanting more."

If the above examples have convinced you of the value of sticking to schmoozing and avoiding flagrant selling, here are some guidelines for promoting yourself unobtrusively and staying out of trouble:

- **Do** ask questions that enable you to describe what you do. It's fine not to know everything. Just make sure your questions aren't too elementary and don't cast doubt on your ethics. Investment banker Fred Richards says he sometimes sees questions "so basic that it's obvious the person asking has no experience whatsoever, like 'Is it cheaper to send things by mail or by UPS?' Just call and ask!" Another time, someone in mail order was asking, about having to pay sales tax to other states, "Can I get around this?" Richards remembers giving this person a stern warning about the consequences of not going by the book.

- **Do** answer questions from others you're qualified to address. Even when the topic isn't smack on target with your service or product, your reputation with the group rises whenever you demonstrate that you know your stuff. Generosity makes a good impression too. Paradoxically, in this medium, selfless sharing of information sells.
- **Do** contribute to discussions that put you or your business in a favorable light. Taking a strong stand is fine so long as you can back up your position with facts or experiences and stay in control of your responses.
- **Do** be constructive in tone. Avoid sarcasm, put-downs, and personal attacks—even if someone throws verbal digs your way.
- **Do** stay focused on the announced topic. "Nothing is more irritating than to go into a thread marked 'FREELANCE WRITERS NEEDED' and find a discussion about restaurants in Omaha," says CompuServe member Kathy Sena, who adds that the problem has a name: "thread corruption."
- **Do** offer valuable information. Ron could have turned his "vacation ideas" solicitation into a solid discussion starter by continuing after "there's no friendlier, more interesting destination in Florida than Key West" with a description of its attractions: the Hemingway connection, its typical February temperatures, the tolerant lifestyle, its accessibility by car and air, etc. By setting himself up as someone knowledgeable about Key West, he's more likely to make a memorable impression in this medium than by pushing his bed and breakfast directly.
- **Do** balance getting with giving and showing off with humility. Although author Charlotte Libov spends a good deal of energy online sniffing out publicity opportunities, she says she deliberately tries to give back as much help as she's received. "I share my contacts with people who have similar interests, and I take part in nonpromotional discussions," she says. "If I feel I've been promoting myself a lot lately, I'll hold back or approach someone privately, by e-mail."
- **Do** check messages frequently. Glassblower Strat McCloskey of Newcastle, Delaware, got the opportunity to present a seminar when someone else couldn't make it at the last minute because he was the first out of fifty people to respond to the online appeal for a replacement.
- **Don't** expect results from vague questions or answers. "Nobody is going to respond helpfully to a question like, 'I need some help with taxes.' It looks lazy, as if you haven't put any energy into it yet at all," says Alice Bredin. "But if you make your question more specific—as specific as you can—people will respect that and put energy back toward you." Likewise, the

more examples and details you can offer as advice, the more you showcase your expertise.

- **Don't** use all capital letters, even in your headline. Online, people consider over-excitement the equivalent of shouting, and it makes them want to cover their ears—oops, their eyes. An extended patch of upper-case letters also slows down reading.
- **Don't** irritate discussion participants with gratuitous exclamation marks, empty superlatives, self-serving exaggerations, unsubstantiated boasts, and other symptoms of hype, such as words like "amazing," "revolutionary," "breakthrough," "unique," "fabulous," or "extraordinary." Avoid any sort of promise or offer, so that you keep a safe distance from the verboten territory of advertising.
- **Don't** post the same message repeatedly. Charlotte Libov recalls getting her knuckles rapped when she posted announcements about the appearance in paperback of her book, *The Woman's Heart Book*, in several sections of the same forum. The forum guardian objected not to the content of the message, but to its repetition. While Libov is correct that some people have automated software set up so that they read only certain sections, it is also true that some folks would encounter her note over and over. A solution: stagger the timing of multiple postings and vary the wording appropriately for each site.
- **Don't** carry out "bombing runs." Several CompuServe veterans use some variation on this term to denote the practice of scattering one message almost indiscriminately throughout the service and then ending with, "If you want to know more, please e-mail me rather than reply here." The impersonality implied in such scatterfire is offensive enough. It's also insulting to the regulars to say you're too busy or not interested enough to hang around their neighborhood for responses.
- **Don't** expect instant results. "I've seen people come on a board, introduce themselves as a hotshot and two weeks later they're gone. A week after that someone has a question for them, and they're not there," says Peggie Hall, owner of Peal Products in Atlanta, which sells marine sanitation products. "After I first went on the Sailing Forum on CompuServe, introduced myself, and started answering questions, it was three or four months before someone requested a catalog. In a year, though, we've done more than enough business to justify the expense of being online."
- **Don't** mention fees or prices unless you are asked. Even then, you might be better off providing them privately. A reasonable

rule of thumb: if you don't normally include fees or prices in ads or a brochure, don't quote them publicly even when you're asked. One exception is a response to a discussion concerning prices. For example, no one will object if someone has asked, "Anyone know where I can buy quality bulk 3.5 inch disks for less than fifty cents each?" and you respond, "We sell name-brand disks, guaranteed, in lots of one hundred for 32 cents each."

- **Don't** ask for the order. Lawrence Seldin, author and publisher of *Power Tips for the Apple Newton*, got reprimanded several places online for using the words, "to order . . ." Complaints vanished when he said, "for more information, please contact me by e-mail." Instead of asking for the order, slip in some information that would catch the interest of someone in your target market, and let them approach you if they want more information. If Ron Tyler added just a little to Netiquette Schmooze #1 above, he'd probably inspire someone to respond, "You're in Key West? We were just talking the other day about what's going on there. Can you send me a brochure?"

14 Taking Advantage of Discussion Groups

"The medium is the message," wrote Marshall McLuhan in his 1964 book, *Understanding Media*, meaning that the same material won't have the same impact on the cover of a magazine as on a flashing neon sign. Not only does every communication medium affect our sensibilities in subtle ways, but also it imposes an invisible grid of possibilities and pitfalls on participants and onlookers. McLuhan's perspective explains why people who listened to the 1959 U.S. presidential campaign debates on radio thought Nixon had won, while those who watched on TV hailed Kennedy as the winner.

To exploit the potential of the medium of Internet discussion groups, you must understand the following characteristics.

Specific Headlines

Participants choose which discussion threads to read by their headings. Unlike newspaper headlines, which appear immediately atop their articles, online headings almost always appear separately first in a list detached from the content of messages. The more your heading points to the specific subject of your post and to your intention, the more likely you are to snag the audience you want. What adman David Ogilvy wrote about ads in newspapers and magazines applies even more online, "On the average, five times as many people read the headlines as read the body copy." A limit of sixteen to twenty-four characters in headings may force you either to use standard spacesaving devices, such as "Q" for "question" and "DTP" for "desktop publishing," or to make some up. Whenever you respond publicly to someone else's message, of course, your reply bears their heading—unless you deliberately create an offshoot with a related heading.

Be Brief

Brevity is at a premium. Not only will you provoke irritation when readers wade through screen after screen of something that could have been stated in two sentences, but also many of those readers will have paid incrementally more to look at or download your bloated timewaster. State your piece simply and clearly and sign off, preferably within twenty lines or less. If you have much more than that to say, either apologize at the beginning of your message or summarize it and invite those interested to ask for more. Avoid the temptation, if your software makes this easy for you, to include the entire message you are replying to before you add your comment. Pare your quote of the previous note to the bone, so that it sets the context, then get to your point.

Be Accessible

Newcomers to the medium and to your discussion can and will look in on an exchange at any moment. This implies two imperatives if you're online to build your business. First, resist the temptation to become too clubby with others who post regularly. Abbreviations and obscure in-group references are fine when you really are hanging out only with each other, or when you only wish to socialize. A public response like "ROTFL—doesn't it remind you of Saratoga?—H.H." may make its recipient smile, but it sends the message to others that you're online for fun and relaxation, not for business. I'm going to take a strong position on this and recommend that you never use special online slang like "ROTFL" for "rolling on the floor laughing" or "< BG >" for "big grin," no matter how widely understood you believe they are. Be inclusive rather than exclusionary, and you'll reap the rewards of a welcoming attitude. Second, try to restate your business identity or business message in every follow-up post. You have tossed away a valuable opportunity when people come across a message from you like, "Sure, I'll be glad to send you a copy. What's your address?" or "It costs only $20 a month for as much time as you want." Compare the effect of rewording those replies as "Sure, I'll be glad to send you a copy of our free report on keeping your tropical fish healthy. What's your address?" or "The Internet access provided by our company in seventy-five major metropolitan areas costs only $20 a month for as much time as you want." And unless your online area discourages the practice (see below, Local Differences), sign every post with at least your whole name and your business name, business slogan, or a revealing occupational title. For example, "Norris Kruntz, Financing for 'Unfinanceable' Upstart Businesses."

Never assume the entire audience knows what you do just because the regulars do. Take a cue from skilled radio talk show guests who know that listeners are continually leaving and joining them—they always toss in phrases like, "As I'm always careful to tell my therapy clients," or "As I explain in Chapter 2 of my book, *MegaBusiness Secrets* . . ." Sandwiched amidst substantive information, this slides by as a clarification rather than as huckstering. Recognize that even the regulars may have only a sketchy understanding of your scope of business. Over the space of a month or two, I interacted with a fellow named Dan Veaner, from Lansing, New York. Although I connected him with the product he had created, called Catalog-on-a-Disk, until we exchanged e-mail messages, nothing he said led me to understand that this was a program for creating a catalog on disk rather than a singular disk-based catalog for specific products. It's a good idea to develop and test a brief spiel that truly communicates what your company does and then insert it as appropriate. For instance, "As you may know, we have created a program that anyone can use to place their catalog, complete with interactive order form, attractively on an IBM-compatible disk."

Establish Your Reputation

Unlike online conferences, which may have a host, a guest, and ordinary participants, in a forum or newsgroup all contributions appear, at least initially, equal to each other. That means that until people stop and ponder it, an uninformed or misinformed response carries the same weight as an informed response. Anyone can comment or criticize. Don't depend on any authority you may have outside of the group to add clout to your message. Instead, count on your online readers to be skeptical and irreverent. Only two factors make your contribution believed more than a competitor's: (1) how well your argument is reasoned or documented, and (2) your reputation for reliability *within the group*. In the latter case, members of the group may urge others to pay attention to you because you have previously demonstrated your trustworthiness. Still, credibility online is short-lived; you'll never be able to coast for a long while without pedaling in additional displays of know-how. In some ways, cyberspace is a radically egalitarian environment. You have the right to mount a soapbox, but any brainless jerk also has the right to either shout you down or ignore your brilliance. Other media upgrade you at least to a podium and a microphone. For example, if you share your information in a newspaper article, people can disagree in a letter to the editor, but not all of those get printed, and you usually get the privilege of the last word. Implicitly the article carries a greater claim to attention than the reply, unlike the free-for-all melee in a forum or newsgroup. Similarly, most promotions you send out into the world lack any sort of talk-back feature. With online schmoozing you can't stop someone from tagging onto your message, "Hey, aren't you the one I sent $30 to last year and wouldn't refund my money?" All you can do is shout back, no! According to Bryan Pfaffenberger, author of *The UseNet Book*, Intel CEO Andy Grove stubbed his toes against the participatory nature of UseNet when he posted a message in newsgroups downplaying the flaw in its Pentium microchips. That message got sent around everywhere with comments attached like, "Can you believe this?" Grove's response might have had a different effect in another medium, Pfaffenberger says.

E-mail, more than snail mail, voice mail, or any other kind of communication, seems to place everyone at the same level. That's great when people respond with interest in how you can help them, not so great when people bombard you—or your suppliers and customers—with complaints for having somehow offended them. I believe this great leveling effect accounts for humorist Dave Barry's comment that he never receives letters through the mail that start off, "Are you the real Dave Barry?" as many e-mail messages that reach him do. If you prefer the role of distant, lofty authority, disconnect your modem immediately.

Context

In discussion groups, any message is fragmentable, and any discussion can get away from you. The ability to take your words out of context is almost built into the technology, where someone can select any portion of a previous message to include in theirs. It's usually more difficult and sometimes impossible for a reader to go back and see those words in context. And since many people follow online discussions on an irregular basis, you can't assume that any rejoinder or correction will get seen by everyone who saw the unfair response. "UseNet in particular is like a yard full of snakes—at any time a snake can come up out of the grass and bite you," says Pfaffenberger. John Glenn, publisher of a guide to translation agencies, heard those snakes hissing after he posted a very casual comment in CompuServe's Foreign Language forum, his prime pond for prospects. In a thread titled "pornography," someone asked a question about Japanese pornography that commonly appears in that country on CD-ROM. "I chimed in to say that they had them in the United States as well, I'd seen them in a CD store the other day. I didn't add, 'Glenn's Guide to Translation Agencies' after my name as I usually did, but I'd joined the forum as 'John Glenn/Glenn's Guide,' and CompuServe added that automatically in the header of my reply." Of the droves of people reading that thread out of curiosity, one asked, "What is 'Glenn's Guide'?" and suddenly everyone drawn there was learning about his product in the puzzling context of pornography. "I got about twenty inquiries from that thread, but it was uncomfortable for me. Someone even suggested it was a good idea to get attention with the word, 'pornography,' and I had to keep explaining that I hadn't done that."

Scheduling

Contributions can and do show up twenty-four hours a day. You're courting disaster if you expect the online world to have any consideration for a nine-to-five, Monday-through-Friday, two-weeks-off-in-summer schedule. One of the most dramatic examples of this I've seen occurred when Sheridan, Indiana–based CBSI agreed to participate in a dialogue on Prodigy about its high-priced business start-up packages. The kick-off announcement went up on a Friday at noon, and it wasn't until almost forty-eight hours later that the CBSI representative showed up online. In the meantime, some extremely damaging claims about the company and numerous "Where are they?" notices remained visible to every Prodigy member without any company response. Where participation is international, those sorts of allegations could build to crisis proportions even overnight. I'm not saying not to sleep, just to be aware that rumors, inquiries, and complaints take no account of your convenience. As a corollary to this, if you're soliciting business online, respondents will be getting in touch twenty-four hours a day, 365 days a year. Since telephone calls and faxes will come in day and night, weekday and weekend, be prepared. Turning off your company's fax machine when you go home for the night or the holiday is unacceptable—people in Europe who don't know that it's Thanksgiving, or in Nova Scotia who don't realize you're in Hawaii, may simply conclude you've gone out of business. The same goes for companies that allow phones to ring forever after office hours. Yet if you're a home-based business and allow your business line to ring in your bedroom, the impression you give could be even worse. Before breakfast one morning I called an 800-number for a sample copy of a newsletter I'd seen discussed on America Online. From the sleepiness of the "hello?" it was obvious I'd awakened the publisher. I wondered about the viability of a publication whose creator had either no money or no business sense.

Adequate Response

A public question requires a public answer. When CBSI finally did show up on Prodigy, the owner of the company, George Douglass, responded again and again to specific, pointed questions with "Call our 800-number and get our tapes." Frustrated participants rejected that answer and repeated their questions, to more frustration. Whatever the rationale, this kind of behavior appears evasive, shady, and manipulative to onlookers. Maintain your credibility by providing as much information as you can, along with appropriate qualifiers, such as, "Our literature contains full details, but basically with the XYZ program a purchaser receives a 486 computer, a modem, five proprietary software programs, a 453-page manual, and unlimited telephone support for $10,329." Or, "According to the ground rules of this forum I cannot give you specific legal advice. However, I can say that in several jurisdictions petitioners have gotten the courts to overturn prohibitions against giving Tarot and astrology readings for pay in one's home."

Think Before You Post

Where you can delete messages, be aware that they may never entirely vanish. They may already have found their way into the archives of the system or of individuals, and system administrators may have easy ways of restoring deleted material, as we learned in the case of Lt. Colonel Oliver North in the Iran-Contra affair. Just how hard it can be to recall or correct misinformation online we know from the Federal Communications Commission, which is still dealing with protests stemming from an unfounded 1986 "modem tax" rumor. "Some days we get dozens of messages about the tax, sometimes just a few," sighs an FCC spokesperson. The best policy here: think before you post!

Local Differences

At a Chamber of Commerce luncheon people may be visibly impressed when you refer to your little law firm as a $4 million business, while at the Bar Assocation dinner, any mention of dollar figures may provoke raised eyebrows and significant glances. Similarly, the online medium is not monolithic, so figuring out one outpost's ground rules doesn't mean you've scoped out all of cyberspace. A method of schmoozing that works perfectly well in one locale may violate the norms in another province. The members of the group may be different, or distinctive traditions may be involved. You have to remain observant. Online, Bryan Pfaffenberger illustrates this principle with the example of the newsgroup *rec.backcountry,* for avid mountain climbers. "If someone dies climbing, a friend is supposed to post an obituary of a certain type because in this group death while climbing is noble, a kind of victory," he says. "If you didn't understand this and said how terrible the death was, you'd find yourself at the wrong end of flames."

Be especially sensitive to expectations about so-called signature files. Sometimes nicknamed ".sigs," on the Internet, these function as the electronic equivalent of a business letterhead. Once set up by the user, they get inserted automatically at the foot of all of his or her postings, the signature.

Since professors and researchers started this tradition, on the Internet this format doesn't usually count as commercial promotion, unless you take it too far. How far is too far? Even the most staid newsgroups and mailing lists seem to tolerate four-line signatures and regard eight lines as too much, and accept a simple description of your line of business but not necessarily a brazen sales pitch like "Call IDP for the best desktop publishing in Iowa!"

However, on the commercial online services you'll have to tone down a signature or leave off everything but your name and a minimal identifier. "We had to make a rule against the Internet kind of signatures because they were abused," says Janet Attard, a sysop on GEnie and America Online. "People were posting one-line messages and ten-line signatures." I was severely chastised on a Prodigy bulletin board for mentioning one of my book titles along with my name, though on CompuServe this was not usually considered overly promotional. When in Rome, you might say, it's safest to observe what the Romans do and follow their example, being perhaps a teensy weensy bit more daring than the norm, if you like.

Another issue over which expectations differ is the extent to which people will put up with the same old questions. Participants in newsgroups and mailing lists are supposed to familiarize themselves with the FAQs—Frequently Asked Questions, available in standard places like "news.answers"—and not to bother the regulars with them. By contrast, on the commercial online services a question that has come up a thousand times before will almost always receive an informative, courteous reply, though possibly a "canned" one. This difference makes sense when you consider that in contrast to the no-one-in-charge, no-one-collecting-fees-for-participation Internet, services like America Online and Delphi make money by catering to newcomers and making sure they feel comfortable spending their time exchanging messages.

Before joining in on discussions, you may want to know how long contributions remain accessible in that online region. Some newsgroups and mailing lists maintain archives of all messages, while others don't. On America Online, GEnie, and The Well, your messages stay visible indefinitely, which feels spooky to me for off-the-cuff conversations. You may also wish to investigate the extent to which postings are screened, sifted, and possibly rejected or edited. Some moderated groups simply include or exclude offerings, while others may trim them in ways objectionable to the one whose name is on it.

Marshall McLuhan coined the phrase "the global village" to describe the effect of electronically linking people all over the world. Jay Linden, an Internet provider and consultant in Toronto, calls the Internet "the world's largest, most diverse small town." Perhaps we just need to change that to "villages" and "small towns" to remind us to check out the local customs before we hang out our shingle and walk up and down Main Street shaking hands.

15 Hiring a Cyber-PR Agent

ERIC R. WARD OF THE WARD GROUP/NETPOST IS AN CYBER-PR AGENT. He helps people promote themselves. Depending on your time and resources, you may choose to hire a Cyber-PR agent to handle all your Internet publicity. Here are Mr. Ward's recommendations regarding what issues you should consider when you are thinking of hiring a Cyber-PR agent to promote your Website:

Automated Submissions

Automated submission services should be used only after careful examination and full disclosure of how they work. Autobots such as Submit-It automatically submit your Website to tens or hundreds of search engines. All are not created equal, and some will ruin your listing attempts. It is always preferred that you use the actual submission form from the site you are submitting to, not someone else's. It takes longer, and yes, it's troublesome, but it is worth it. Ward currently gets new clients every month who used one of these autobots first, and now pay him to resubmit their listings.

Hard Copy Confirmation

Demand that you receive a printout for every single site used. This does not mean a one-page list of all sites, but the actual confirmation for each and every site. Ward's clients receive a seventy-five to one-hundred-page hard-copy report when he's done—tangible proof of each submission. This helps prove that the sites were used one at a time, the right way. If you do not get a copy of every post sent or confirmation screen printout, you should seriously question whether or not you're getting what you paid for.

References

Ask for references. This is so simple, yet overlooked too often. If a company claims that it can help you with building awareness of your site, ask for proof.

Follow-Up Services

Are follow-up services available to verify that your URL made it in, and for free resubmission after thirty days for slow or lagging indexes? We know how slow the directories are to respond to new submissions. Sometimes it seems like they let them slip through the cracks. Why should you have to pay twice for something that should have made it in the first time? Here is what you should get: after thirty days, at least one free resubmission to any directory that has not yet added the listing.

Contacts

Ask them if they locate, keep up with, and maintain ongoing editor and publisher relations with the Internet media folks. Have they ever even talked to a single editor? It is essential that a Cyber-PR agent, just like an off-line PR agent, knows the industry and its decision makers. Make sure that the prospective Cyber-PR agent knows the names of the key Internet media folks. Find out if they attend the trade shows and follow the industry.

Blind Carbons

Never use a service that sends blind carbon copies to a list of names. Blind carbons are the equivalent of an unsolicited phone call to your house to sell you something. They irritate. Have you ever received one? If so, you probably didn't like it much, especially if you didn't ask for it. Then you probably did what we all do with them: hit the delete key. This is the exact opposite of what you want your PR to do. Ward, for example, sends each and every e-mail one at a time, to a specific person, by name. Yes, it is slower, but it has worked for his clients.

Less Is More

More is absolutely *not* better. Some services will resend your information to hundreds upon hundreds of directories or other contacts, bragging about the free link they got you. Baloney. What good is being on thirty obscure hot lists that get three hits a day each? This is nothing but a way of trying to impress you with big numbers of sites used, as opposed to what really matters—the quality, demographics, traffic, and interests of the users of the sites. Also, just because a directory offers a free link to any business does not mean it will be in the best interests of your company to be in that directory. A XXX-rated or fringe-interest directory that offers free links to any business might not be the place you want to see your company. Image and positioning is key. Not every link is a good link; quality beats quantity in the long run.

Target Affinity Groups

Require some effort to look for regional and topical Affinity Internet Audience outlets. If all a PR agent does is stick your URL in all the major general directories they know of, he or she has insulted you and your site. What about the specialized collections and regional Web-zines or e-zines and lists? Yes, they take some time to research. It's worth it. Most awareness services don't even try.

Billing Structure

Be very cautious of those who want to charge by the hour for promotional activity. At least two companies have services that will bill you based on the number of hours they spend each month engaged in "link-seeking" activities for your site. Isn't billing by the hour an invitation for abuse? A way to avoid quantifying performance? If you choose this method, agree to some set of performance goals first, and if you can, get a track record.

Exclusivity

Will they give you category exclusivity, or turn around and promote your competitors at the same time they promote you? Ward says that he offers category exclusivity because trying to increase awareness of two or more similar—and possibly competing—companies is unethical and self-serving, and not in the best interests of the client and the Website. All exclusivity options are for three months, at which time the client has the option to use his services again, thus securing the category for another three months, or release the category back.

16 How to Measure the Effectiveness of Publicity

IS IT POSSIBLE TO MEASURE THE EFFECTIVENESS OF YOUR PUBLICITY ON the Internet? It is difficult, but not impossible. The following chapter outlines several key tools for tracking publicity. Just imagine the Internet being used like print publications; it too contains advertising space, editorial space, and letters to the editor.

The Basics

First, you need to understand that Web pages function to some extent like magazines. Like print publications, the Internet not only has space for paid advertising, but the content of this advertising is kept under your control, barring the activities of hackers. On the Internet you can also find the equivalent of editorial pages. Internet versions of editorial pages appear in the form of UseNet and listserv discussions, which allow you to track what people are saying about your company or product.

You need to monitor such areas of public discussion for the same reason public relations specialists monitor print media. The best example of the need to do so is the recent Intel fiasco. Another company, Intuit, knew better. When problems were discovered in their new tax software, the company proactively offered free upgrades of the package before online incriminations got out of hand. Even if the download took more than two hours to complete, more than 1,500 people took advantage of the offer in the initial week.

When preparing to monitor your public appearance on the Internet, you need to consider several key issues. The biggest problem is: where do I start—Web pages or discussion groups? Perhaps the best thing to do is to continue to carry over the comparison with print media and the Internet. When businesses or organizations release information to the public, certain magazines and newspapers are the first choice because they effectively reach a specific market. Likewise, on the Internet you must present certain types of information in the appropriate venue. This same principle applies when monitoring what other people say about your company in cyberspace. Next, you need to decide how you will monitor online discussions about your company or product. Traditionally one would be forced to choose between clipping newspaper and magazine articles in-house or hiring a clipping service. This is also the case with the Internet: you need to determine whether you have adequate resources in-house to do the necessary online monitoring or whether you need to hire an outside firm.

Regardless of how you get the job done, there are other issues to consider. Always get a second opinion: whoever you hire to monitor online chatter about your company should be a member of your target audience. Because of your perspective as the manufacturer of a product, you tend to see things in a certain way and might miss something that members of your target market see as obvious and crucial. The opposite might also occur: what you think is a disaster might just as easily positively affect your market. It is also necessary to ensure that online monitoring be done constantly. Because the Internet increases the speed of information dissemination, things change quickly and constantly. This speed, characteristic of the Internet, makes the medium both dynamic and malleable: what is the hot discussion one day could be cold and dead the next. For this reason daily monitoring is highly recommended. But you need to know what to look for and where to look as well. For organizational purposes it is necessary to note the location, subject, date, and tone of discussions, as well as to pay attention to what kind of messages appear about your company and its competitors. Ultimately, you should put at least as much effort and concern into recording and evaluating online comments about your company or its products as you would with print media. By doing this, you can eventually develop benchmarks to help you determine which tactics, topics, and techniques work best in each online medium—Web pages or discussion forums.

Once you've gotten this far, you need to keep up your efforts by figuring out who and what's out there. For decades, companies have been plagued with the question of how can they know that their media activities are reaching their audience. The good news regarding this issue is that you can gather this information easily on the Internet. This can be done by simply including a questionnaire on your Website through which you can request visitors to provide some basic demographic information before they get what they are looking for or before they can exit the site. All you need to do is ask. While it is true that these visitors could lie just as easily as they do with traditional demographic forms, if you offer free software or something else that requires mailing addresses and the like, you have a much better chance of receiving accurate e-mail information.

Most servers have software in place to track Web visitations. The problem is, however, that most of the data generated just sits there. It is necessary to analyze and interpret this information. Analyst software packages can take this information and easily convert it into graphs, charts, and tables that can help you identify trends and determine the effectiveness of your online advertising. In the next subsection on Web measuring tools, some of these software packages are discussed.

In terms of monitoring newsgroups and listservs, it is important not only to identify the appropriate forums but also the places from which you can do this. The tool Mailbase makes it possible to research a wide variety of online discussion forums. You can find relevant lists, repositories of archives of past discussions, and more details about any group found there. Another tack is to employ the "UseNet" search function in Digital's Alta Vista search engine (*http://www.altavista.digital.com/*). This handy tool makes it easy to perform searches of the most recent UseNet discussions based on keyword searches. All you need do is enter your company's name or product name and wait for the results. This can be a truly effective means of keeping tabs on the public's reaction to your business. A new product, Echo-Sentinel by Information Cybernetics, Inc. (*http://www. icybernetics.com*), monitors all sorts of discussion forums and can also send e-mail to alert you of any "mischief" going on about your company on those forums.

Measuring the effectiveness of your publicity campaign is a difficult and laborious process, but it can be done. By using the above tools and methods and by putting at least as much effort into researching your online audience and marketplace as you would with print media, you can turn the Internet into an effective public relations tool. The only problem is that as the Internet continues to grow, tracking your online publicity will eventually demand the maturation of available tools and a further growth of your budget for online public relations.

Web Measuring Tools

Commercial Web ventures hope to make money by selling advertisers on the popularity of their pages. Advertisers are attracted to high-volume sites, but want rich demographics about Website visitors instead of the simple hit tallies typically publicized. Looking to service both Web publishers and advertisers, three firms have rushed to offer auditing software and services that at minimum make sense of log file data and in some cases add value by cross-referencing log information with statistical profiles of domain names and users. Internet Profiles Corp. (I/Pro) in San Francisco provides three products/services: I/Count, I/Audit, and I/Code. I/Count enables Websites to analyze Web use and users, including the identity of organizations assigned the IP addresses that access the Website. By tracking IP addresses and matching them against a precompiled database, I/Count attempts to provide additional market intelligence. That includes a usage report extrapolating variables such as company size and geographic location.

The report must be extrapolated due to the inherent problem posed by dynamically assigned IP addresses. Major online services and national Internet access providers continually re-use a large block of IP addresses, and there is no information that can be automatically grabbed to provide more detail. I/Pro's I/Count brackets these users, creates a baseline profile of all other users accessing the site, and then applies the number of visits from the online services according to the established baseline.

An additional service from I/Pro, I/Audit, will analyze usage statistics for a Website and attest to the accuracy of the numbers. The well-known Yahoo site is an early I/Audit customer. Started as the hobby of two Stanford University graduate students, Yahoo is now a commercial venture that plans to generate revenue by selling advertising. According to Tim Brady, Yahoo's director of marketing, advertisers are not yet demanding audited numbers, but he expects they will soon. Yahoo's strategy was to get out in front of the demand and elevate its credibility.

Open Market (Cambridge, Massachusetts) has released Web

Reporter software. This package is designed to make it easier to extract information from Web log files. Unlike I/Pro's I/Count, Open Market does not claim to add information that cannot be obtained from a thorough sifting of server logs combined with common add-on patches. However, Web Reporter does provide a variety of ways to manipulate server log data. For instance, Websites can group pages by user-defined characteristics and then look at global access numbers by category.

Web Reporter understands Open Market's extended log format, says Pierre Bouchard, vice president of Open Market's server products group. Open Market's Webserver replaces the CERN, NCSA, or Netscape server software, and captures additional logging information.

Web Reporter also makes it convenient to concatenate incremental reports into larger data sets without having to regenerate all new reports. "Web Reporter lets us easily get a very high-level view of what is going on with the Website. Rather than giving page-by-page traffic reports, we can define a set of pages that are our core product catalog and get statistics for that set of pages," says Dave Mackie, manager of online technologies for Books that Work, a CD-ROM producer.

Moreover, says Mackie, he can track the percentage of users accessing those pages with a Netscape browser and determine whether or not they should make use of Netscape browser extensions.

Answering such questions was pretty difficult with any product other than Web Reporter, Mackie says. So Web Reporter not only provides usage information, but also helps him make intelligent decisions about the design and operation of the Website. You can find an interactive demo of Web Reporter on Open Market's Website.

A third entry into the Web analysis market is WebTrack in New York. Its WebStat product/service tracks the total number of times each page is accessed, the number of unique sessions in which a page is accessed, or the total number of sessions for the site. It is designed to track domain types and referring URLs. It will also provide an analysis of average session behavior, such as the number of links in an average session, session duration, and common pathways—i.e., the order in which links are selected.

▼

Community

17 State of the Internet Community

IN THIS CHAPTER, I WANT TO REVIEW THE CURRENT STATE OF THE Internet community, how it has grown over the past two years, and its effect on other media. Recently Coopers and Lybrand Consulting (CLC) completed a study that evaluated the "Winners and Losers in the Evolution of the Internet and the World Wide Web." Their research revealed, for example, that the Internet and the World Wide Web are having a negative impact on television viewing, but are actually boosting the sales of print media. In fact, consumers are spending more money on books and magazines covering the Internet than they are in electronic commerce on the Internet. Among the other major findings of CLC's Electronic Access 96 (EA96) study of consumers are:

- Three distinct segments of online users are evolving: communicators, information seekers, and browsers.
- Security concerns are retarding the growth of online commerce.
- The popularity of Internet service provider (ISP) services is continuing to grow in comparison to that of traditional online service offerings
- Consumers continue to show interest in interactive television (ITV); until ITV emerges, consumers show a strong preference for wireless cable over direct broadcast satellite.

Electronic Access 96 was designed and analyzed by the Telecom and Media Practice division of Coopers and Lybrand Consulting and conducted by Response Analysis Corporation. It is the second study CLC has conducted to capture the impact that the Internet and World Wide Web are having on consumers, traditional media, marketers, and access providers. Electronic Access 94 involved more than 1,600 in-home interviews (average length ninety minutes) projectable to 41 million U.S. households with incomes of $35,000 and over. In addition, more than one hundred face-to-face interviews were conducted with industry leaders. EA96 is based on telephone interviews of a subset of 750 of the original 1,600 households. The sample was broken down into subcategories by the age, gender, income, education levels, and geographic region of the participants. Again, industry interviews were also conducted.

Internet's Effect on Traditional Media

As mentioned above, the survey results showed that the Internet has had a favorable impact on the print medium, generating more sales in books and magazines covering the Internet than it has in online commerce. Coopers and Lybrand Consulting estimates that consumers are spending from $300 million to $600 million annually on books and magazines as guides to the Internet. This compares favorably to industry estimates of $200 million to $300 million in electronic commerce actually conducted on the Internet last year. Almost one-third (30 percent) of the survey participants use magazines or books to learn about content on the Web and close to two-thirds (65 percent) of those who have looked at an online publication consider it as a complement rather than substitute for the print version.

At the other end of the spectrum, the Internet is having a negative impact on television. A majority (58 percent) of Internet users indicated that the time they spend online is shifted directly from time previously spent watching television.

Profile of Internet Users

EA96 shows that three distinct clusters of online users are evolving. Communicators and information seekers are the most active segments. Communicators, who make up 22 percent of online users, are innovators that began using the Internet back in 1994. They tend to be well-educated males who do some work from home and are very comfortable with technology. This group is especially interested in activities involving communication with others, such as chat, e-mail, bulletin boards, meeting people. Information seekers make up 24 percent of online users. Similar to communicators, these early adopters tend to be males who do some work from home. However, unlike communicators, they are less technologically adept and are likely to have young children. They spend most of their online time getting information, downloading software, and reading online magazines.

A majority (54 percent) of users are browsers. This group of light users is split almost equally between males and females. Like information seekers, they also tend to be less technologically adept than communicators and are more likely to have young children. Browsers take part in far fewer online activities than the other groups. Their primary interests seem to be general information, e-mail, databases, or just browsing.

Marketing and Advertising on the Internet

In addition to traditional media (39 percent), Internet users cite word-of-mouth (44 percent) and browsing (32 percent) as the most common ways that they learn about Websites to visit. Only 10 percent learn of Websites through links with other sites. According to CLC Telecom and Media partner Bill Battino, "Marketers must consider how they can attract visitors while they are browsing the Web. This can be accomplished by establishing links with other Websites and directories, in addition to promoting the site through such traditional media as newspapers, magazines, and television. The biggest challenge is to sell subscription and *à la carte* services to consumers."

Consumers expect to use the Internet for purchases once security is in place. However, Internet commerce will not take off until consumers are satisfied that this new medium has effective security safeguards. According to the study, only a small minority of consumers, 15 percent of direct Internet users and 19 percent of commercial online subscribers, have already used credit cards to make purchases online. More than three-quarters (80 percent) of Internet users indicate that they are concerned about the security of financial data. These security concerns are most prevalent in conducting banking and brokerage transactions.

Many consumers are resistant to advertiser supported content on the Internet. In fact, 37 percent of Internet/online service users are opposed to advertising as a way to reduce the cost of Internet services. However, among the remaining users there is strong interest in various forms of interactive advertising. Participants showed a preference for certain types of advertising on the Internet. "Advermation" (ads with detailed information) would be used by 41 percent of all consumers interviewed. Close to one quarter of the participants would make use of "customization" (ads targeted to meet that consumer's interest) and "advermarts" (ads that facilitate ordering). Only 9 percent were favorably inclined toward "advertainment" (interactive ads that are primarily entertaining).

PC Usage and Growth

While the recent slump in computer sales will slow the growth of the Internet somewhat, EA96 shows continued rapid growth of Internet and World Wide Web usage among existing computer owners. More than one-third (37 percent) of U.S. households and a majority (58 percent) of survey participants have at least one computer, the latter representing an increase of 23 percent from 1994.

However, growth in PC penetration appears likely to slow. Of the 28 percent of targeted households ($35,000 and over) who plan to purchase a computer in the next year, only 12 percent will be first-time buyers rather than replacement buyers. In addition, past experience suggests actual purchases will be lower than consumer estimates. Ten percent of the target consumers use both methods of access. Both types of access providers are experiencing high growth in subscribers and each is used primarily for communications and information gathering.

Interactive Television

Consumers still show strong interest in interactive television (ITV) despite roll out delays. When study participants were given a description of ITV, 58 percent indicated at least a moderate interest in purchasing the service at a level of $50 a month. Individual electronic access applications appeal to the same target segments as they did in the 1994 study. The most valued applications of those consumers "very likely to use ITV" include time-shifting (viewing favorite television programs at more convenient times) and video-on-demand (movies available at any time). This same group showed a strong preference for wireless cable (42 percent) over direct broadcast satellite (21 percent). Regional Telecom providers are expected to be offering wireless cable service in the very near future.

While the Internet community appears to be growing in various dimensions, many have also spoken about the need for ubiquitous access in order to ensure that growth. The Internet is only going to become a great vehicle for marketing and publicity as the mass of people on it continues to grow.

18 Building Critical Mass

IF THE INTERNET IS TO BE THE CATALYST FOR A COMMUNICATIONS revolution, it is important for everyone to demand access to the Internet or work creatively in their communities to obtain such access. Access is one of the most critical issues determining the future of the Internet and the leveling of the playing field for all. Independent businesses and individuals have much to gain by the ubiquity of access to the Internet.

Potential Benefits

The Internet is not controlled by anyone. Therefore, the success of the Communications Age will be up to us. Consider the potential benefits, some of which are already available. With ubiquitous access, these benefits would be available to even more people.

With access for all, people could live practically anywhere they want without sacrificing opportunities for fulfilling employment by "telecommuting" to their offices via the Internet. This feature raises several environmental issues. Telecommuting would allow business owners to service a global clientele from their homes. The best schools, teachers, and courses would be available to all students, regardless of location, resources, or disability. Professionals could share knowledge and techniques with each other. They could "distance learn" and teach diverse groups of students from anywhere in the world.

Art, literature, science, and technology would also be freed from physical spaces. Art would not have to be only in museums and galleries. Literature would not have to be bound in libraries, bookstores, and archives. Science would be made available outside of the laboratories and research institutions. Small businesses could get orders electronically from all over the world. Movies, video games, banking, and shopping could all be accessed from the comfort of one's home.

What Kind of Access?

Access to the Internet can mean many things. Many people have erroneously considered access to mean physical access to the Internet. I believe there are actually three important aspects of access to the Internet. The first is the physical connection to the Internet via phone lines, cable, optical fiber, etc. The second is the ability to access and find information. The third is friendly, easy-to-use hardware and software user interfaces.

Physical access to the Internet requires three components: a computer, a modem, and an Internet provider. Each of the three components has a price tag. Fortunately, the price of hardware drops every year. Modems and computers have become relatively inexpensive commodities. For less than $1,500, you can get a decent computer with fast access to the Internet. Local Internet access providers charge between $15 to $20 a month for dialup access to the Internet. However, in this competitive environment, many of these local providers are going out of business. In the United States, I have found NETCOM Online Communication Services, Inc., to be the best. NETCOM, furthermore, is dedicated to the growth of Internet usage among local communities and schools. They provide nationwide Internet dialup access. Nationwide Internet dialup access means access to the Internet with a local phone call from anywhere in the United States. Local providers usually offer only local access, meaning that if you are away from your home base or out of the area code of your home base, you need to make a long distance call to get on the Internet. More than one thousand people a day are signing up to the Internet through NETCOM. I am confident that NETCOM will be in business for a long time. Furthermore, they are laying down transatlantic cable to Britain and Europe. This means that you can get on the Internet in London or France via a local phone call.

Physical access to the Internet can also be accelerated through the development of public access networks. In various small towns in New Zealand, small businesses, arts organizations, and artist cooperatives have joined together to buy computers and access to the Internet. Others in the community have begun to build public access networks that are available to anyone in the local community. Public access networks help build the critical mass of users and services that will make interactive communications more valuable. These networks focus uniquely on the needs of local people and communities. They have the potential to grow into a sophisticated, low-cost distribution system for the information and services of individuals, microenterprises, arts, and public service organizations.

In the town of Blacksburg, Virginia, a major public access network has been organized. After nearly two years of operation, Blacksburg's Electronic Village is already linking more than a third of the population and a third of the local shops and businesses. The network also provides access to healthcare information, job referrals, local mail service, movie schedules, and the ability to apply for municipal permits. "What we're re-creating is the old village square where people get together with their neighbors," says Andrew M. Cohill, project director of the Electronic Village. "Everyone else in the country is fixated on the concept of global connectivity. What people here are saying is, 'We don't care. We want to do Blacksburg stuff.'" Larger networks help create so-called virtual communities in which people who are separated by long distances can be linked by issues or interests. These virtual communities are valuable, but they can't go far enough to help citizens in the very real community of Denver, Colorado, for example, who are trying to solve the city's homeless problem. Connecting local groups and organizations takes a communications system that provides access to the requisite local information and to the right people. The Denver Free-Internet is placing terminals linked to its network in area homeless shelters through which people can access job listings, social service agencies, and other services.

Many public access networks take the next step as well, such as one in New Zealand, by providing physical access through donated equipment, subsidized public kiosks, or terminals. Many nonprofit organizations, in particular, can benefit from such proactive methods. Organizations that are short on funding should work with local businesses to trade advertising space on the organization's Website in exchange for funding to access the Internet. This can also help local businesses get free or low-cost access to the Internet.

Finding information is another aspect of access. From the beginning of civilization, priests, learned scholars, and archivists have played a role in preserving our history. Information was given special value. It was denied to some members of society and reserved as part of rituals belonging to an elite. Thus, we cannot simply look at the machinery of access without considering the ability to find information as a part of the access problem. If few people can find your Website on the WWW, or if it is very difficult to find relevant information, then the value of your physical connection to the Internet is reduced.

Most search engines on the Internet use keyword searching. Keywords are used to describe information objects such as text, images, audio, and video files on a Website. The search engines use the keywords to locate these objects. However, my doctoral research at MIT, and that of others, in the areas of keyword searching, term frequency, co-occurrence, and other statistical techniques have proven that keyword searching is a passable solution for some disciplines with highly specific vocabularies, but nearly useless in all others.

Keyword searching doesn't take into account different terms for the same concepts. It also doesn't take into account information in other languages or the different levels of user access to that information. Searches for information by children, for example, will probably be different than searches by adults. Libraries already use different subject-access schemes for children's materials. Furthermore, nontextual items, such as software, graphics, sound, and video do not respond at all to keyword searching.

There is no effortless way to create an organization for information. The best tools for accessing relevant information are a clearly defined classification scheme and a human indexer. A classification or indexing scheme gives the searcher a chance to develop a rational strategy for searching. Arts-Online, for example, is an Internet art project organizing a large part of the Web's art-related Websites into a conceptual framework using both conceptual terms and keywords. This project involves the initial work of many expert human indexers who are knowledgeable in the diverse fields of art. The resulting conceptual index of Arts-Online will enable users to find more relevant and conceptually based information. The advanced conceptual indexing of Arts-Online will be superior to the WWW directories and search engines of Yahoo!, WebCrawler, etc., which rely solely on keywords.

The importance of new organizational tools for finding and accessing information cannot be overstated. It all comes down to the fact that if we can't find the information we need, it doesn't matter if it exists or not. If we don't find it, it isn't information. There are undoubtedly millions of bytes of files on the Internet that are, for all practical purposes, nonexistent.

Thus, it becomes imperative that new search engines, new search methods, indexing techniques, and advanced searching tools are a part of the public resource. If not, then there will be no real and equal access to information. Those who want to find you, regardless of their connection to the Internet or their hardware, may not be able to simply because they do not have the search tools to locate you. Education and training in learning how to use search technology and classification methods will be essential for success in finding the right information. I highly recommend that those of you who are serious about using the Internet as a research tool take an introductory course in library science or information retrieval. Such education will result in skills that will be highly valued.

Usable and friendly interfaces are the third aspect of access. Many experts today talk about their concerns for the "last mile." The term last mile refers to the last mile of wire and/or cable to deliver information into every home. I think we should be concerned about the last few feet. We can easily move information from one computer to another, but how do we get it from the computer to the human being in the proper format? Not all information is suited for electronic use on the current hardware mediums. Think of the small books you like to curl up in bed with. It's not that fun to curl up with a computer—not now, at least.

Even the Library of Congress has announced that it is undertaking a huge project to digitize five million items from its collection. Then what? How will we make use of those materials? Sitting down in front of a fourteen-inch computer screen with really bad flicker to read a novel is really no fun. I don't know of anyone who reads novels on their computer screen. Many people will simply not do it. There are high-definition screens and other devices that are being developed that will make the computer more visually appealing. Such devices need to be made more accessible. Even using a mouse and a keyboard is not the most natural way to interact. The ultimate user-friendly way for humans to interact with a computer would be with voice and gestures. The mouse and keyboard are intermediaries of human interaction with the computer.

There are many commercial products on the market today that enable users to use both speech and gestures. In the last decade, major advancements have been made in speech recognition technology. Apple and IBM are already releasing products to households that allow users to give simple voice commands to their computers. NASA's original development of the data glove is also reaching the market. The data glove enables users to send inputs to the computer with hand gestures. The fusion of speech recognition and gestural technology will make human interaction with a computer far more natural and easy.

Thus, user interface design and development will be a key aspect of access. Many of my friends who are not computer-savvy don't look forward to using their computers. That's primarily because the user interface for computers is not at all natural. Most systems require you to know how to type and use a mouse. I believe that ordinary people need to use computers and to tell us why they are bad. Such feedback can help us design more friendly and creative interfaces. Technophobia keeps many away from the computer. Friendly and easy-to-use interfaces can change that.

Why Universal Access?

Now that we understand what access means, we can say why universal access is important. In addition to the potential benefits outlined above, ubiquitous access at an affordable cost is a necessary starting point, not necessarily for ideological or egalitarian reasons, but for very practical ones and for the common good. Unless every individual, organization, and community has access to interactive communications and the opportunities it offers, the Communications Age will never realize its potential.

Interactive communications is made possible by myriad interconnected networks. Ubiquitous access to these networks is essential in establishing the critical mass of users required to realize its value. This was also true of previous communications networks, such as railroads, telephones, and interstate highways. As the number of people they could reach increased, their value grew exponentially.

The availability of interactive communications can and should be as common, affordable, and essential as the availability of electricity was during the industrial revolution. As David Hughes, a pioneer in public access networks, has pointed out, "There's no reason in technology or economics why 100 percent of the population shouldn't be connected." Today, knowledge and education are the predominant indicators of individual success. As we progress more deeply into the Communications Age, the skills of network usage and information management will become as essential as the ability to use keyboard and software are today. There are, even now, hundreds of journals and other information sources that are only available online. More importantly, some of the forms in which information can be presented on the networks, using interconnected links and multimedia for example, make these documents nearly irreproducible on paper. Without access to interactive communications, and without education in its use, groups of people will be cut off from this knowledge-rich world and from the ability to succeed in the information economy.

Consider the other side as well: network users may never learn from the wealth of knowledge and experience held by those who lack access. Despite legitimate cautions about creating an information underclass, it is to some degree the wrong way to frame the issue. We already have such divisions in society today. These divisions have less to do with technological "haves" and "have nots" than with "who can?" The real question is: Will we use the potential of interactive communications to close the gaps in knowledge and opportunity, and to cross lines of traditional prejudices and discrimination, or will we widen them?

19 Demographics

LET'S TAKE A CLOSER LOOK AT WHO IS ON THE INTERNET AND PROFILES relative to their marketing efforts and their successes. According to a case study done by *Activ*Media, Inc., almost one quarter of World Wide Web marketers (23 percent) are trying to sell products or services from their Websites. Yet, 31 percent of respondents described their Websites as "profitable now." In fact, more than one added a note saying, "We've been profitable from the very beginning." How can this disparity be explained?

The research shows that another 25 percent of marketers on the Web do not offer products for sale at their sites. Instead, they use the sites for product literature, technical support, or other applications. Many of these companies consider themselves successful online marketers. In fact, one quarter of those who offer nothing for sale described their sites as "profitable now," apparently from the expense side of the balance sheet. These companies, added to the quarter that are trying to sell but sold nothing, make up almost one half of those on the Web!

Among the remaining half of companies who are actually selling something, 18 percent sold less than $1,000 during the previous month. Few of these consider their sites "profitable now." Another 13 percent of companies, some of whom consider their operations "profitable now," brought in only $1,000 to $9,999 in revenues last month, attesting to the importance of a few thousand dollars to a small operation.

Another 9 percent of online marketers brought in $10,000 to $99,999 during the previous month. Most online revenues, however, are split among the top 2 percent of marketers. This handful of companies brings in anywhere from $100,000 to a few million dollars in a month. Remembering that most of these online operations are less than one year old, and that many are selling expensive goods with a long sales cycle, these results are impressive.

Many people notice the disparity between the mass of online marketers with almost no sales and the few with very strong sales and conclude that only certain types of products are selling. In the report Trends in the WWW Marketplace, there is a detailed discussion of each product and service type and its relative success. The dramatic differences in Website marketing and management between successful and unsuccessful marketers (described in Who's Succeeding on the Web and How?) also affect results. In addition, marketing savvy, opportunity, technological know-how, and, occasionally, luck, all play a part in the mix, as the case-by-case analyses of "successful" companies in this study demonstrate.

In both surveys of online marketers to date, it was found that companies of all sizes are nearly as likely to consider their sites successful or profitable. Case Studies in Successful Online Marketing shows that the way companies determine success or profitability varies quite a bit by company size, however.

Medium-sized companies (100–499 employees) also appear to expect increased revenues from their online ventures, tying profitability to sales. Annual sales fall in the $3 million to $20 million range. Some of our mid-sized examples profit from an exquisite fit with online users; others are working furiously to build the back-end infrastructure that will make them attractive buyout candidates when the heavy-hitters enter the game.

Large companies (greater than five hundred employees) appear to view profitability with the expense side of the ledger in mind as much as revenues. They also have a keen eye toward the future and consider their current projects as valuable strategic investments toward a future world of wired households. And, of course, the importance of an attractive Website for shareholders and the public does not go unnoticed. Still, even among large corporations, online revenues are beginning to flow here and there.

Even while large corporations are the least likely to consider revenues significant, in many ways they have far more at stake as telecommunications, computer, software, financial services, and many other industries become inextricably wedded. Opportunities are increasing in size, but decreasing in variety and quantity. As the advantages of size are somewhat ameliorated by global communications, many of the international giants will be thrown into mortal combat. North American companies may have an early advantage in experience, but that far from assures their success over the longer term. The large companies in these case studies are as notable in their maneuvering for position as future online contenders as they are for the more immediate consequences of their operations.

How Many on the Internet?

How many people are on the Internet and what are they like? Those two questions are a major source of controversy right now. It seems that everyone wants to know who's using the Internet and what they're using it for. Madison Avenue is especially concerned with the Information Superhighway; they can't sell ads unless they come up with some numbers for the size of the audience.

The problem with calculating Internet demographics is that the Net is decentralized. No one controls access to the Internet, so it's very hard to estimate the number of users. Below, we'll examine the three most-quoted surveys on the Internet and the World Wide Web. The numbers are rough estimates and they're often used inappropriately. But the trends they show are useful for making marketing decisions.

The MIDS Survey

This survey was conducted by Matrix Information and Directory Services (MIDS) in early 1996. It is the most reliable of all Internet surveys I've seen, in part because it was sent to Internet service providers rather than people on the Net. MIDS received 1,463 responses from organizations that represent roughly 10 percent of the people on the Internet.

The MIDS survey came up with the following numbers: 27.5 million people can exchange Internet e-mail. Roughly half of these people (13.5 million) have access to the Internet, and half again (7.8 million) have direct Internet accounts via SLIP/PPP. These are the most accurate numbers yet on the size of the net.

One problem with the MIDS survey is that it tallies accounts rather than people. As many as one-third of the people using the World Wide Web have multiple Internet accounts, according to one directory service. Therefore, the number of people on the Internet could be much lower than the number of accounts reported by MIDS.

Other interesting figures from the MIDS survey involve growth and gender. The Internet has been doubling in size every year for the last six years. While this growth rate will eventually slow, the popularity of the World Wide Web is attracting more people than ever to the Internet. MIDS shows a dramatic narrowing of the Internet gender gap. The ratio of males to females is often quoted as ten to one; the new MIDS survey pegs this at two to one.

After looking at all the data I could find, I feel most comfortable with the following numbers, as of the summer of 1996: thirty to forty million people have e-mail, about twenty-five to thirty million people are on the Internet, and about eleven million people have access to the World Wide Web.

I have recently cruised more than one hundred malls on the World Wide Web. Mall owners sell Web storefronts to people who want to do business on the Internet. Almost without exception, the mall owners were quoting a potential audience of thirty to forty million people, even though only a fraction of those people can access the Web.

For those trying to do business over the Internet, one thing is clear: you need to make product information available via e-mail. If you are relying on the Web to reach your audience, you are missing as much as 90 percent of the market. E-mail isn't as sexy as the Web, but it's still the most effective sales tool in the Internet kit.

Web Surveys

Two other recent surveys deal with World Wide Web users only. Both surveys are flawed; they were posted on the Web and relied on voluntary compliance. I haven't seen any attempt to subject these surveys to statistical modeling, so please take the numbers with a shaker of salt.

The Hermes survey was conducted by the University of Michigan Business School in spring 1995 and received thirteen thousand responses. The people who responded are well educated (80 percent had some college education) and surprisingly well off (more than 50 percent had incomes over $50,000). A similar Web survey was conducted in fall 1994 by the Georgia Institute of Technology. Of the eighteen thousand people who responded, nearly half were between twenty-six and thirty years old and 90 percent were male. (UPDATE: Hermes and Georgia Tech have merged and now produce one survey, the GVU Web Survey, at *http://www.cc.gatech.edu/gvu/usersurveys/*

UserSurveyHome.html. Another excellent Website for learning about Internet demographics is CyberAtlas at *http://www.cyberatlas.com/.*)

I don't want to quote these surveys at length because the numbers are so unreliable, but there are some interesting indicators. The good news is that people use the Web mostly for entertainment or research. They enjoy reading magazines and looking at cool Websites, and they specifically cruise the Web looking for product information.

The bad news is that they don't buy online. As a reason for using the Internet, shopping has finished dead last in every survey I've seen. People prefer to buy in person. They even like direct mail better than the Internet. Part of the reluctance to buy is due to security. The preferred way to close an online purchase is through a toll-free phone call.

With so many Internet vendors now offering "secure transactions," there's more than fear behind the weak retail performance of the net. Part of the problem is the culture on the Internet, where almost everything is free. Another problem for retailers is that most people are logging onto the Internet from work. They might not mind planning their vacations on company time, but they feel uncomfortable closing transactions right there in the office.

Demographics of Purchasing

According to Mecklermedia Corporation, in the August 19, 1996, issue of *Web Week*, longtime Web users are more likely to make purchases online than are newcomers, according to findings from Nielsen Media Research. Also, the profile of netizens is getting closer to resembling the general population, and Internet access is up by 50 percent compared to a year ago, according to the study. The new Nielsen report, commissioned by CommerceNet, an industry consortium based in Palo Alto, California, is part of a six-month follow-up to the ambitious study of Internet demographics released last year. More than 2,800 respondents to the earlier Nielsen study were contacted for the follow-up. "The Internet marketplace is beginning to cross a chasm from the early-adopter stage to mass-market deployment," said Asim Abdullah, executive director of CommerceNet.

Changes in the profiles of netizens from September 1995 to April 1996 showed decreasing percentages in the number of computer-industry professionals, males, college-educated people, and those who live in high-income households. The percentage of computer professionals in the earlier survey was 23 percent; now it's 11 percent. Males represented 67 percent of netizens last year compared with 60 percent now. College-educated people had represented 56 percent of Internet users; now they comprise 39 percent. And households with incomes over $80,000 formerly accounted for 27 percent of

Internet users, compared with 17 percent now, the study said.

"These falling ratios are all indications that users now on the Internet are becoming closer to the norm," said Abdullah. He also said that the study showed that newcomers are lighter users, and usage builds up over time. The percentage of users who have made purchases through the Web has remained stable at 14 percent. Saying that Nielsen overestimated usage, critics had challenged the earlier study's conclusion that 37 million Americans and Canadians ages sixteen and older had Internet access. The scrutiny has helped redefine how best to conduct this type of research, said Paul Lindstrom, vice president and senior researcher at Nielsen Media Research, New York.

20 Intelligent Agents

INTERNET PUBLICITY CAN ALSO BE SUPPORTED THROUGH THE USE OF intelligent agents. Just as many businesses use intermediaries called agents to help them find new opportunities, on the Internet the term "agents" refers to software programs that find information, respond to information, or translate information. The term "intelligent agents" refers to those tools or programs that do these tasks with greater ease and intelligence.

Why Intelligent Agents Are Needed

Given the sheer volume of information on the Internet, it is becoming more and more imperative to find what you are looking for, and have what you are looking for find you. The features of the Internet encourage the exploration of information. Thus, many people hop from site to site on the WWW. With new sites coming on the Internet each day, it is increasingly complicated for anyone intelligently to find sites that are useful. While exploration of information can be fun and entertaining, it can also be time consuming. Intelligent agents serve not only to explore information, but also behave almost like a personal cybersecretary. Intelligent agents are servants for information retrieval and organization. These servants can make connections for you and provide you with advice and other useful information, without taking the 15 to 60 percent cut that human agents might ask for. Specifically, intelligent agents can serve to send you specific information on a daily basis, take care of your correspondence, and even find new opportunities for work.

Agents for Hire

Today, many on the Internet spend hours surfing and finding information. For those running businesses on a tight budget, surfing on the Internet should be a means and not an end in itself. Intelligent agents can make your online time more efficient. Intelligent agents, moreover, are not new to computing; the Internet has had such agents for some time. The first intelligent agent was the listserver.

A listserver is a program hooked up to an e-mail address. Sending e-mail to the address activates the program, which looks at your e-mail message and fulfills requests it finds in the message. The nearest equivalent to a listserver in the real world is perhaps fax on demand (FOD) systems. FOD is implemented in various ways; in the simplest case, a prospective client dials the phone and requests a fax by talking to a human being or using the buttons on a touch-tone phone.

FOD is a wonderful marketing tool; however, it costs several thousand dollars. A listserver, on the other hand, can be set up for about $100 and run for $50 a month or less. Using a listserver, you can set up a catalog, list upcoming events, and automatically respond to prospective clients who e-mail you at the listserver address. This can save you the time of sending a handcrafted e-mail message to everyone who calls you. The listserver can become your electronic clearinghouse for sending out standard information to prospective clients.

Search engines are also a type of intelligent agent. Search engines were developed to find things on the Internet. Typically, a search engine requests a keyword or a series of keywords. When you type the keyword, the agent searches the Internet or an index and attempts to find all sites on the Internet that have that keyword. Archie, for example, is a search engine for finding files. Other search engines include WebCrawler and Alta Vista. The problem with current search engines is that they are keyword-based. This means that they search Websites with a particular word. While this will obviously return lots of documents with the word in it, many of those documents may be irrelevant. In the future, search engines will perform searches on concepts, not just words.

One of the most important intelligent agents being developed is the cross-language translator. This agent will be similar to the universal communicator in *Star Trek*; it will break down the walls of language. People will not have to learn English. Such technology will have great ramifications for maintaining both cultural and linguistic heterogeneity.

Other intelligent agents appearing on the market are being called information filters. These filters are enabling people to receive personalized information automatically, without having to do manual searches using search engines. Every day new Websites are developed. Wouldn't it be great to receive a daily list of all the Websites that just went up? Or how about a list of Websites related to particular interests? Or what about a list of paintbrushes, shoes, or anything that has just gone on sale worldwide? Information filters will automatically deliver such information to your computer every time you log on, based on your personal tastes and profile. Such agents can make online time far more efficient and worthwhile.

21 Internet Directories and Communities

WITHIN THE INTERNET THERE ARE BOTH GEOGRAPHICAL COMMUNITIES such as Harvard-Square.Com *(http://www.harvard-square.com)* and functional communities such as E-Trade.Com *(http://www.e-trade.com)*. The former, geographic, community serves the area of Harvard Square in Cambridge, Massachusetts. The latter, functional, community serves the interests of online traders. Many of these communities are also referred to as Internet directories.

There are many different types of directories and communities burgeoning on the Internet. Locating and deciphering all of them can be a confusing and time-consuming process. It is, however, important to build a relationship with these communities as a part of your Internet publicity campaign. To save you time and help you understand these communities, I have divided them into seven categories: announcement sites, search engines, general directories, guides and cool sites, geographic directories, business directories, and product directories.

Announcement Sites

The explosion of sites being added daily to the Web has created a need for announcement sites that track all of these new sites that join the Internet. Announcement sites are not only useful for Web masters and marketers to kick off their online promotion campaign, but also for users to keep current with what's happening on the WWW. Virtually anything can be announced—new Web pages and articles, as well as new resources. How new a site should be and how long it will be posted differs from announcement site to announcement site, but all announcements are posted for a limited period of time.

- *NCSA's What's New.* The What's New page is a joint project of the National Center for Supercomputing Applications (NCSA) and the Global Network Navigator, Inc. This announcement service is highly visited. All submissions to What's New are automatically sent the *WIC Select Catalog.*
- *Net Happenings.* Net Happenings is a service of InterNIC Directory and Database Services and the list moderator Gleason Sackman. Materials are segmented by information entered that day and those entered during the current month. They are archived by month and year thereafter.
- *Netscape's What's New.* Netscape's announcement site reviews submissions and presents sites that are not only new to the Internet, but also that use or advance the technology of the Net in new ways.
- *What's New Too!* Manifest Information Services posts an average of five hundred new announcements every day usually within thirty-six hours of submission. In addition, all announcements are posted and none are turned away. The information is not filtered, which means any announcement from a personal home page to an informational text file is posted. While screening doesn't take place by What's New, it does occur during the announcement searching process. Users can select the announcements category of interest or by length of time that an announcement has been posted.
- *What's New in Europe.* What's New in Europe, part of The U.K. Shopping Centre's European Directory, posts all newly developed Websites or services of the European Internet community. The main What's New in Europe listing displays sites announced over the last twenty-four hours as well as the sites and services that have been introduced weekly to the Internet over the last six months. Once announcements are submitted, they are displayed within twenty-four hours. Announcements can be made in any language of your choosing.

Search Engines

Search engines catalog Websites by visiting them periodically. They work by following URLs around the Web, copying the contents of the pages they find, indexing each page, and searching through the generated index.

- *Alta Vista.* DEC's AltaVista is a fast search engine powered by the DEC Alpha chip. It has a Web index of more than 16 million Web pages made up of 8 billion words. A full-text index of more than thirteen thousand UseNet newsgroups is also available.
- *Comprehensive List of Sites.* The World Wide Web Wanderers Index with more than twenty thousand registered hosts. It is managed by net.Genesis.
- *Excite.* Architext Software's Web database consists of more than 1.5 million pages. Excite specializes in contextual searches.
- *GTE SuperPages.* GTE's search engine has a database of more than 10 million U.S. businesses and fifty thousand Websites.
- *Harvest.* Colorado University's Harvest Broker currently has indexed seventy thousand WWW home pages.
- *InfoSeek.* InfoSeek Corp's directory has both a free and a pay service.
- *Inktomi.* This Web index is part of a Web server research project at the University of California at Berkeley. It's database consists of 2.8 million documents.
- *Lycos.* Lycos originated at Carnegie-Mellon University and is now owned by CMG Holdings. Lycos has cataloged more than 10 million sites, representing nearly 92 percent of the World Wide Web.
- *Open Text.* Open Text's Web index contains about 2.5 billion words of text and more than 27 million hyperlinks. Users can perform simple, power, and weighted searches on the Web with Open Text's search engine.
- *Tribal Voice.* Tribal Voice are developers of PowWow, an Internet program that allows people to chat, send and receive files, and cruise the World Wide Web together as a group. In addition, they also maintain the Internet Trailblazer Search Engine.
- *WebCrawler.* America Online's search engine has explored and indexed information on more than 1.8 million different documents. WebCrawler also posts a list of what they consider to be their top twenty-five sites.
- *WWW Worm.* The WWW Worm has a database of three million URLs and their home page states that two million visitors a month make use of its search engine.

General Directories

Almost any company, person, or organization can post a Website to the general directories. Most of these directories support both drilldown by category and general keyword searches.

- *ALIWEB.* ALIWEB is a public service provided by NEXOR. ALIWEB's main advantage is that it allows for a great deal of control over how your site is described in its directory. You set up an index file in a standard format and place it on your server. ALIWEB will access it regularly and you can make changes to your file as often as you like.
- *Linkstar.* LinkStar is owned by LinkStar Communications. It is positioned as being not only an Internet directory, but a facilitator of communication between listed individuals and companies. If you have an e-mail address, you can register by filling out an electronic business card or "e-card." When performing a search, a user is provided with both e-mail and Web location information. Adding and editing data on your e-card can be done very easily.
- *The Huge List.* This is an up-and-coming directory site provided by 3W Media with more than 1.5 million hits per week. The Huge List also provides links to the more popular Web, file, and domain searching sites.
- *Starting Point.* Starting Point is designed to make your daily Web experience more productive. Starting Point helps you manage Web resources by combining a powerful, centralized Web searching tool with quality, subject-oriented Web resources you need every day—all combined in an easy-to-use, comprehensive, and well organized starting point.
- *Tradewave's Galaxy.* Formerly EINet, this is Tradewave Corporation's Internet directory service. Sites that are less than seven days old are located in a "What's New" section.
- *Yahoo.* Yahoo was one of the first directories to catalog the Web. Be sure to give a great deal of thought in choosing categories when you register. Enter your site under more than one category, however, there is no guarantee your site will be listed under all of the headings you request. Yahoo! puts a limit of about two or three categories per site. If all goes well, you should be added to Yahoo! about two weeks after submission.

Guides and Cool Sites

Guides are quickly becoming an important source for finding interesting and useful sites on the Web. In general, guides review and rate only a small percentage—3 to 5 percent—of all sites submitted.

Therefore, make sure your site is rate-worthy before posting. Most of the guides allow reviewed sites to use their special icons as a sign of quality. Cool sites usually select one new Website every day. Getting selected as a cool site attracts high traffic for a short time.

- *Cool Site of the Day.* Every day InfiNet introduces its choice for "Cool Site" of the day and every business day provides its pick as the "Categorically Cool" site of the day. Categories change on a weekly basis. There is also a "Still Cool" section where Cool Sites of previous days can be accessed. You can go all the way back to August of 1994. If you think your site is cool, InfiNet takes suggestions. If you're nominating your own site, you can include your phone number and they'll notify you if your site is chosen.
- *Excite NetDirectory.* Architext Software's database consists of more than 1.5 million pages, fifty thousand of which have been reviewed and are located in the NetDirectory section. These reviewers search the Web for pages to critique, but also take a look at the pages submitted by the "Suggest Site" button at the bottom of the page.
- *Magellan.* McKinley's directory, Magellan, reviews and rates Internet sites. Reviewers evaluate each site on a variety of criteria and provide an overall rating of one to four stars. In the near future, McKinley will begin awarding a fifth star to those they consider to be the "best of the Net." Because of the high volume of submissions, McKinley cannot guarantee that all sites will be reviewed. They currently have an unrated database containing 1.5 million sites. If your site is critiqued, you can download the "Reviewed by Magellan" award logo. Use the Feedback section to notify Magellan editors of any corrections or updates to your site.
- *InfoSeek Guide.* InfoSeek Guide reviews sites in twelve categories. Referred to as the "InfoSeek Select Sites," the guide includes what InfoSeek considers to be the more interesting and useful Websites. Recommendations for inclusion into the Select Sites are accepted by InfoSeek. In addition to searching InfoSeek's Select Sites from the InfoSeek Guide search engine, you are also able to search the entire World Wide Web, UseNet newsgroups, and e-mail addresses.
- *inSites by iGuide.* iGuide's inSites currently includes seventeen thousand site reviews organized by sixteen categories. Site reviews and rankings are made at the discretion of the iGuide editorial team so, as with other guides, there's no guarantee that they will review or list yours.
- *Point.* Owned by Lycos, Point rates and reviews the top 5 percent of all Websites and lists them by category. You can

nominate your site for the top 5 percent badge, but there is no guarantee it will be listed. Fortunately, you can always nominate your site again after it has been updated and you think the site has improved.

- *Spider's Pick of the Day.* Bob Allison provides the Spider's Pick of the Day. In addition to being resourceful, the Spider is pretty long. Bob selects a new site every day. According to the Spider site, SPoD "likes new, content-rich, graphically cool, unusual, helpful, interactive pages and tries not to put on pages that have already been picked by the others."
- *WIC Select.* The Whole Internet Catalog Select is a hand-picked collection of the best sites the Internet has to offer. Each of the two thousand sites in the WIC has been reviewed and categorized by subject by the WIC Select editorial team. WIC Select receives their submissions via NCSA's What's New.

Geographic Directories

Some people feel that search engines and directories yield results that contain a strong bias toward U.S. Web pages. Hence, geographic-based directories grew out of a desire to have access to resources pertaining to specific parts of the world. These directories restrict submissions to companies and organizations based in their geographic area.

Asia/Pacific

- *ABC-Asia Business Connection.* ABC's directory is a business resource center for Asia. Website submissions are only accepted from countries in Asia and the Pacific. Searches, performed either by subject or by country, can be used to collect information on doing business in Asia or information on companies in Asia.
- *Australia Announce Archive.* Australian Announce Archive (AAA) is located on the same page as World Announce Archive (WAA). AAA is made up of Australian and New Zealand Websites while every other part of the world falls into WAA. Both directories are updated several times a day. The main attraction of the archive is that all announcements are posted within four hours of submission. Therefore, do not announce your site until it is complete. A user can perform a one-word search of sites or browse through the list of most recently posted sites.

Europe

- *The European Directory.* The U.K. Shopping Centre claims its directory is the largest European-specific directory on the Web.

Before adding your URL, be sure to check that you are not already listed on the directory. The reason you may find your Website is because What's New in Europe is located within The European Directory. You can expect URL submissions to be added within five working days.

- *PRONET.* PRONET, provided by PRONET Enterprises Ltd., is a global business resource covering all parts of the world. Information can be accessed in six languages—English, French, Dutch, Portuguese, Italian, and Spanish.
- *Yelloweb Europe.* Officially online as of the first of February 1996, Yelloweb Europe provides the European community with a directory of exclusively European-based Websites. A benefit of Yelloweb is that it is available in six European languages—English, Dutch, French, German, Italian, and Spanish.
- *UKdirectory.* UKdirectory has more than 3,500 U.K. Websites listed throughout forty-five categories. It is free to list a U.K.-based Website under one category. For a fee, you can choose to put multiple entries under different categories, have your link appear as the first entry of a search result, increase the font size, or add a few extra lines to your company description.
- *UK Index.* UK Index Ltd. provides a directory of sites located in the United Kingdom. The UK Index also welcomes new site submissions, regardless of where they are based, if that site directly pertains to the U.K. and/or its surrounding area. When submitting your site, you'll have little problem finding an appropriate category to place your Website. U.K. Index divides Web resources into thirty-one categories. There is even a category called "Weird," which contains eccentric and fringe resources as well as creative uses for the Web.
- *The U.K. Web Library—WWLib.* This catalog is operated by WebWise. It is run at, but not supported by, the School of Computing and Information Technology at the University of Wolverhampton. WWLib is a classified catalogue of more than three thousand U.K. Web pages and organized using the Dewey Decimal Classification. As a search engine, many of the U.K. Web pages are acquired by a robot. However, new entries can be also be submitted for inclusion in the main catalogue. Such sites are differentiated through various symbols that appear after the Dewey code. A "!" means the entry was entered via a user, whereas a "+" means the entry was acquired via the robot.
- *U.K. Yellow Web.* British Telecommunications offers a comprehensive directory to U.K. sites on the World Wide Web. You can use the directory if you want to look for information under a classified heading or use the search engine if you want to find Websites relating to a particular word.

- *The Dutch Yellow Pages.* Digital Market Opportunities provides the Dutch Yellow Pages, which lists more than a thousand WWW pages of companies, academic institutions, and government organizations based in The Netherlands. All sites located within this region can fill out a form found on the Dutch version of the guide.

The Americas

- Canadian Internet Business Directory. Despite finding the word "business" in the directory's name, the Canadian Internet Business Directory does include nonbusiness categories, such as government, universities, and travel. After you submit your URL, 9 to 5 Communications will review it and decide where the best place is for your site to be linked. Suggestions for category placement are also taken in the add-URL form. 9 to 5 tries to notify companies when their URL has been added, a much-appreciated feature.

Business Directories

Business directories provide searchable databases and other informational material that pertain specifically to the world of commerce. They are used most frequently for research and to locate information on companies, services, or products within the business sector. You can usually search by business name, type, and/or location.

- *Apollo.* Apollo Advertising offers a searchable database of businesses worldwide. You can search by continent anywhere around the world. It was the first directory of its kind to charge for site submission, which is now $8 (in U.S. currency) for businesses and organizations.
- *BizWeb.* More than two thousand companies are listed on BizWeb's directory and are categorized by the goods or services they provide.
- *Industry.Net.* Industry.Net provides a business directory, but is really an online marketplace. You can locate thousands of companies with the business center directory located in the Marketplace. Searches can be made by company name or by the product or service they provide. You can visit these companies to gather information or even choose to conduct business with them online. You can also access product information that is divided by "floors" and then by industry segment. Membership is free to join Industry.Net. However, in order to advertise your services within a business center, you need to contact one of the regional business centers.

- *The European Business Directory.* Eurédit's business directory allows you to search from among 150,000 European suppliers. Searches can be performed by company, product, or service, and in a language of your choosing. To have your company listed in Europages, you need to send an e-mail with your address and company details. The e-mail automatically comes up when you click the "How to Appear in Europages" button. The site also contains information about business in Europe and is a resource on European markets.
- *Innovators Network, LLC.* Innovators Network provides a directory of yellow pages and offers one free listing. Additional fee-based services are available such as having the option to display company or product icons and to establish a Web link by category or by subject.
- *New Riders Yellow Pages.* This is Macmillian Publishing's searchable directory of WWW sites. Getting listed is a matter of filling out a form. You're notified if your entry is approved and the site is posted a couple of business days later.
- *NYNEX Interactive Yellow Pages.* The NYNEX directory consists of 16 million businesses. Essentially if you have a telephone number, you're in the Yellow Pages directory. You can also link your Website to the NYNEX Interactive Yellow Pages listing. If you do this your business listing will appear at the top of a search-results file. To establish a link, you fill out a link form and a NYNEX business representative will contact you within a week's time.
- *Virtual Yellow Pages.* This is Interactive Marketing Services' directory of Websites and other information.
- *WWW Yellow Pages.* This directory of WWW business sites is provided as a service to the Internet community by the UH College of Business Administration. Listings are organized by category.

Product Directories

Internet malls and some commercial directories take a retail approach to the Internet, but opportunities do exist to post your business-to-business listing as well. Their directories provide links to products and services that you can buy or use.

- *iMall.* There is a great deal of traffic at iMall, Inc.'s online shopping mall. The mall directory provides links to a variety of products and services. To list your product or service on iMall, there is a form to fill out which will be followed by a call from an iMall sales representative. This commercial mall is fee-based.

- *Internet Mall.* Intuitive Systems' Internet Mall is a very busy mall. Each day, more than six thousand visitors browse through the eight thousand different stores listed. If you don't want to try to tackle the mall alone, you can use the searchable database to locate shops or search for particular companies in the alphabetical index. There is no charge for a basic listing in the Internet Mall, but there are fees for sponsorship of a department or floor.
- *Open Market.* Open Market is a directory of commercial services, products, and information on the Internet. At this time OpenMarket has suspended all submissions.
- *NetMall Directory.* American Information Systems has created a searchable index of more than ten thousand businesses on the Internet. The number of listings in the database is growing at 1,200 per month. You can search through NetMall's Directory as often as you like for free. Adding a listing to NetMall is also at no charge. All you need to do is fill out a form and you should be listed within two days.

22 Internet Publicity Resources

THIS CHAPTER IS A COMPREHENSIVE DESCRIPTION OF ALL INTERNET publicity resources available online. These resources fall into the following groups:

- advertising rates, guides, site selection, cooperatives
- advertising information resources
- advertising management software, banner ad placement, banner rotation
- advertising content and image protection, content and ad blocking filters, banner creation tools
- Website ad sales representation
- offline browsers, intelligent agents, banner ad tracking agents
- business and media mailing lists and guides
- public relations, marketing, Website promotion, listing, submission
- full service marketing/PR firms and submission services, Website promotion, marketing, traffic development

- submission services
- other PR, marketing, e-mail
- PR news release distribution wire services
- Website traffic counters, tracking, audit services
- Web usage statistics, demographics, research
- e-mail, e-mail auto responders, e-mail address services, e-mail software, e-mail lists
- e-mail address services
- e-mail utilities, auto-responders, fax, e-mail list software, services
- e-mail list creation, acquisition software, services
- e-mail list providers
- e-mail, netiquette, spamming, censorship
- general Internet information for advertising, PR, marketing
- Internet periodicals and other news sources
- lists of lists (e-mail mailing lists for advertising, marketing, sales)
- legal
- calendar of events and trade shows—commerce, electronic payment, shopping cart, wallet systems, checks by wire, merchant systems
- Website award designations
- association
- search engines for Websites, e-mail, UseNet, reference, research, lists, and more
- telemarketing, call center, voice messaging
- software—windows, Internet, utilities, advertising, Web page validation
- keynote speaker sources
- personalized news home pages and delivery services
- personalized home pages
- personalized news delivery
- Internet publications and periodicals in print

Each of the above groups are explored in detail in the subsections below. The goal is to offer actual URLs that service the various areas.

Advertising Rates, Guides, Site Selection, Cooperatives

http://www.sisoftware.com SI Software presents information, resources, and software tools designed to maximize the utility of Web advertising (buying and selling), marketing, PR, and e-mail. Featuring *The One-Stop Directory Of Advertising, PR, Marketing and E-Mail links*; *Web Ad Rate Guide*; and Ad Watch Surfbot—a Web surf agent. SI Software offers other custom value-added search agents with the Surfbot Offline

Browser from Surflogic, which can be scheduled automatically to surf selected sites and track banner ads by monitoring Web page updates. Media Watch Surfbot and many other specialized agents are offered.

http://www.eads.come/eAds Our definition of eAds simply means that the site that hosts the eAd (the "host site") gets paid based on the number of responses the ad generates, not the number of impressions provided. We find advertisers that want to promote their products and services on the Net, then we go to Websites that have the kind of traffic that would be interested in the particular product or service being marketed and offer them a fee per response. Our staff designs and places the eAds, manages the database that tracks the click information the eAds generate, and distributes month-end statements and checks to host sites.

http://www.resource-marketing.com/banner.html Resource Marketing Inc. TradeBanners Program: Don't get knocked out on the information highway, advertise your site by trading hot-link banners free!

http://www.resource-marketing.com/IBM As a Web page owner, it's easy and *free* to join the Internet Banner Network. The Internet Banner Network (IBN) delivers the most highly targeted and flexible advertising on the Internet. The IBN allows advertisers the unique ability to deliver banner advertising messages to users who are most appropriate for their products and services.

http://www.swwwap.com/ SWWWAP! allows you to target exactly where you want your banners to run, by geographic location and by Website type (i.e., reference, sports, arts, etc.). There is also a free banner ad exchange program.

http://www.imgis.com/ IMGIS Network AdForce: It's easy to affiliate your Website with IMGIS and start making money by delivering targeted advertising. Our AdForce software does it all. It identifies the proper visitor to your site, serves the proper ad, selects the format for advertising on your site, tracks the ads placed, accounts the revenue due to your site, and handles payment to the proper CyberCash or traditional account.

http://owa.com/wave/ Wave Power is an advertising co-op created to give powerful publicity to Websites of all sizes. Wave Power will place your banner ad on hundreds of Websites, absolutely free.

http://www.ipgnet.com/bannerad/ Banner Ad: Banner Ad link exchange program.

http://www.jjj.com/webvert/ Owners of popular Web pages place an advertisement on top of their sites. Every time the page is visited an ad of "webvertizing" will be shown. The owners of these sites get a great deal of the advertising costs.

http://www.narrowcastmedia.com/ NarrowCast Media (NCM) provides you with the fastest and easiest method to reach your target market with precision and consistency, buy and sell your ad space, exchange your ad space for space on other sites free, and track your site's statistics and demographics.

http://www.worldata.com/rcard.htm Rate card area of this Website. WebConnect, the media placement service of the Internet, will generate qualified traffic to your Website. WebConnect sells bundled ad hyperlink services and lists rates for Websites, (about one thousand smaller sites) that apparently have an exclusive media placement contract. The service accepts ad agency commissions.

http://www.fwy.com/ The Web Ad Space Registry: If you're buying or selling ad space on the Web, begin here. This service is free to all users.

http://www.focalink.com Focalink is a new fee-based service specializing in online Web media resource guides and Web advertising campaign management (ad server).

http://www.trafficresource.com Offers online media planning, Website ad rates, and some fee-based services.

http://www.webtrack.com Offers news, ad rates, databases, and ad services for Web advertisers and marketers—some fee based.

http://www.netcreations.com/ipa/adindex Interactive Publishing Alert's Online Advertising Index (pricing database) and guide to selling advertising.

http://www.directrix.com Directrix Advertising is a comprehensive solution provider for advertising on the Web. It features a large directory of Websites that have advertising and sponsorship opportunities, as well as general reference information for Web advertising.

http:///.linkexchange.com If you have your own Website and want to become a member, we invite you to explore the rest of our Website and learn more about our exciting new service. Remember, the Internet Link Exchange is a free public service that allows you to advertise your Website through banner ads—a luxury previously available only to those with money.

http://www.intermotion.com/parade/bannermenu.htm "BannerBase!" is a database of sites that offer banner advertising or sponsorship. Wherever possible, links to additional sponsor or advertising information has been provided. Prices, if available, are in columns with a low price, high price, along with the type (monthly or impression).

http://delph.sponsor.net/auction The SponsorNet Media Market is a new way to purchase Web advertising space, bringing together Websites that sell ad space with businesses looking to advertise. Click on a category to see the Websites in that category with advertising space for sale. (This site may find a new home—stay tuned.)

http://www.cris.com/-raydaly/sponsors.shtml Sponsor of the day promotes new sponsors and sponsored WWW sites every business day. It highlights the sponsors of Internet publications, resources, information, and other sites. OnServices produced this site to promote sponsorship of Internet services and to provide an index of advertisers on Internet.

http://www.envision.net/marketing/inet/inetdata.1.html Four-star reviews of 150 marketing sites with hyperlinks to the site page that begins the ad-banner URL-submission process.

http://commonwealth.riddler.com The Commonwealth™ Network is a global community of Website owners and developers supported by advertising revenue. To join, all you have to do is register as a Commonwealth Network member and make a simple change to the HTML code on the page(s) where you want to display ad banners. We'll do the rest, dynamically changing the contents of the banners and tracking the number of unique-host visitors to your pages. At the end of the month, we'll pay you three quarters of a cent for every unique host impression generated by your Commonwealth Pages. Participation in the Commonwealth Network is totally free!

http://www.sandbox.net Sandbox, an entertainment-oriented site, utilizes product placement, integrating ads into the story lines of online serials and treasure hunts.

http://www.avenue.com/about/ads.html Sponsoring mailing lists, newsletters, and newsgroups, this is a compilation of links to mailing lists, newsgroups, etc. that accept advertising—many offer excellent target marketing opportunities.

http://www.srds.com Standard Rate and Data Service (SRDS) is America's premier provider of media and marketing information—print guide only.

http://www.ca-probate.com/comm-net.htm Web Site Banner Advertising provides information about Internet Website banner ad servers. This information is written for Web masters, but advertisers may also find it useful.

Advertising Information Resources

http://www.utexas.edu/co/adv/world/ University of Texas Advertising World (Ad Agencies Websites) is the most extensive collection of advertising-related links on the Web for advertising and marketing professionals and academics.

http://www.telmar.com/ AMIC, Telmar Advertising Media Internet Center, "Gateway to Advertising and Media Information," offers free and fee-based information from Telmar Media software provider.

http://www.admarket.com/ Ad Market is primarily a directory of ad agencies and PR agency Websites, and some additional marketing and media content. Its biggest sponsors are *Ad Age* and *Hot Wired*.

http://www.amic.com/amic-mem/research/hits.html A pricing Website advertising the media buyer's view.

http://www.adage.com/IMM/ *Ad Age* Interactive Media and Marketing.

http://www.interbiznet.com/ibn.nomad.html *First Steps* marketing and design daily.

http://www.sjmercury.com/help/advertise.html Mercury Center covers advertising on the World Wide Web with topics such as: things you need to know about Web advertising, measuring and auditing Websites, caching, site mirroring, firewalls, vulnerability to tampering, protecting the privacy of users, ways of measuring analyzing server log files, registering users, understanding audits, comparing print and Web advertising, comparing Websites to one another, and why advertisers should pay based on performance.

http://www.nytimes.com/library/cyber/week/0526measure.html *New York Times* Cybertimes Article: "Hits, Views, Clicks, and Visits: Web Advertisers Face Data Jungle"—requires site registration.

Advertising Management Software, Banner Placement, Banner Rotation

http://www.netgravity.com/ NetGravity Web Advertising Management: place, rotate, report, and track ads with their automated ad server.

http://www.netcreations.com/admagic/ AdMagic is an innovative way for Web publishers to boost their ad space instantly! Features include rotating sponsorship banners, change the length of time the banner stays on screen, the number of banners in the rotation, and the background colors and textures, and for any banner on any page on your site. Better traffic data for your advertisers. Bill and track by impressions and click-throughs. Generate daily and monthly reports by advertiser. A billing reminder service assigns each advertiser several thousand impressions. When the advertiser's "impressions account" runs low, AdMagic automatically notifies the advertiser by e-mail. If the advertiser wants to continue, the new allotment of impressions are simply added to the existing ones with no disruption in service.

http://www.online.paracel.com/home.html Paracel develops and markets advanced filtering and categorization solutions for high-volume, dynamic information. Our unique approach to text searching and retrieval enables organizations to deploy highly personalized one-to-one publishing solutions that meet the specific requirements of their target audiences.

http://www.directchoice.com DirectChoice is Web-based relationship marketing software designed to transform your Website from an inbound presence to an outbound powerhouse. It is designed to allow users to register and build a personal profile and enables the Website to publish personal, proactive, individualized e-mail messages.

http://www.ad-network.com/ad-master The complete electronic advertising management solution, Ad-Master™ does it all. Rotate ads, any shape, any size, and guarantee each and every page view, with or without borders! Rotate your graphics, like logos, page headers, photos, and illustrations, with or without hyperlinks! Rotate text for sponsors, quotes, contests, trivia, stories, and results, with or without hyperlinks! Rotate HTML, a whole page or just parts, rotate your backgrounds, your links, sites of the day. Rotate multiple sections of your page when multiple copies of Ad-Master™ are installed on your Web server!

http://www.bellcore.com/sample-datea/advertiser-html/advertiser.html Bellcore Adapt/X Advertiser allows you to present your ads according to the consumer's profile, usage patterns, or the subject the consumer is viewing. The selection and placement of the actual ads is controlled by contracts with the advertiser that specify the set of conditions, such as frequency, coverage, or fairness, in which to show them. Your ads are targeted to interested consumers. Also allows executable ads, or agents, which connect the user to services related to the advertisement. Executable ads allow a consumer to proceed to the next step of a transaction; for example, an automobile advertisement may include an executable ad for registering a new car.

http://www.networkingwizards.com/products/on-target.html On Target Internet Advertising Server is sold as part of CommerceSuite.

http://www.66west.com/adjuggler/ Ad Juggler is a powerful Web tool for displaying randomly rotating banner ads hyperlinked to advertiser's Websites. Each time the page is loaded a new randomly selected banner is displayed. Impressions count, clicks count, domain name, and date statistics, client account information, and more—all effortlessly managed right from your Web browser. Ad Juggler may be incorporated in any static or dynamically created HTML document.

http://www.ipe.com/home/current/html/demo2.html IPE™ (U. S. patent pending) was designed from the ground up to enable advertisers and content providers to communicate better with their customers. IPE allows for the dynamic presentation of both advertisements and content based upon virtually any criteria and format desired.

Advertising Content and Image Protection, Content Blocking Filters, Banner Creation Tools

http://maximized.com SiteShield is an exciting new concept in Web content protection. Content providers can employ SiteShield as a deterrent against copyright infringement and easy theft of images and other content.

http://www.privnet.com Internet Fast Forward, Information Filtering, Banner Ad Blocker, Personal Image Blocking: right-click on any image you no longer wish to see, select "Block this Image" and you won't see or download it again unless you want to!

http://www.mindworkshop.com/alchemy/alchemy.html GIF Construction Set takes advantage of the full feature set of the GIF89a file structure—transparent backgrounds, interlaced GIF graphics, and rotating and animated banners in a single GIF file with timing control and palette manipulation generate quick, painless animations.

Web Ad Sales Representation

http://www.wwwebrep.com WebRep serves as national sales representatives for Websites interested in generating revenue from online advertising.

http://www.i-traffic.com The first and premier inbound link placement firm, I-traffic is helping marketers and publishers generate online traffic, and offers an array of services including: media plan development, assistance, and support through paid links; media planning and buying; banner development; nonpaid links; online publicity traded links; and crosslinking campaigns.

http://www.worldata.com/webcon.htm WebConnect, the media placement service of the Internet, allows advertisers to control the placement, reach, frequency, and cost of advertising on the Web. WebConnect concentrates on generating targeted traffic to an advertiser's Website by placing your advertising message (in the form of banners and links) on strategically selected sites.

http://www.burstmedia.com BURST! is building a network of independent Websites ranging in size, sophistication, and content. We're going to represent that network to advertisers who are more eager than ever to bring their message to the Web. By aligning your Website with other independent sites on the network, you'll be part of a powerful block that will draw advertisers' attention, and money.

http://www.realmedia.com Real Media in New York City is focused on providing newspapers and other local Web publishers with the tools and expertise they need to build dominant positions within their markets in the delivery of locally targeted advertising, and on making those sites conducive to national and regional advertising. Real Media is also focused on providing advertisers with a flexible, cost-effective, and powerful network for sending their advertising messages to a multitude of Websites. Real Media's first offerings are MediaExpress™, a network of Web publishers' sites; and AdStream™, a Web-ad placement system.

http://www.doubleclick.net DoubleClick and doubleclick.net deliver the most highly targeted advertising available on the Internet. DoubleClick has created the world's most comprehensive database of Internet user and organization profiles—Poppe Tyson subsidiary.

Websites that want to display ad banners must first join DoubleClick. Next, you make a simple change to all HTML pages where you wish to include DoubleClick ad banners. With DoubleClick, you can keep your existing advertisers and supplement your ad banner revenue with DoubleClick ad banners. DoubleClick verifies that everything is all right and activates your site. When your site begins displaying DoubleClick ad banners, you begin generating revenue.

http://www.interactive.line.com Sponsorship Opportunities can help you to reach your Internet customers by placing sponsorship hyperlinks on some of the most highly trafficked and targeted sites. Also handles Web sweepstakes and promotions.

http://www.katz-media.com Katz Media is a large media representative firm.

http://www.reedref.com/nrp/flagship.html Standard directory of advertising agencies contains listings of ad agency media planners who typically are the buyers of ad space.

http://www.mediacentral.com/index/ InsideMedia's *Inside Media* magazine is a source of media planner lists.

http://www.narrowcastmedia.com NarrowCast Media advertising space brokerage and exchange provides you with the fastest and easiest methods to reach your target market with precision and consistency, buy and sell your ad space, exchange your ad space for space on other sites free, track your site's statistics and demographics.

http://www.mckinley.com McKinley Group sells and buys ads. Contact Cindy Martin.

http://www.cks.com CKS Partners places ad banners with appropriate sites.

http://www.ad-network.com/what.html Ad-Net is in an advertising network for the media known as the World Wide Web. Ad-Net is a network of member Website publishers that we call affiliates. Affiliates agree to host advertising sold by Ad-Net sales reps on their Web pages. Ad-Net contracts with media sales reps all over the world to sell the available advertising space of Ad-Net affiliates to companies looking to purchase advertising banners on the Web.

Offline Browsers, Intelligent Agents, Banner Ad Tracking

http://www.sisoftware.com SI Software presents information, resources, and software tools designed to maximize the utility of Web advertising (buying and selling), marketing, PR, and e-mail. Featuring the one-stop directory of advertising, PR, marketing, and e-mail links; Web ad rate guide; and Ad Watch Surfbot, a Web surf agent. SI Software offers other custom value-added search agents with the Surfbot Offline Browser from Surflogic which can be scheduled to surf automatically selected sites and track banner ads by monitoring Web page updates. Media Watch Surfbot and many other specialized agents are offered.

http://www.surflogic.com Surfbot, from Surflogic, is the number one rated offline browser, unattended Web surfer, HTML page and graphics grabber, updated URL checker, and personalized news and information retriever.

http://www.hpp.com Invoke Go.Fetch to find, read, filter, match, then fetch the contents of the global Internet that meet your requirements. Go.Fetch is the world's first personal agent software for business and research on the Internet. On your command, Go.Fetch systematically collects information for you from the entire World Wide Web and/or more than thirteen thousand UseNet groups. You may set Go.Fetch for multiple simultaneous tasks. Launch up to ten sessions at the same time. Collect data on multiple words/subjects/phrases with accuracy and ease. You may exclude unwanted matches. For example, you could ask Go.Fetch to ignore all ".edu" documents.

Business and Media Mailing Lists and Guides

http://www.parrotmedia.com Parrot Media Network contains listings of TV stations, radio stations, cable systems, and newspapers, with valuable market data and key personnel by name and title—seventy thousand key media execs!

http://www.rtvf.nwu.edu/links.html The Mega Media-Links index is the best electronic media index on the Web. It contains thousands of film, video, radio, television, cinema, and new-media site listings conveniently categorized with brief site descriptions.

http://www.webcom.com/-nlnnet/yellowp.html A listing of professional media Websites, e-mail addresses and more.

http://www.islandnet.com/-deathnet/media-e-mail.html Media E-mail Directory lists newspapers, magazines, radio, and TV outlets that accept electronic submissions.

http://www.gugerell.co.at/gugerell/media Use E-mail Media List to find all media on the World Wide Web.

http://www.smartbiz.com/sbs/sw/sw.10.html Profile and order information for Bacon's 1996 Media Directory. No other source provides as much information as Bacon's does on every U.S. and Canadian daily newspaper, all U.S. weeklies, plus business, trade, and consumer magazines, and newsletters, new services, and syndicates. The CD-ROM features information about more than twenty thousand media outlets.

http://www.dmnews.com *Direct Marketing News* covers regular mail lists offered for sale as well as a wealth of other direct marketing news and information.

http:///www.abii.com American Business Information, Inc., offers a wide range of products and services designed to help you make the most of our information: business directories, consumer lists, business credit service, sales leads, maps, customer profile analysis, Infoaccess online list service, special markets, and Canadian business information.

http://www.newslink.org/ *American Journalism Review* lists three thousand media links.

http://www.asiresearch.com The Internet Market Research/Advertising Industry E-Mail Directory sends its list periodically (approximately monthly) to all members.

http://www.whatson.com/ukmedia An Internet directory of U.K. media.

http://www.mcs.net/-kfliegel/media/wmg-con.html Kurt Fliegel's Web media guide

http://tvnet.com/guestbook/e-mailpost.html TV Net offers TV-related media e-mail listings. PR-ProfitCenter includes addresses, editors, fax numbers, e-mail, etc., for magazines, syndicated columnists, TV, and radio, all broken down into specific categories.

Public Relations, Marketing, Website Promotion, Listing, Submissions

http://www.mmgco.com/webstep.html Public relations, marketing, and news release services as well as Website submission services—free and fee—are available from the MMG Top One Hundred Free Listings Master Index. MMG maintains a database of more than three hundred sites that will accept a listing for your Website for free, such as search engines, databases, and yellow pages. MMG is run by John Audette, moderator of the highly acclaimed Internet-Sales List.

http://www.usa.net/wolfbayne WolfBayne Communications is a marketing consultancy specializing in high technology business-to-business communications. Our strengths include strategic and tactical public relations, marketing communications management and logistics, and Internet marketing planning and implementation.

http://www.bayne.com/wolfBayne/htmarcom/default.html HTMARCOM Communications is a high-tech marketing communications list, Website, and newsletter. President Kim Bayne is moderator of the highly acclaimed HTMARCOM Marketing Discussion List.

http://www.netpost.com Netpost by Eric Ward of The Ward Group Inc. offers Internet publicity and media services, including Website promotion and submission.

http://www.tenagra.com An Internet marketing, public relations firm (site offers useful Internet marketing and PR advice).

http://www.newstips.com/newstips/ Newstips Inc. is a public relations company that specializes in companies related to the computer industry. In addition to performing traditional publicity services, Newstips Inc. produces media receptions at trade shows through its Newstips Events Division. Newstips also traffics more than five hundred review requests in a typical month through Product Sweep electronic editorial review solicitations. The flagship of Newstips Inc. is its weekly Newstips Electronic Editorial Bulletin, which reaches some three thousand computer industry journalists every week.

http://www.interbiznet.com/promophop.html Promophobia: The Concept—an operating division of IBN (the Internet Business Network) specializing in Website promotion, marketing, and traffic development.

Submission Services

http://www.homecom.com/global/pointers.html Homecom Pointers to Pointers service: a list is provided to direct users where they can go on the Internet to submit their sites. Every site we find that performs this service will be welcomed as an addition to Pointers to Pointers.

http://www.iTools.com/promote-it/promote-it.html Promote-It: Click on "submit-it" then follow the instructions to register your site with all the catalogs and search engines listed.

http://www.submit-it.com/ Submit-It is one of the best known submission services.

http://rampages.onramp.net/-cscanlan/Webpromo.html There is no more comprehensive listing of free Web ad/classified promotion sites on the Internet. A tested collection of 558 free ads! Links are regularly maintained (free to nominal charge).

http://www.webpost96.com/ WebPost96™ is the only tool for promoting your Website that lets you track, save, verify, or change your listings, receive new listing opportunities, print client reports, and offers more than sixty places to list your Website and with more coming.

http://www.envision.net/marketing/inet/inetdata.1.html Four-star reviews of 150 marketing sites with hyperlinks to the site page that begins the ad banner or URL submission process.

http://dfrontier.com/starting-pts.html More than one hundred popular sites where you can list your URL; the hyperlinks lead directly to URL-submission forms. Digital Frontiers also offers link-up and traffic builder fee-based submission services.

http://www.netcreations.com/postmaster/ Use Postmaster online application to submit your information to several hundred spots automatically, with accuracy, accountability, and choice. You can try submitting to a small subset of spots for free, or you can buy the application if you are serious about promoting your site.

http://www.mgroup.com/freelinks/ FreeLinks categorizes databases, search engines, and links pages where you can list your site for free.

This is a free service to aid and simplify your Website promotion efforts.

http://www.dev-com.com/-expose1.htm Expose's free Website promotion center allows you to choose from hundreds of free Website promotion resources as well as our paid service of up to five hundred possible postings! Search engines promotional sites link classifieds, business indexes, and regional indexes.

http://www.wgi.com/webster Internet Blitz Pro promotes your Website to up to 201 promotional engines, and also nominates your Website to fifty review and critique sites, such as Point Top Sites, Cool Site of the Day, etc.

http://www.netcom/-karyntag/web.html Announce-It will submit your Website for listing to the top fifty, one hundred, or two hundred directories and search engines. Fee based.

http://www.eze.com/confederacy.html The Internet Confederacy will currently submit your site to more than twenty-nine search engines and indexes for free.

Other PR, Marketing, and E-Mail

http://www.cyberstop.com/secretary/hiresec.html The Virtual Secretary can develop and maintain e-mail lists, promote your Website, prepare reports, take orders, and electronically deliver your existing newsletter. The Virtual Secretary can keep you informed about the competition and up-to-date on new Websites.

http://www.westworld.com/-ah.ha/optimizms.html Surprise someone with an electronic postcard.

http://www.prnewswire.com PR Newswire is an inexpensive service that will distribute your news releases to a large audience.

http://www.hnt.com/bizwire/ Business Wire will distribute your news releases to a large audience.

http://www.access.digex.net/-usnwire U.S. Newswire provides electronic distribution of press releases, advisories, and statements. By using proprietary network connections to newsrooms across the country, Washington-based U.S. Newswire gets your news to the media faster and more effectively than either e-mail or fax services.

http://www.gina.com Global Internet News Agency (GINA) has been at the forefront of Internet press release distribution, Website promotion, and other public relations industry services.

http://www.lucepress.com/www/clip/online.html Luce Online, a division of Luce Clipping Service, now provides wire services and print media directly to your e-mail and via fax faster and at lower cost than any other database, plus comprehensive monitoring of the Internet exclusively for public relations clients.

http://www.pressline.com/homepage.html PRESSline is an international Internet press release submission/distribution service.

E-Mail, E-Mail Autoresponders, E-Mail Boxes, E-Mail Software, E-Mail Lists, E-Mail Address Services

http://www.NetBox.com NetBox is a permanent electronic mail address that lets you forward e-mail to and from any Internet address or access mail directly on the server. Optional private domain names, POP3 access, Mailbot autoresponders, World Wide Web hosting, or redirecting and password-protected FTP services are available.

http://netaddress.usa.net With NetAddress, you'll never again have to change your e-mail address just because you move or switch to a different Internet Service Provider.

http://www.juno.com Juno, America's first free Internet e-mail service.

http://www.freemark.com Take a look at Freemark Mail, the world's first totally free Internet e-mail service.

http:///www.goldmail.com GoldMail is a free personalized mailbox where you can receive promotional offers and electronic advertising. Why read advertising? When you enroll in GoldMail, you help determine what you will see. You tell us about yourself, your activities, and your lifestyle. Advertisers then send offers that match your tastes and activities. Read the messages, then get rewarded. Reading promotions enables you to accumulate points that can be traded in for merchandise awards, gift certificates, travel, and more.

http://www.hotmail.com What does HoTMaiL have to offer? Never change your e-mail address again. Accessible worldwide from any computer—one Web, one e-mail, one stop, no installation required, and it's free!

http://www.connectsoft.com E-mail Connection, the only universal electronic-mail in box, provides a central location for people to send and receive messages. E-mail Connection also supports Internet mail, CompuServe®, America Online, Prodigy®, RadioMail, and MCI® Mail; and provides gateways to AT&T EasyLink®, AppleLink®, fax services, GEnie®, postal, and X.400 addresses; and is compatible with most local area network-based systems, including cc: Mail and Microsoft Mail.

E-Mail Utilities, Auto-Responders, Fax, List Software Services

http://www.faxsav.com/faxsavinternet/html/welcome.html The FaxSav for Internet Suite of services offers convenient ways to send faxes straight from your computer desktop, either from e-mail or directly from an application, over the Internet to any fax machine worldwide via the FaxSav network.

http://www.westworld.com/-ah.ha/optimzms.html Surprise someone with an electronic postcard—free.

http://www.silverquick.com SilverQuick Communications are specialists in supplying automated e-mail services, such as autoresponders, mail list management, electronic newsletters, and automated information servers.

http://www.autoresponders.com The place to visit for instant information retrieval via e-mail! In most instances, just click and send and the information is instantly on its way to your e-mailbox!

http://www.netcreatoins.com/web/ WebList is the easiest way to manage a distribution list. Frustrated with inadequate mailing list software? Ever have it go ballistic, spewing multiple messages to everyone, and then sending the recipients' angry responses to the same list, multiplying it, too? Between the difficulty in installing and setting up mailing lists and the difficulty of administering them on a daily basis, traditional mailing lists (majordomo, listserv, listproc) are disasters waiting to happen.

http://homepage.interaccess.com/-arachnid/taul.html The Arachnid Utilities mailto: series—mailto: Formatter, converts mailto: responses into standard text or database-delimited records. mailto: Manager, offers simple database management for formatted mailto: responses.

http://www.sledge.com/solution/index.html More than simple e-mail-on-demand, EMOD provides your customers and business prospects access to your entire library of text files, word processing, and graphics documents, even complete multimedia presentation sent automatically to the e-mail address of their choosing. The Digital Librarian saves you time and money by automating your marketing reply tasks.

http://www.jan-lind.com Faxaway: Email-to-Fax, and Email-to-Fax Broadcast Service offers rates as low as five cents per fax! Take a free test drive to experience the ease of use. Your fax can be "printed" on your own letterhead, with your scanned signature, and the name of the recipient can be merged throughout the document if you like!

http:www.directchoice.com DirectChoice is Web-based relationship marketing software designed to transform your Website from an inbound presence to an outbound powerhouse. It is designed to allow users to register and build a personal profile and enables the Website to publish personal, proactive, individualized e-mail messages.

http://www.w3.org/pub/WWW/MailRobot/Help.html Web3 Servers is a robot that maintains the W3 mailing lists, and allows W3 documents to be retrieved on request. You can subscribe or unsubscribe to any of the various WWW mailing lists by sending e-mail to the robot *listserv@info.cern.ch.*

http://www.wbm.ca/visions/auto An autoresponder.

http://www.internet-tools.com/it-html/mail-list.html Do you have a Web page? Then you should be asking visitors to sign up for your mailing

list. This will allow you to communicate with them at a later date. Also offers a mail robot (a.k.a. mailbot or autoresponder) that will automatically reply with your prepared text when an e-mail message is received.

E-Mail List Creation, Acquisition Software, Services

http://www.wishing.com/webaudit/wa.html Wishing's Web Snoop grabs the e-mail addresses of your Website visitors and runs as a CGI on your Website.

http://www.tesser.com/ma/spnage.htm SPNage software program builds e-mail lists from UseNet groups.

http://www.floodgate.com Floodgate! is the ultimate in e-mail programs. Open the floodgates and let the e-mail flow.

http://206.151.751166/index.html Freedom is so named because it is designed to simplify your use of e-mail and free you from the traditional costs and labor of snail mail. You will be able to build and maintain a database of e-mail addresses from various sources on the Internet and online services, such as America Online and CompuServe.

http://www.alphasoftware.com/netmailer Netmailer is a contact manager and an e-mail program wrapped into one. Half of the program is dedicated to collecting and managing the names, e-mail addresses, and personal information about the people with whom you like to keep in touch. The other half is dedicated to the creation and merging of e-mail messages with contact information.

http://www.roverbot.com Rover is a unique Internet research tool that generates custom e-mail mailing lists by exploring Web pages that meet your criteria. Rover can use Web page indexes, search engines, and other popular Internet site indexes as starting points, allowing you to pinpoint just the companies and individuals you want to reach with your message.

http://www.hpp.com/ Go.Fetch™ is the world's first professional personal agent software for the Internet. Designed for business and high-speed research, Go.Fetch is far better than using manual search engines, instantly revolutionizing the way you gather information from the Internet. Go.Fetch will streak through the Internet and bring you back every e-mail address at each WWW site and at each UseNet group. You will rapidly and automatically build a high-powered mailing list.

E-Mail List Providers

http://www.aracnet.com/-starr/bulk1.htm Aracnet sells large bulk e-mail lists.

http://www.uni.com/bizemail.html Using bizEMail™ Services will let you reach more than three hundred thousand online users with your promotional message.

http://www.internetmedia.com Internet Media is a direct marketing resource for the Internet offering category-based e-mail lists, e-mail mailing services, e-mail list property management, automated list generation, e-mail software design, hit statistics and site auditing, and bulk e-mail franchise opportunities.

http://www.teleport.com/-web/dmgwho.html We are a list brokerage firm that provides the highest quality mailing and telemarketing lists available on the market today. There are more than fifty thousand lists to select from.

Website Traffic Counters, Tracking, Audit Services

http://www.internet-audit.com/ Internet Audit Bureau.

http://www.accessabc.com/ Audit Bureau of Circulations is the world's largest circulation-auditing bureau.

http://www.nielsen.com A. C. Nielsen.

http://www.ipro.com/ Nielsen's I/PRO, I/COUNT, I/AUDIT, I/CODE, I/MAIL, Java Count first audit tool for Java Applets, and WebPartner are trademarks of Internet Profiles Corporation.

http://www.nielsenmedia.com Nielsen Media Research.

http:/www.100hot.com or **http://www.web21.com** Paid ranking service of the one hundred most popular Websites based on number of page requests. Intended to compete with I/PRO.

http://www.pcmeter.com PC Meter attaches a device to the participating personal computers of users to track online activity. One thousand households are enrolled, ten thousand are planned. Eight ad agencies are paying subscribers.

http://www.npd.com/swps2.htm PC Meter sweeps of top twenty-five Websites.

http://www.openmarket.com/reporter Open Market's WebReporter is a comprehensive and versatile tool that lets you analyze your Website's server activity.

http://www.andromedia.com/ Andromedia's software is designed for Web masters and corporate marketing departments. Users can generate detailed, graphical reports on the activity of a particular Website, Web page, content element, advertising banner, user profile, or visit profile. Advertising or content management software will be able to access the data in real time to generate custom pages or rotate ad banners.

http://www.wishing.com/webaudit/wa.html Wishing specializes in making your Website profitable! You can have instant statistics with Web audit, guestbook, e-mail snoop (grabs e-mail address of visitors), and site history, and by simply adding our Plug In CGI into your Web pages!

http://www.interse.com/marketfocus/ Intersé Market Focus™ is an off-the-shelf solution that lets you conduct Website analyses at your place of business.

http://www.WebTrends.com/ WebTrends offers statistics, marketing, and traffic reporting for Web servers.

http://www.netcount.com The NetCount basic service provides unlimited access to a securely protected online report summary of the participating site's weekly activity with a free sixty-day introductory period (partly owned by Price Waterhouse).

http://www.cortex.net/sitetrack/ SiteTrack 1.03 continues to extend the lead Group Cortex has established as the premier provider of user-tracking systems for Netscape servers.

http://www.bienlogic.com/Perl/ Unix-based SurfReport™ provides statistical reports with the following information: access to the Website, number of accesses on a particular page, total number of hosts who have connected to a Website, list of the top hosts that most often access your Website, list of the pages that are most often looked at within your Website.

http://www.webtrack.com WebTrack.

http://www.xmission.com/-dtubbs/ Statbot is a WWW log analyzer, statistics generator, and database program. It works by snooping on the logfiles generated by most WWW servers and creating a database that contains information about the WWW server. This database is then used to create a statistics page and GIF charts that can be linked to by other WWW resources. Because Statbot snoops on the server logfiles, it does not require the use of the server's CGI-bin capability.

http://www.outreach.com With an account at the Outreach Counter Service, you can keep a running count of the number of times your page has been accessed, with the count currently displayed when they view your page. Then, you can click on the counter image for a more detailed report of who has been accessing your page and when.

http://www.digits.com/ WebCounter can be used by anyone on the Internet to maintain a count of the number of people who have accessed your site. It makes use of the GIF-manipulating GD library written by Tom Boutell.

http://www.maximized.com/ FlashStats is a program that will enable you to analyze statistics about the Websites that you host on your server. Great for internal Websites, corporate Websites, and Website providers. ISP's can easily configure FlashStats to allow secure access to real-time statistics for clients.

http://streams.com:80/lilypad/ What's the difference between Lilypad and all the other Web-auditing programs and services? Most focus on the measurement of events within a Website, offering information about file transfer or "hits," peak times, and your most popular areas. Lilypad measures none of this data but rather reports how visitors found out about your site in the first place. It measures how well your Internet promotions are performing.

http://www.netgen.com/ The best method for determining the effectiveness of your Website is net.Analysis 1.0 from net.Genesis. The first real-time Website usage analysis package, net.Analysis brings the power of Website usage reporting to your Windows NT or UNIX desktop.

http://W3.com/ Personal Web Site (PWS) is a visitor tracking program that complements a standard Web server by offering powerful tracking, customization, and administration features. A full featured server extension, it is designed for UNIX platforms.

_http://www.merc-in.com/products/WebTest/ Website usage capacity testing, WebTest is a new technology extension designed to be used with Mercury Interactive's Automated Software Quality (ASQ) client/server testing tools—WinRunner, XRunner, and LoadRunner. This Web extension automates testing of your corporate Website's functionality, performance, and capacity while integrating easily with your client/server testing tools.

http://www.boutell.com/wusage/ Wusage 4.1 is a server-based statistics system for Windows and Unix that helps you determine the true impact of your Web server. By measuring the popularity of your documents, as well as identifying the sites that access your server most often, Wusage provides valuable marketing information.

http://www.allen.com/ GuestTrack is Website profile and tracking software. Gather and store information about each visitor to your Website and personalize your presentation on the fly.

http://www.radzone.org/gmd/trakker Track incoming hyperlinks to your Website and unlock a host of information about how people find your pages. With LinkTrakker's fast spider technology, incoming hyperlinks are confirmed and categorized for easy analysis!

http://netpressence.com/accesswatch/ AccessWatch is a World Wide Web utility that provides a comprehensive view of daily accesses for individual users. It is equally capable of gathering statistics for an entire server. It provides a regularly updated summary of WWW server hits and accesses, and gives a graphical representation of available statistics.

http://www.usadata.com/demo/overview.htm AdLab is the first competitive tracking service specifically designed to monitor brand advertising within Internet media vehicles. It will tell you what brands are aggressively using Internet advertising and the Internet media vehicles they are employing.

Web Usage Statistics, Demographics, and Research

http://www.nielsenmedia.com/commercenet/ CommerceNet/Nielsen Internet Demographics Recontact Study (March/April 1996 Executive Summary). The initial survey was designed to assess the dimension of the new medium in terms of personal access and usage patterns, while the objective for the recontact survey was to identify behavioral changes over time.

http://www.boardwatch.com/mag/95/dec/bwm1.htm Definitive analysis of Web usage as of December 1995. Requires free registration to *Boardwatch* magazine.

http://www.cc.gatech.edu/gvu/user-surveys/User-Survey-Home.html GVU's WWW user survey results.

http://www.cyberatlas.com/ CyberAtlas from I/Pro offers Internet statistics and demographics.

http://www.ora.com/survey/ O'Reilly Internet Research Studies.

http://www.findsvp.com FIND/SVP, Worldwide Research and Consulting Firm.

http://www.mit.edu/people/mkgray/growth A report by Matthew Gray measuring the growth of the Web, June 1993 to June 1995.

http://www.echonyc.com/~parallax/interfacts.html Internet facts and statistics from Parallax Webdesign.

http://www.interlog.com/~bxi/size.htm BXI offers information on the size of the Internet with additional information on domains, browsers, and links to many of the other Internet demographic sites.

http://www.demon.co.uk/mediamgc/custinfo/analysis.html A critique of Internet surveys, May 1996 (focus on Britain).

http://www.yahoo.com/Computers/Internet/Statistics and Demographics Yahoo's list of demographics.

http://www.census.gov/ The U.S. Census Bureau.

http://govinfo.kerr.orst.edu/ Government Information-Sharing Project.

http://www.demographics.com/ *American Demographics* magazine/ marketing tools.

http://www.npd.com/todsp.htm "Research in the Future: the Role and Measurement of the Internet," presented by Tod Johnson, chief executive officer of The NPD Group, Inc.

http://www.asiresearch.com/ ASI Advertising/Marketing/Media Decisive Survey is a Windows-based application that completely automates the survey process by enabling the user to create a questionnaire, e-mail it, parse the responses, and perform in-depth analysis or export results to other applications.

http://www.openmarket.com/intindex/ Open Market Internet Index is an occasional collection of facts and statistics about the Internet and related activities.

http://www.femina.com/results.html Survey of Women on the Web.

http://www.webcom.com/walsh/stats.html InterNet Info specializes in the analysis of the commercial domains registered with the InterNIC.
http://www.gallup.com/ Gallup Organization.

E-Mail, Netiquette, Spamming, Censorship

http://www.tenagra.com/net-acceptable.html Links to netiquette and spamming articles.
http://www.cco.caltech.edu/-cbrown/BL/ Blacklist of Internet advertisers; clearinghouse, blacklist, and mediation for complaints about improper usage of net advertising and e-mail.
http://www.mci.com/about/info/policy/home.shtml MCI policy on spamming.
http://www.fdma.com/-news/advert.faq FAQ on posting anything that is commercial onto UseNet.
ftp://rtfm.mit.edu/pub/usenet-by-group/news.answers/usenet/what-is/part2 "FAQ: Advertising on UseNet: How to Do It, How Not to Do It."
ftp://rtfm.mit.edu/pub/usenet-by-group/nes.answers/usenet/primer/part1 Rules for posting to UseNet.
http://www.isa.net Proposed junk e-mail guidelines of the ISA (Interactive Services Association) and the Direct Marketing Association.
http://www.safesurf.com/index.html Safesurf is an organization dedicated to making the Internet safe for your children without censorship. We've developed and are implementing an Internet rating standard that is bringing together parents, providers, publishers, developers, and all the resources available on the Internet to achieve this goal. It involves marking sites with the SafeSurf Wave.

General Internet Information for Advertising, PR, and Marketing

http://www.bnet.att.com AT&T Business Network welcomes you to a free gold mine of business news and information. Offering more than one thousand free industry reports, Marketing Center is the place to turn for market analysis.
http://www.vip.at/cfeichtner Internet Information Center is a resource for beginners seeking to understand and use various Internet features—primers, history, introduction, netiquette, hotlist, search engines, etc.
http://www.wwinet.com Worldwide Internet Network: whereas Websites acting independently may be too small to sell their own advertising space, or to sell space at a reasonable price, when they join WWIN, they become part of a large that is extremely attractive to advertisers.
http://www.internic.net/ Internic Directory and Database Services home page.

http://www.shoppingdirect.com/ The Shopper is a directory of four hundred Internet malls.

_http://www.ecola.com/ Internet Publishing Access for simple and helpful guides to the Internet. Ecola's thousands of links are presented on Web pages designed for speed and utility.

http://www.hoovers.com/ Hoover's ten thousand companies—directories, databases, profiles.

http://www.mediacentral.com A Guide to Media Central News Digest is a daily compendium of Media Central News—sites, forums, folios, commentary, columns.

http://www.tippecanoe.com/activmed.html Use ActivMedia's Online Marketer Resource Locator to search for Web tools, designers, marketers, ad space, market research, free directory listings, and other resources.

http://www.planetdirect.com/low/facts.html Planet Direct delivers an enhanced suite of products and services, such as both public and private personal home pages, 3-D (VRML) chat, advanced personal messaging, localized electronic yellow pages, customized news and information retrieval, Web searches, directories and site reviews, accelerated Web browsing, and e-mail all free and packaged to help ISPs generate new revenue and attract new customers. Leveraging CMG's background in database marketing, Planet Direct will offer advertisers and direct marketers the world's largest demographic clickstream database of Internet customers and usage patterns. Information analysis provided on this database will provide advertisers with greater targetability, enhanced local presence, and broader reach than that achieved by working directly with any single ISP.

http://www-e1c.gnn.com/gnn/wr/96/01/26/features/bestads/index.html GNN features the best Web ads of 1995.

http://www.portfolios.com The Portfolios Online site includes portfolios and detailed work profiles of photographers, illustrators, graphic designers, art directors, animators, industrial designers, advertising agencies, copywriters, multimedia artists, and surface designers.

http://www.gagme.wwa.com/-boba/masters1.html Bob Allison's Web Masters Page! is a comprehensive source for information and links for Web masters and Web page designers on style, searching for material, browsing for material, seeing what's new; spotlight on Web-Oriented newsgroups; random inspiration; keeping your pages inviting and easy to read; spotlight on GIFs and icons; transparent GIFs; clickable pictures, Imagemaps; using backgrounds textures and patterns; background colors; HTML links; HTML Editors; HTML converters; using ALT tags, using ASCII Art; CGI; PERL; more tools; SGML; VRML and information and techniques; spotlight on browsers; announcing your Web page; and spotlight on publicizing your page.

http://www.wilsonweb.com/webmarket/ Wilson Internet Services: a small business and effective Web marketing information center. You'll find links to more than 225 online articles about effective Web marketing and online resources for business. The focus is on small business, though some articles and links reflect applicable lessons from larger firms. It also offers *Web Marketing Today,* an e-mail newsletter, and miscellaneous Internet services.

http://www.curtin.edu.au/curtin/dept/designs/STOCKPHOTO/StockWeb Siteshtml Stock photography Websites.

http://www.wmo.com/Articles/Release/PR.html E-mail Releases: the good, the bad, and the awful—from who's marketing online to a fun Web review/analysis site with a marketing angle.

http://www.ifi.uio.no/-terjen/interaction Interaction/IP™ provides your Web server with advanced dynamic services that support interpersonal communication and make your Website into a social place. As early as 1994, the software provided one of the first threaded conference systems on the Web so visitors could browse or post messages from their Web browser. The Threaded Discussion Forum is still a core service of Interaction. The application also integrates highly customizable chat rooms and other services. Interaction is highly extendable with services such as a shopping cart feature so you can tailor a shop on the Web.

http://pub.savvy.com Newsletter Library is your source for free newsletters. The Internet Newsletter Library is your guide and source to the wealth of information contained in newsletters. With a comprehensive list of topics and more than eleven thousand newsletters, the Newsletter Library is bound to include a newsletter that helps you do your job better and enjoy your leisure time more fully.

http://pwer.com/creative Creative Exchange lists graphic and advertising professionals.

http://www.cybergold.net/home-page.html CyberGold™ has a unique approach to delivering both mass market and highly targeted ads to Internet users. CyberGold recognizes that the resource in shortest supply on the Internet is attention. There is simply more stuff on the Internet that requires attention than there is attention to pay. CyberGold makes a market in attention, connecting those who want attention to those who are willing to pay attention. Specifically, if an advertiser wants to deliver a message to a consumer, the advertiser offers to pay a consumer directly to watch an ad. The money earned can be used to pay for content, services, or even hard goods on or off the Internet using CyberGold's patent-pending technology.

http://haven.ios.com/-freelans Freelance Online is a professional online service for freelancers in the publishing and advertising fields. It serves as a directory for employers and as a resource and information center for freelancers.

Internet Periodicals and Other News Sources

http://www..pressline.com/homepage.html Pressline is a multilingual database archive of more than twenty thousand press releases.

http://www.magic.ca/majicmedia/adrap.html Ad Rap by Peter Mosely is a regular Internet column on advertising with good advice and insight.

http://www.interbiznet.com/ibn/nomad.html *First Steps* is a marketing and design daily.

http://www.infi.net/naa/edge.html Subscriber-based, The Digital Edge shows the interactive world from the precipice, and gives you the edge you need to compete successfully in this new medium.

http://www.adage.com *Advertising Age.*

Legal

http://www.webcom.com/-lewrose/home.html The Advertising Law Internet Site is maintained by Lewis Rose, an advertising and marketing law partner with the Washington, DC–based law firm of Arent, Fox, Kintner, Plotkin, and Kahn. Cyberspace Law is a free e-mail Internet seminar for nonlawyers. It will send out one message every two to three days about the basic principles of the law of copyright, free speech, libel, privacy, contract, and trademark, as they apply on the Internet. It's a distribution list, not a discussion list. We currently have more than 9,700 subscribers. To subscribe, send the message SUBSCRIBE CYBERSPACE-LAW yourfirstname yourlastname to LISTPROC-REQUEST@COUNSEL.COM, Owner: Jake Vogelaar.

http://infolawalert.com Information Law Alert covers emerging issues involving computer and communications technology and intellectual property. Its coverage ranges from software patents and cryptography to copyright in a digital environment.

http://www.eff.org/pub/Legal/ One of the best places to find out what's going on in terms of legal regulation of the Internet is the Electronic Frontier Foundation. Articles and links relating to BBS liability.

http://www.gahouse.com/docs/whatsnew/parsons.htm Entry point with good links to bill and commentary on HB 1630, Georgia's Internet Police intellectual property bill.

http://www.law.georgetown.edu/lc/internic/domain1.html This Website offers background and information concerning trademarks, the Internet, and domain names. It examines conflicts between domain names and traditional trademark law, and offers solutions for solving these problems.

Calendar of Events and Trade Shows

http://www.expoguide.com EXPOguide Calendar of Trade Shows, Conferences, and Expositions, also offers exhibition, conference, and meeting halls, show services, and other resources.

http://www.kweb.com/ The Computer Events Directory.

http://marketing.pcworld.com/mktg/Events/index.html *PC World* Online.

Commerce, Electronic Payment, Shopping Cart, Wallet Systems, Checks by Wire, and Merchant Systems

http://www.mindthestore.com Virtual Store from Mind the Store offers complete POP and Internet merchant management systems; conducts real-time electronic commerce.

http://www.openmarket.com/products Open Market offers a suite of products that enable Internet commerce. OM-Transact can host an electronic marketplace, enable business-to-business transactions, and offer home banking or bill-payment services. Open Market Merchant Solution is the first complete business solution that allows merchants to run their business securely on the World Wide Web.

http://www.sbt.com SBT Internet Systems' Web Trader 2.0 storefront creation software captures sales orders, leads, and product registration.

http://www.outreach.com MallManager™ software is an electronic real-time payment system! It offers software delivery, software keys, club memberships, online donations, and online Web tools.

http://users.mwci.net/-tnc/payment.htm "Paying for Products and Services on the Internet" by Anton Holzherr is an article for the layman about internet payment issues from the international point of view.

http://www.absbank.com Web Pay allows Web merchants to accept checks and credit cards on the World Wide Web. Online Checks Direct (OCD) is a service that allows Sysops to accept checks online via their bulletin board systems. Checks Direct for "Over the Phone" Sales Checks Direct is a service that allows businesses to accept checks over the phone or fax from their customers. Merchant Account Services are available.

http://www.checkfree.com The system for secure Internet transactions with CheckFree Wallet and a major credit card. You can buy goods, services, or information from online merchants.

http://www.checkmaster.com/internetchecks With Checkmaster, your customers can authorize you as a merchant to print a check for them. It's called a pre-authorized draft and requires no signature.

http://www.cybercash.com/cybercash/who-we-are/overview.html Cybercash: There are more than 400,000 CyberCash Wallets in the distribution channel, including CyberCash, Checkfree, and Compuserve wallets. Connected to 80 percent of the banks in the United States.

http://www.digicash.com Digicash: Ecash is a software-only form of electronic money that provides all the advantages of cash, and then some. It is *the* money for the Internet.

http://www.fv.com/ This is the first virtual Internet payment system enabling simple, secure, online transactions.

http://www.redi-check.com Redi-Check's unique payment system enables anyone to accept payment online from customers who use standard bank checks.

http://www.verisign.com VeriSign's mission is to provide trusted digital identification services in support of secure electronic commerce solutions. Markets: digital authentication of individuals, entities, and content for Internet access and communications, electronic commerce, and corporate Intranet solutions. Digital IDs, commonly referred to as digital certificates, are used in much the same way as conventional forms of identification, such as a driver's license or passport, to provide irrefutable evidence of the owner's identity and, in some cases, authority in a given transaction. Digital IDs are issued by VeriSign, a trusted third party which verifies the identity of a subscriber.

http://www.clickshare.com/ Clickshare from Newshare is for Internet users who are tired of remembering multiple registration IDs and passwords as they move among their favorite Websites. Many would like to be able to purchase information by the click without having to use their credit card numbers each time. The Clickshare Access and Payment System enables multisite user authentication, microtransaction billing and settlement, and cross-site access measurement. Clickshare registration will provide you access to a universe of information content offered by independent publishers. A single registration will allow you access to any of the cooperating publishers with only a single authentication per session.

http://www.natlcard.com Merchant account systems provider.

http://www.e-com.com-buyersguide/ Published in hard copy format since 1987 by Electronic Commerce Strategies, Inc., the *Buyer's Guide to Electronic Commerce* is the most complete listing and description of e-mail, EDI, and electronic re-engineering products and services in the marketplace.

http://worldmart.com/scripts/ Shopping cart software scripts.

http://www.eff.org/-erict/Scripts/ Shopping cart software scripts.

http://www.ifi.uio.no/-terjen/interactoin/ Interaction/IP™ provides your Web server with advanced dynamic services that support interpersonal communication and makes your Website into a social place. As early as 1994, the software provided one of the first threaded conference systems on the Web so visitors could browse or post messages from their Web browser. The Threaded Discussion Forum is still a core service of Interaction. The application also integrates highly customizable Chat Rooms, and other services. Interaction is highly extendable with services such as a shopping cart feature so you can tailor a shop on the Web.

http://www.eastland.com/shopping.html Java shopping cart applet.

http://www.releasesoft.com/ Let people download fully featured software from your Website—for free. Let them try it. Let them fall in love with it. Let them get addicted to it. When they can't live without it, make them pay for it. A/Pay is an embedded sales agent that transacts the user purchase of your software after a free trial period. The transaction process is then handled by Release Software Comp.

http://www.mercater.com Mercantec develops and markets SoftCart, a virtual storefront application. SoftCart is the missing link between the World Wide Web technology, secure payment systems, and back-end commercial applications.

http://www.webmate.com/wm/newsite/webmate/page/newsite/welcome Develop, deploy, and manage your own Website with WebMate software. WebMate is a comprehensive suite of tools and a server-based platform that includes built-in database functionality, a powerful yet easy-to-use scripting language, browser, and e-mail interface for rapid update of Web page content, plug-in modules for electronic commerce, interface to external SQL databases, and enhanced security features such as full data encryption. WebMate runs with all popular HTTP servers, on most UNIX® and NT® platforms. WebMate comes with ready-to-go applications that you can customize and put into actual use—at a fraction of the cost of a custom-built solution. For example, one application lets you build and manage an electronic storefront for selling your products and services—complete with an integrated secure credit card transaction capability.

Award Designations

http://www.tenagra.com/awards.html The Tenagra Awards for Internet Marketing Excellence (annual).

http://www.pointcom.com Point Top 5 percent of Websites—reviews by category.

http://www.spt.com/award.html Starting Point Directory Choice Site Awards.

http://www.infoseek.com Infoseek Cool Site by category.

http://www.owi.com/netvalue Netvalue Interesting Business Sites.

http://www.mckinley.com Magellan Internet Site Ratings Award.

http://www.vmedia.com/cat/press/store/business/ Ventana Internet Business 500 Most Essential Business Sites.

http://www.mainstreetearth.com/ Main Street Web Site Ratings Award.
http://www.tricky.com/liz/ NBNSOFT Content Awards.
http://webcrawler.com/Webcrawler/Top25.html WebCrawler Search Engine Top 25 Linked Sites Award.
http://www.lycos.com Lycos 250 Award—Top 250 Hot List.
http://www.isisnet.com/paula/ Mylo's Pick of the Week, Cool Site, Spider's Picks.
http://www.interedge.com Interedge Top Ten Sites.
http://www.web100.com The Web 100: The Web's Best Sites.
http://www.riddler.com/ Riddler's Choice Game and Puzzle Site.
http://www.cciweb.com/ Iway 500: The Best 500 Sites on the World Wide Web.
http://www.gnn.com GNN Best of Net Winner NCSA.

Associations

http://www.ama.org/ American Marketing Association.
http://www.commercepark.com/AAAA/ American Association of Advertising Agencies.
http://199.1.171.82/Ad Council The Ad Council is a volunteer organization that creates public-service advertising.

Search Engines for Websites, E-Mail, UseNet, and Others

http://www.metacrawler.com Metacrawler Parallel Engine Search Service.
http://www.altavista.digital.com Altavista Parallel Engine Search—Web and UseNet.
http://www.hotbot.com Hotbot sponsored by Hotwired and Inktomi—massive meta search.
http://www.dejanews.com Deja News UseNet Search.
http://okra.ucr.edu/okra/ OKRA: a powerful e-mail search engine—5.4 million names.
http://www.nlightn.com NlightN is a powerful database retrieval system and one-stop search site. Information is available from a periodical database, news retrieval systems, Internet search engine, reference library, and bookstore.
http://www.elibrary.com Electric Library Monster search engine (fee based).
http://www.iTools.com/find-it/find-it.html Find-It lets you find what you're looking for, no matter what it is.
http://www.liszt.com/ Liszt: looking for an e-mail discussion group? Enter any word or phrase to search the world's largest directory of mailing lists (by a long shot!)—48,234 listserv, listproc, majordomo, and independently managed lists from 1,473 sites.

http://www.tricky.com/lfm/niches.htm *Niche Search Engine Resource Guide* compiled by Paul "the soarING" Siegel. The purpose of this guide is to help us do research on the Internet. It is organized according to the general steps we follow in the search for information: Universal Search Engines; Building Bibliographies; Libraries; Locating Experts; Universities Government Institutes and Nonprofits Business Associations Email; Finding Expertise; Media Data Bases Discussion Groups; Locating Products and Services; Locating Regional Resources.

http://www.hpp.com/ Go.Fetch scheduled for July 1996 availability, is the world's first professional personal agent software for the Internet. Designed for business and high-speed research, Go.Fetch is far better than using manual search engines, instantly revolutionizing the way you gather information from the Internet. At your command, this loyal dog automatically finds, reads, filters, and returns documents matching your requirements. We call Go.Fetch the "browser buster" and you will too. For entertainment, use your favorite browser. For everything else, use Go.Fetch.

http://www.directory.net Open Market's Commercial Sites Index.

http://www.whowhere.com/ Directory Search of e-mail addresses, phone numbers, and addresses of companies on the Internet Yellow Pages.

http://www.excite.com Excite.

http://ugweb.cs.ualberta.ca/-mentor02/search/search-all.html One hundred twenty-eight search engines linked on a single page.

http://www.webcrawler.com WebCrawler.

http://www.lycos.com Lycos.

http://www.yahoo.com/ Yahoo!

http://apollo.co.uk/ Apollo International Directory.

http://www.stpt.com/ Starting Point—meta search.

http://www.cs.colostate.edu/-dreiling/smartform.html Savvy Search searches multiple search engines.

http://www2.infoseek.com InfoSeek.

http://inktomi.berkeley.edu/query.html Inktomi—UC Berkeley.

http://www.mckinley.com/ Magellan: search the Web or just the Magellan Diretory of Reviewed Sites.

http://www.opentext.com/omw/f-omw.html Open Text.

http://guano.cs.colorado.edu/wwww/ World Wide Web Worm.

http://worldmail.com/wede4.shtml WED: world e-mail search engine.

http://www.bigfoot.com/ Bigfoot is a global white pages, which has been purpose-built to help you find that elusive someone. We travel greatly, all around the planet, and have found it hard to keep in touch with our friends. Bigfoot helps us do just that.

http://maxonline.com/webmasters/ The Webmaster's guide to search engines and directories.

http://www.search.com/ Welcome to personalize search.com. You can put all your favorite searches onto your own personal page in three steps.

http://www.hotwired.com/wired/4.05/indexing/index.html *HotWired* article on search engines—requires registration.

http://www.dis.strath.ac.uk/business/search.html Links to eight search engine review articles.

http://www.avenue.com/search/ Aquinas's Avenue search engine front-end requires Netscape Navigator 2.0. Frontend for search engines, news, resources, magazines, UseNet, etc.

Telemarketing, Call Center, Voice Messaging

http://www.telepro.com/tel-buy.hmtl TeleProfessional's 1996 Vendor's Index to Products and Services mainly lists company names only and very few direct links. The Vendor's Index is a generic listing of companies and organizations in the call center and telemarketing community.

Software for Advertising and Web Page Validation

http://www.redalert.com RedAlert monitors your Websites throughout the day and notifies you of down sites with details on type of problem.

http://www.jumbo.com Shareware, freeware.

http://sage.cc.purdue.edu/-xniu/winsock/ws-ftp-f.html Xiaomu Niu's Internet application collection.

http://www.tucows.com Tucows shareware and freeware.

http://www.shareware.com Large shareware collection.

http://ntserver.psl-online.com/ Public software library offers shareware, CD-ROM collections, and provides an order-taking service (charge card, 800 number, etc.) for shareware software developers.

http://www.amic.com/telmar Telmar Information Services Corporation, the world's leading creator of software for the advertising media industry since 1968.

http://www.javaworld.com/ *Javaworld* magazine.

http://www.gamelan.com Largest selection of free and fee-based Java applets.

http://home.caravelle.com/ WebWatcher, the real-time monitoring and alerting tool that puts Webmasters in control of their sites by monitoring the availability of key Internet and intranet services, such as HTTP, SMTP (mail), FTP, DNS, and others twenty-four hours a day, seven days a week. A "must have" for anyone serious about maintaining their credibility on the Web!

http://www.webaid.com/ Ultimate HTML and GIF file resource for Website creation.

http://www.unipress.com/cgi-bin/WWWeblint With UniPress' WWWeblint Web page validation service, you simply supply the URL of a page anywhere on the World Wide Web and the Weblint program checks your HTML code for you.

http://www.webtechs.com/html-val-svc/ The WebTechs HTML Validation Service is intended to be used by folks who are wondering whether some idiom or syntax is legal according to the HTML 2.0 specification.

http://ugweb.cs.ualberta.ca/-gerald/validate/ This is a friendly, easy-to-use HTML validation service based on a real SGML parser. It is similar in function to the WebTechs validator (which is more commonly known as the "HALSoft validator"), but the returned errors are (hopefully) easier to figure out.

http://imagiware.com/RxHTML/ Doctor HTML retrieves a Web page and performs several tests to see if your document is in tip-top shape.

http://www.webgenie.com/software/cgistar.html CGI*Star is a Windows 3.x and Windows 95 application that allows the easy creation of CGIs for either Unix or Windows NT servers to process HTML forms in Web pages.

http://worldwidemart.com/scripts Matt's Script Archive contains many free Perl and CGI scripts to benefit the Internet and WWW community.

http://www.clickables.com Clickables are plug and play CGI software. Our goal is to develop software that adds power to Internet Websites: Page Launcher, Marketplace 2000 B-Boards, New Global Mall Data Catcher, One-Page Cart, Arturo's Maui Onion Salsa MultiCart.

http://www.mindworkshop.com/alchemy.html GIF Construction Set takes advantage of the full feature set of the GIF89a file structure—transparent backgrounds, interlaced GIF graphics, and rotating and animated banners in a single GIF file, image blocks, text blocks, control blocks, manage palettes.

http://www.coder.com/creations/banner/ The Banner Generator creates free advertising banners automatically in various standard sizes. Provides banner backgrounds, special effects, and more.

http://cws.wilmington.net/cwsa.html Stroud's Consummate WinApps List.

http://www.windows95.com/ The Best Windows 95 Information, Drivers, and Shareware on the Internet!

Personalized News Home Pages and Delivery Services

http://www.infoseek.com Infoseek Directory—create a personalized home page.

http://www.excite.com Excite Directory—create a personalized home page of hyperlinks and convenient news.

http://www.netscape.com Netscape—create a personalized home page of hyperlinks.

News Delivery

http://www.pcfn.com Pointcast freely distributed "Screen Saver" personalized news delivery software supported by advertising—must see.

http://www.infosage.ibm.com IBM Infosage Personalized Web or e-mail daily delivery service.

http://www.atg-dynamo.com/dynamo/main/ Using Dynamo, you can create customized pages. Dynamo allows your site to build pages on the fly for every user in real time! When a page is created, the data on the page can come from internal or external databases. A thousand users can be looking at the same Dynamo page and each see different customized content.

http://www.search.com/ Welcome to personalize search.com. You can put all your favorite searches onto your own personal page in three steps.

http://www.newspage.com/ Thousands of categorized news stories updated daily, NewsPage is the Web's leading source of daily business news. Simply select an industry and drill your way to today's news in 2,500 topics from more than six hundred information sources. The services will send personalized daily e-mail of selected news.

http://www.webhitz.com/ "Your Front Door to the Web"™ WEBHITZ™ should be your preferred home page upon startup of your Web browser. It's fast!

http://www.merc.com Mercury Mail is a free personalized daily news delivery service.

▼

Epilogue

THE INTERNET IS CHANGING THE NATURE OF PUBLICITY ITSELF. THIS BOOK hopefully has elucidated this point. The Internet, from its beginning, was developed for communication between groups of people with similar interests. Today, for example, there are over ten thousand newsgroups catering to a host of narrowcasted interest groups. The principle of localization cannot be overlooked in planning a publicity campaign. This principle requires understanding the nature of online communities, which serve particular geographic or functional interest groups.

Unlike the broadcasting approach to publicity, Internet publicity needs to be based on operating and influencing these narrowcasted online communities. While the ideas in the book have given you a host of techniques and information to operate within this new sphere of online communities, there are still many new methods to be developed. As the Internet evolves, you will develop your own creative methods, which will be tested and found to be successful or not. I look forward to hearing your stories and hope you will share them with me. Feel free to e-mail me at *shiva@icybernetics.com.*

Appendix

Media List

Daily Newspapers

Albany *Times-Union* (New York). Letters: *tuletters@aol.com*; Newsroom: *tunewsroom@aol.com*; Capitol Bureau: *tucapitol@aol.com*; Library: *tulibrary@aol.com*

Arkansas *Democrat-Gazette* (Little Rock). *news@arkdg.com*

Atlanta *Journal-Constitution*. Specify in your message whom the message is for: *gpph16a@prodigy.com*

***The Baltimore Sun*.** To reach reporters or comment on the paper (letters to the editor or subscription requests): *baltsun@clark.net*

***Boston Globe*.** Story Ideas: *news@globe.com*; Circulation Requests: *circulation@globe.com*; Letters to the Editor: *letter@globe.com*; Submissions to "Voxbox" Column: *voxbox@globe.com*; Comments on Coverage/Ombudsman: *ombud@globe.com*; "Ask the Globe": *ask@globe.com*; Thursday Calendar Section: *list@globe.com*; Health and Science Section: *howwhy@globe.com*; Confidential Chat: *chat@globe.com*; City Weekly Section: *ciweek@globe.com*; Real Estate

Section: *lots@globe.com*; Religion Editor: *religion@globe.com*; Arts Editor: *arts@globe.com*; "Plugged In": *plugged@globe.com*

Boston Herald. Political Comments: *heraldpol@delphi.com*; Other Op-Ed Comments: *heraldedit@delphi.com*

Cape Cod Times (Massachusetts). *cctimes@delphi.com*

Champaign-Urbana News-Gazette (Illinois). Comments on local news only: *gazette@prairienet.org*

Chicago Tribune. *tribletter@aol.com*

Christian Science Monitor. Op-Ed: *oped@rachel.csps.com*

Elyria Chronicle-Telegram (Ohio). *macroncl@freenet.lorain. oberlin. edu*

The Columbus Dispatch (Ohio). *crow@cd.columbus.oh.us*; Letters to the Editor: *letters@cd.columbus.oh.us*

Contra Costa County Times (California). Letters to the Editor: *ccletrs@ netcom.com*

Corvallis Gazette-Times (Oregon). *74250.2373@compuserve.com*

Daily Citizen (Washington, D.C.). *ben@essential.org*

The Daily Telegraph (London). *editor@telegraph.co.uk*

Dallas Morning News (Texas). *74774.2236@compuserve.com*

Des Moines Register (Iowa). *dsmreg@delphi.com*; *:76247/2367. compuserve.com*

Fairfax Journal (Virginia). *journalexp@aol.com*

Flint Journal (Michigan). *fj@flintj.com*

Gazeta Wyborcza (Poland). *gawyb@ikp.atm.com.pl*

The Guardian (United Kingdom). Letters: *letters@guardian.co.uk*; "Notes and Queries": *nanq@guardian.co.uk*; Computer Page: *computerg@guardian.co.uk*; "Online": *online@guardian.co.uk*

The Independent (United Kingdom). Computer Page: *comppage@ independent.co.uk*

International Herald-Tribune. *iht@eurokom.ie*

Irish Times. *computimes@irish-times.ie*

Jerusalem Post (Israel). *ipost@zeus.datasrv.co.il*

Journal American (Bellevue, Washington). *jaedit@aol.com*

The Knoxville News-Sentinel (Tennessee). Newsroom: *kns-news@ use.usit.net*; Letters: *kns-letters-to-editor@use.usit.net*

Middlesex News (Framingham, Massachusetts). *mnews@world. std.com*

Minneapolis Star Tribune. Letters to the Editor: *opinion@startribune. com*; Minnesota Politics Feedback, etc.: *politics@startribune.com*

Morgenbladet (Oslo, Norway). *truls@telepost.no*

Morning Journal (Lorain, Ohio). *mamjornl@freenet.lorain.oberlin.edu*

The Morning of Russia (Utro Rossii). *utro@belik.msk.su*

The Namibian (Windhoek, Namibia). *tom@namibian.com.na*

The News & Record (Greensboro, North Carolina). Letters: *edpage @nr.infi.net*

Norwich Bulletin (Connecticut). *norbull@aol.com*
The Olympian (Olympia, Washington). *olympian@halcyon.com*
Philadelphia Inquirer. Editorial Page: *editpage@aol.com*
Phoenix Gazette. No press releases: *phxgazette@aol.com*
Portland Oregonian. *oreeditors@aol.com*
Prague Post. *100120.361@compuserve.com*
Reno Gazette-Journal (Nevada). *rgi@libcom.dps.com*
Sacramento Bee (California). Letters, Op-Ed Pieces: *sacbedit@netcom.com*
St. Petersburg Times (Florida). *73174.3344@compuserve.com*
Salt Lake Tribune (Salt Lake City). *the.editors@sltrib.com*
San Francisco Examiner. *sfexaminer@aol.com*
San Jose Mercury-News. General: *sjmercury@aol.com*; Letters to the Editor: *letters@aol.com*
Santa Cruz County Sentinel (California). Letters to the Editor: *sented@cruzio.com*; News Desk: *sentcity@cruzio.com*
Seattle Times. Op-Ed: *opinion@seatimes.com*; Personal Technology: *ptech@seatimes.com*
Spartanburg Herald-Journal (South Carolina). *73511.522@compuserve.com*
Springfield News-Leader (Missouri). Letters to the Editor: *nleditor@ozarks.sgcl.lib.mo.us*; Press Releases: *nlnews@ozarks.sgcl.lib.mo.us*
The Sunday Times (London). Innovation: *innovation@delphi.com*
Sun-Sentinel (Broward County, Florida). Grapevine: *vineeditor@ aol.com*
Die Tageszeitung (Berlin). *briefe@taz.de*
Tallahassee Democrat. *letters@freenet.fsu.edu*
Toronto Sun. "Page Six": *pagesix@aol.com*
Tucson Citizen (Arizona). Letters to the Editor: *tcnews@aol.com*
USA Today. Letters to the Editor: *usatoday@clark.net*
Vancouver Columbian (Washington). *vanpaper@aol.com*
Wall Street Journal. Subscription services only: *wsj.service@cor.dowjones.com*
Winnipeg Free Press (Winnipeg, Manitoba). News Tips: *city desk@freepress.mb.ca*; Library: *library@freepress.mb.ca*; Letters to the Editor: *letters@freepress.mb.ca;* Computer Columnist: *pihichyn@freepress.mb.ca;* Computer Editor: *minkin@freepress.mb.ca*

Weekly/Alternative Newspapers

The Anarchives (Toronto). *yakimov@ecf.utoronto.ca*
Austin Chronicle (Texas). *xephyr@bga.com*
Bay Windows (Boston). *baywindo@world.std.com*
Boston Phoenix. *71632.63@compuserve.com*
Channel (Point Richmond, California). *channel@calon.com*
CityPages (Minneapolis). *citypages@igc.apc.org*

City Sun (New York, New York). Computer column: *sysop@f206.n278.zl.fidonet.org*
Eye (Toronto). *eye@io.org*
Hill Times (Ottawa). *hilltimes@freenet.carleton.ca*
Icon (Iowa City). *icon@igc.apc.org*
The Irish Emigrant. For sample of printed edition: *connell@world.std.com*; for a sample e-mail issue: *ferrie@iol.ie*
LA Weekly. *laweekly@aol.com*
Los Gatos Weekly-Times (California). *lgwt@livewire.com*
The Met (Dallas, Texas). *74742.1401@compuserve.com*
The Mirror (Montreal, Québec). *mirror@fc.bablon.montreal.qc.ca*
Ottawa X Press. *xpress@freenet.carleton.ca*
NuCity (Albuquerque, New Mexico). *nucity@swcp.com*
Palo Alto Weekly (Palo Alto, California). *paweekly@netcom.com*
Ridgefield Press (Connecticut). *71052.3315@compuserve.com*
The Riverfront Times (St. Louis, Missouri). *rft@plink.geis.com*
Saratoga News (California). *sn@livewire.com*
The Stranger (Seattle). *stranger@cyberspace.com*
Sunday Times of London. Innovation: *innovation@delphi.com*
Tico Times (Costa Rica). *ttimes@huracan.cr*
Tucson Weekly (Arizona). Letters to the Editor ONLY: *71632.105@compuserve.com*
Twin Cities Reader (Minneapolis). *sari23@aol.com*
The Village Voice (New York, New York). *voice@echonyc.com*
Voir (Montreal). *voir@babylon.montreal.qc.ca*
Washington City Paper. *washcp@aol.com*
Weekly Mail & Guardian (Johannesburg, South Africa). *wmail-info@wmail.misanet.org*
Willamette Week (Portland, Oregon). *mlzl@aol.com*
XS (Broward County, Florida). *xsmag@satelnet.org*

College Newspapers

Algonquin Times (Algonquin College, Nepean, Ontario, Canada). *times @algonquinc.on.ca*
The Anarchives (University of Toronto). *yakimov@ecf.utoronto.ca*
BG News (Bowling Green State University, Ohio). *bgnews@andy.bgsu.edu*
The Bucknellian (Bucknell University). *bucknellian@bucknell.edu*
Cavalier Daily (University of Virginia). *cavdaily@virginia.edu*
CM-LIF. (Central Michigan University). Letters to the Editor: *cmlife@cmuvm.csv.cmich.edu*
The Cornell American. *ca-l@cornell.edu*
Cornell Daily Sun. *Cornell.Daily.Sun@cornell.edu*
The Daily (University of Washington). *daily@u.washington.edu*

Daily Bruin (University of California at Los Angeles). Viewpoint (Op-Ed): *viewpoint@asucla.ucla.edu*
The Daily Northwestern (Evanston, Illinois). *daily@merle.acns.nwu.edu*
Daily Pennsylvanian (University of Pennsylvania). *dailypenn@al.relay.upenn.edu*
Daily Texan (University of Texas-Austin). *texan@utxvms.cc.utexas.edu*
The Daily Universe (Brigham Young University). Op-Ed Submissions: *letters@byu.edu*
The Dialogue (Duke University). *mockg@mail01.adm.duke.edu*
Gair Rhydd (Cardiff University, Wales). *gairrhydd@cardiff.ac.uk*
GW Hatchet (George Washington University). *hatchet@gwis.circ.gwu.edu*
The Hustler (Vanderbilt University). *hustler@ctrvax.vanderbilt.edu*
The Iowa State Daily. *daily@iastate.edu*
Kansas State Collegian (Kansas State University). *rjohnso@ksu.ksu.edu*
The Medium (Rutgers University). *mvalenti@eden.rutgers.edu*
Minnesota Daily (University of Minnesota). *network@edit.mndly.umn.edu*
The Muse (Memorial University, Newfoundland). *muse@morgan.ucs.mun.ca*
National College University Magazine. *umag@well.sf.ca.us*
The Oxford Student (Oxford University). *theoxstu@sable.ox.ac.uk*
The Peak (University of Guleph, Canada). *peak@uoguelph.ca*
Planet Communications (University of Toronto). *editor@planet.org*
The Post (Ohio State University). *an790791@oak.cats.ohiou.edu*
Redbrick (University of Birmingham, United Kingdom). *redbrick@bham.ac.uk*
The Reporter (Polytechnic University of New York). *reporter@photon.poly.edu*
The Sagebrush (University of Nevada, Reno). *sgbrush@shadow.scs.unr.edu*
The Sewanee Purple (University of the South, Tennessee). *purple@seraph1.sewanee.edu*
The Shield (University of Southern Indiana). *janderso.ucs@smtp.usi.edu*
The Student Movement (Andrews University, Michigan). *smeditor@andrews.edu*
The Tartan (Carnegie-Mellon University). *tartan@andrew.cmu.edu*
The Tech (MIT, Cambridge, Massachusetts). Letters to the Editor: *letters@the-tech.mit.edu*
The Troubadour (Franciscan University, Steubenville, Ohio). *74143.2374@compuserve.com*
Washington Square News (New York University). *nyuwsn@aol.com*

Magazines

Adbusters. *adbuster@wimsey.com*
Advertising Age. Letters to the Editor: *ehbu73a@prodigy.com*; Interactive Media and Marketing: *ywkj04a@prodigy.com*
The Advocate. Letters: *letters@advocate.com*; Info-server: *info@advocate.com*
Allure. *alluremag@aol.com*
The American Prospect. *tap@world.std.com*
American Journalism Review. Letters to the Editors/Queries (*no press releases*): *editor@ajr.umd.edu*
The American School Board Journal. *asbj@aol.com*
The Annals of Improbable Results. *air@mit.edu*
Arcana. *david@hslc.org*
BioScience. *aibs@gwuvm.gwu.edu*
Brown Alumni Monthly (Providence, Rhode Island). *bam@brownvm.brown.edu*
Budapest Business Journal (Hungary). *100263.213@compuserve.com*
The Business Journal (Portland, Oregon). *pdxbj@teleport.com*
Business Week. *bwreader@mgh.com*
Chronicle of Higher Education. *editor@chronicle.merit.edu*
Canadian Treasurer (Toronto). *mcdouga@ecf.utoronto.ca*
Cause/Effect. Submissions for Peer Review: *jrudy@cause.colorado.edu*
Claustrophobia. *phobia@bronze.coil.com*
Clinical Data Management. *anneb@delphi.com*
Classroom Connect (Lancaster, Pennsylvania). *edit@wentworth.com*
Colors (Rome, Italy). *colors.mag@agora.stm.it*
CM Magazine (San Francisco). *cmmag@aol.com*
Daily Pacific Builder (San Francisco). *dbuilder@aol.com*
Delta (Poland). Mathematics, physics, chemistry: *delta@plearn.edu.pl*
DePauw Magazine (Greencastle, Indiana). *mlillich@depauw.edu*
Details. *detailsmag@aol.com*
Earth First! Journal. *earthfirst@igc.apc.org*
Electric Shock Treatment (United Kingdom). Innovative and experimental music: *bdl@mm-croy.mottmac.co.uk*
Electronic Music Magazine. *emeditorial@pan.com*
The Executive Educator Magazine. *execeduc@aol.com*
Final Frontier. *72075.516@compuserve.com*
Frank Magazine (Ottawa, Ontario). *ag419@freenet.carleton.ca*
Focus (United Kingdom). *focus@focus2.demon.co.uk*
Focus (Munich, Germany). *100335.3131@compuserve.com*
Forbes. *5096930@mcimail.com*
Free Times. *71632.165@compuserve.com*
Glamour. *glamourmag@aol.com*
Go World. *ishius@ishius.com*

GQ. *gqmag@aol.com*
Head Magazine (United Kingdom). *100344.1203@compuserve.com*
Illinois Issues. Letters to the Editor ONLY: *plong@eagle.sangamon.edu*
Infowar Review. *gldneaglpr@aol.com*
Inside Media. *mediaseven@aol.com*
InterFace Magazine (Victoria, BC). *jedi@dataflux.bc.ca*
International Business Magazine. *emmervosh@ibnet.com*
Internazionale (Italy). *r.internazionale@agora.stm.it*
Interrace Magazine (Atlanta). *73424.1014@compuserve.com*
Kurier Chemiczny [Chemical Courier] (Poland). *kurier@chem.uw.edu.pl*
Lambda Book Report (Washington, D.C.). *lambdabookreport@his.com*
Liberty Issues. *liberty@prostar.com*
Link, The College Magazine (New York). *editor@linkmag.com*
Living Marxism (United Kingdom). *lm@camintl.org*
Mademoiselle. *mllemag@aol.com*
Media West (West Vancouver, BC). *shyba@wimsey.com*
Medical Laboratory Observer. Letters to the Editor: *editor.mlo@medtechnet.com;* Tips and Technlogy: *tips.mlo@medtechnet.com*; Computer Dialog: *computer.mlo@medtechnet.com;* Management: *management.mlo@medtechnet.com*
Metropulse Magazine (Knoxville, Tennessee). *metropulse@aol.com*
Midwifery Today and Childbirth Education. *midwifery@aol.com*
MiniWorks. *miniworks@genie.geis.com*
Mondo 2000. *mondo@well.com*
Mother Jones. *x@mojones.com*
Ms. Letters to the editor: *ms@echonyc.com*
Multichannel News. *higgins@dorsai.dorsai.org*
The Nation. *nation@igc.org*
New Church Life. *david@hslc.org*
The New Republic. *editors@tnr.com*
New Scientist (United Kingdom). U.S. bureau: *75310.1661@compuserve.com*; "The Last Word": *newscl@stirling.ac.uk*
Newsweek. Letters to the Editor: *letters@newsweek.com*; "Periscope": *ghackett@newsweek.com*
NOW Magazine (Toronto). *news@now.com*
Oberlin Alumni Magazine. *alummag@ocvaxc.cc.oberlin.edu*
One Country (Baha'i International). *1country@bic.org*
Ottawa Magazine (Ontario). *aq060@freenet.carleton.ca*
Ottawa Business Magazine. *aq060@freenet.carleton.ca*
OutNOW! (San Jose, California). *jct@netcom.com*
Physicians's Office Laboratories (POL) Advisor. Letters to the Editor: *editor.pol.mlo@medtechnet.com*; Problem Solver: *problem.pol.mlo@medtechnet.com*
Playboy. *edit@playboy.com*; Playboy Forum: *forum@playboy.com*; Dear Playboy: *dearpb@playboy.com*

Political Science Quarterly (New York). *psq123@aol.com*
Popular Science. *75140.1732@compuserve.com*
Postepy Fizyki [Advances in Physics] (Poland). *postepy@fuw.edu.pl*
Private Eye (United Kingdom). *strobes@cix.compulink.co.uk*
The Progressive (Madison, Wisconsin). *progmag@igc.apc.org*
Real Goods News. *realgood@well.sf.ca.us*
Reason. *70703.2152@compuserve.com*
Red Pepper (United Kingdom). *redpepper@gn.apc.org*
Rolling Stone (New York). *rollingstone@echonyc.com*
Running Wild Magazine (Lincoln, Massachusetts). *runwild@world.std.com*
St. Charles Countian (Missouri). *pacmosteve@aol.com*
S.F. Examiner Magazine. *sfxmag@mcimail.com*
Security Insider Report. *p00506@psilink.com*
Self. *comments@self.com*
Science. General Editorial Inquiries: *science_editors@aaas.org*; Letters to the Editor: *science_letters@aaas.org*; Manuscript Reviews: *science_reviews@aaas.org*; General News: *science_news@aaas.org*
Silueta (Santa Rosa, California). *silueta@wave.sci.org*
Soundprint. *soundprt@jhuvms.hcf.jhu.edu*
Sky & Telescope (Cambridge, Massachusetts). *skytel@cfa.harvard.edu*
Southwestern Union Record. *72734.1717@compuserve.com*
Spectrum (New York). *n.hantman@ieee.org*
Der Spiegel (Germany). *100064.3164@compuserve.com*
Stern Hamburg (Germany). *100125.1305@compuserve.com*
3D-Magazine. *3dmagazin@stereo.s.bawue.de*
Streetsound (New York). *streetsnd@aol.com*
Time. *timeletter@aol.com*
Training Magazine (Minneapolis). *trainmag@aol.com*
Transitions (University of Southern Indiana). *jwolf.ucs@smtp.usi.edu*
U. Magazine. *umag@well.sf.ca.us : umagazine@aol.com*
Ultramarathon Canada. *an346@freenet.carleton.ca*
Urb (Los Angeles). *urbmag@netcom.com*
USA Weekend. *usaweekend@aol.com*
U.S. News and World Report. *71154.1006@compuserve.com*
Utne Reader. *editor@utnereader.com*
VeloNews (Boulder, Colorado). *velonews@aol.com*
Vibe. *vibeonline@nyo.com*
Video Magazine. *75147.1255@compuserve.com*
Virus (alternative music), (Bratislava, Slovakia). *virus@cenezu.sk*
Vogue. *voguemail@aol.com*
Washington Technology. *technews@access.digex.net*
West Countian (Missouri). *pacmosteve@aol.com*
Whole Earth Review. *wer@well.sf.ca.us*
Wired. *editor@wired.com*

Z (Sweden). *z.mag@zine.se*
Zielone Brygady [Green Brigades] (Poland). *zielbryg@gn.apc.org*
Zurnal UP (Palacky University, Czech Republic). *veselovs@risc.upol.cz*
Zyzzyva (San Francisco). *zyzzyva@tmn.com*

News/Media Services and Press Associations

Associated Press. "On the Net" column ONLY, no general messages: *weise@well.sf.ca.us*
Conus Washington/TV Direct. *conus-dc@clark.net*
Cowles/SIMBA Media Daily. *simba02@aol.com*
Croatian Journalists' Association, Zagreb, "Novinar" Monthly Magazine. Letters to the Editor: *mario.profaca@public.srce.hr*
Greenwire. *greenwire@apn.com*
Katolicka Agencja Informacyjna (Poland). *kai@ikp.atm.com.pl*
Media Page. *mpage@netcom.com*
M2 News Agency (United Kingdom). *satnews@cix.compulink.co.uk*
National Press Photographers Association. No press releases: *loundy@plink.geis.com*
Newsbytes. *newsbytes@genie.geis.com*
Telecomworldwire (United Kingdom). *satnews@cix.compulink.co.uk*
World Association of Community Radio Broadcasters (Montreal, Québec). *amarc@web.apc.org*

Radio and Television Networks

BBC Television. Ceefax Travel: *travel@bbc.co.uk*; Children's BBC: *childrens@bbc.co.uk*; Points of View: *pov@bbcnc.org.uk*; See Hear: *bryn@cet.education.bbc.co.uk*; The Net: the-net@bbcnc.org.uk; Open University: *info@oupc.bbc.co.uk*
BBC East. *lookeast@nc.bbc.co.uk*
BBC Radio 3. Open University: *info@oupc.bbc.co.uk*
BBC Radio 4. Today: *today@bbcnc.org.uk*; New Ideas: *newideas@bbc-sci.demon.co.uk*; Womans Hour: *womanshour@bbc.co.uk*
BBC Radio 5-Live. The Big Byte: *big-byte@bbc.co.uk*
BBC Radio Hereford & Worcester
BBC World Service. *iac@bbc-ibar.demon.co.uk*
CBC TV. "All in a Day": *allinaday.cbc@uniboard.synapse.net*; "Prime Time News": *ptn@toronto.cbc.ca*; "Front Page Challenge": *front_page_challenge@mindlink.bc.ca*; "Open Wide": *open@winnipeg.cbc.ca*
CBC Radio. "Brave New Waves": *bnw@babylon.montreal.qc.ca*; "Cross-Country Check-Up": *checkup@babylon.montreal.qc.ca;* "Definitely Not the Opera": *opera@winnipeg.cbc.ca*; "Gabereau": *gabereau@*

mindlink.bc.ca; "Marg Meikle—The Answer Lady": *marg_meikle@mindlink.bc.ca*; "Morningside": *morningsdie@hookup.net*; "Real Time": *realtime@mindlink.bc.ca*; "Sunday Morning": *sunmorn@hookup.net*; CBC Radio Research Vancouver: *cbc_radio_research@mindlink.bc.ca*

CBC Toronto. "Radio Noon": *radio.noon@canrem.com*

CBS. "Late Show with David Letterman": *lateshow@pipeline.com*

Channel 500. *fitv@aol.com*

C-SPAN. Requests for coverage: *cspanprogm@aol.com*; Questions during live call-ins: *cspanguest@aol.com*; Viewer services and questions: *cspanviewr@aol.com*

Channel 2, "Rapport" (Sweden). *twonews@basys.svt.se*

FilmNet (Europe). *70671.1624@compuserve.com*

Fox TV. *foxnet@delphi.com*. "Encounters": *74663.3011@compuserve.com*

Maine Public TV. "Media Watch": *greenman@maine.maine.edu*

Monitor Radio (Boston). *radio@csps.com*

MTV Europe. Most Wanted: *mostwanted@mtvne.com*

Nebraska Educational TV (Lincoln, Nebraska).*etv@unlinfo.unl.edu*

Namibian Broadcasting Corporation. Head Office: *marietha@nbc_hq.nbc.com.na*

Nexus International Broadcasting Association (Milano, Italy). *press@nexus.qnet.bull.it*

National Alternative Network (Minneapolis). *nanrev@aol.com*

National Public Radio. "Talk of the Nation": *totn@npr.org*; "Talk of the Nation/Sci.Friday": *scifri@aol.com*; "Fresh Air": *freshair@hslc.org*; "Weekend All Things Considered": *watc@clark.net*; "Weekend Edition/Sunday": *wesun@clark.net*; "West Coast Live": *owner-west_coast_live@netcom.com*

NBC. "Dateline": dateline@news.nbc.com; "Late Night with Conan O'Brien": *conanshow@aol.com*; Nightly News: *nightly@news.nbc.com*; "Today": *today@news.nbc.com*; "TV Nation": *tvnatn@aol.com*

New England Cable News (Needham, Massachusetts). *necn@aol.com*

Ohio University Public Radio. *radio@ohiou.edu*

Ohio University Public Television. *tv@ohiou.edu*

Polskie Radio Program I (Poland). *radio1@ikp.atm.com.pl*

Polska Telewizja Kablowa (Poland). *ptk@ikp.atm.com.pl*

PBS "POV": *povonline@aol.com;* "Radio Graffiti" *alan@panix.com*

Public Radio International (formerly APR). "Marketplace": *market@usc.edu*

Radio Nederland. *letters@rn-hilversum.nl*

Red Sox Radio Network (Boston). *bosoxradio@aol.com*

Rush Limbaugh Show. *70277.2502@compuserve.com*

Spectrum (Holmdel, New Jersey). *spectrum@overleaf.com*

TV Ontario. "The Future": *the_future@tvo.org*

Voice of America/Worldnet Television. From outside the U.S.:

letters@voa.gov; from within the U.S.: *letters-usa@voa.gov*; QSL reports, outside U.S.: *qsl@voa.gov*; QSL reports, inside U.S.: *qsl-usa@voa.gov*; Agriculture Today: *agri@voa.gov*; VOA-Europe (English): *voa-europe@voa.gov*; VOA-Morning Program: *voa-morning@voa.gov*

Radio and Television Stations

Brunel Radio B1000 (United Kingdom). *brunel.radio.b1000@brunel.ac.uk*
Community Radio 3CR (Australia). "Careering Arts Australia": *vincent@journalism.ss.rmit.oz.au*
Radio Havana (Cuba). "DXers Unlimited": *radiohc@tinored.cu*
CHVC-TV (Valemount, British Columbia, Canada). *ad274@freenet.unbc.bc.ca*
CJLB Radio News (Thunder Bay, Ontario). *an80386@anon.penet.fi an69041@anon.penet.fi*
CJOH-TV (Ottawa, Ontario, Canada). *ab363@freenet.carleton.ca*
KARK (Little Rock, Arkansas). *newsfour@aol.com*
KFJC (Los Altos, California). *kfjc-publicity@wiretap.spies.com*
KGTV (ABC, San Diego). *kgtv10@aol.com*
KHOU-TV (Houston). *khou@neosoft.com*
KING-AM (Seattle). *king1090@aol.com*
KIRO-AM/FM (Seattle). *kiro@halcyon.com*
KJR-FM (Seattle). *normg@halcyon.com*
KKSF-FM and **KDFC-AM/FM** (San Francisco). General Comments: *comments@kksf.tbo.com*; News Releases: *news@kksf.tbo.com*
KOMU-TV (NBC, Columbia, Missouri). *swoelfel@bigcat.missouri.edu*
KOIN (Portland, Oregon). *koin06A@prodigy.com*
KPIX-TV (San Francisco). *kpix@aol.com*
KREV-FM (Minneapolis). General: *rev105@aol.com*; "Moonlight Meditations": *lunarev@aol.com*
KRON-TV (San Francisco). Gardening segment: *garden4@aol.com*
KUAT-TV (PBS, Tuscon, Arizona). *comments@kuat.arizona.edu*
KUOW Radio (Seattle). *kuow@u.washington.edu*
KWMU-FM (St. Louis, Missouri). *kwmu@umslva.bitnet*
KWTV (Oklahoma City). *tv9@aol.com*
KXTV-TV (Sacramento, California). *kxtv@netcom.com*
KYTV (Springfield, Missouri). News Releases: *kytvcom@sgcl.lib.mo.us*; Editorial Comments: *kytvnews@sgck.lib.mo.us*
KZSU (Palo Alto, California). *releases@kzsu.stanford.edu*
WAGA-TV (Atlanta). *wagatv@america.net*
WATE-TV (Knoxville, Tennessee). *watetv6@aol.com*
WBBM-TV (CBS, Chicago). *wbbmch2@aol.com*

WBCN-FM (Boston). *wbcn104fm@aol.com*
WBFO-FM (NPR, Buffalo, New York). *wbfo@ubvms.cc.buffalo.edu*
WBNQ-FM (Bloomington, Illinois). *radiobn@heartland.bradley.edu*
WCBS-AM (CBS, New York). *news88a@prodigy.com*
WCVB-TV (Boston, Massachusetts). *wcvb@aol.com*
WCCO-TV (Minneapolis, Minnesota). *wccotv@mr.net*
WCKY-AM (Cincinnati). *550wcky@iglou.com*
WDCB Radio (Glen Ellyn, Illinois). *scotwitt@interaccess.com*
WOR-AM (New York, New York). "Rambling with Gambling": *bcastboy @aol.com*
WEOL-AM (Elyria, Ohio). *maweol@freenet.lorain.oberlin.edu*
WEOS (Geneva, New York). *weos@hws.bitnet*
WEEK-TV (Peoria, Illinois). *xxweek@heartland.bradley.edu*
WFAA-TV (ABC/CNN, Dallas/Ft. Worth). "Computer Corner" only: *news8@onramp.net*
WFIU-FM (Bloomington, Indiana). "Friday Edition": *friday@indiana.edu*
WFLA-AM (Tampa). *wfla97b@prodigy.com*
WFMJ-TV (Youngstown, Ohio). *news21@yfn.ysu.edu*
WFNX-FM (Boston). *wfnxfm@aol.com*
WGN-TV (Chicago). *wgntv@aol.com*
WGNO-TV (New Orleans). *wgnotv@aol.com*
WHDH-TV (CBS, Boston). *74201.2255@compuserve.com*
WHO-AM (Des Moines, Iowa). *news@who-radio.com*
WHTZ-FM (New York). *z100radio@aol.com*
WICB (Ithaca, New York). *wicb@aol.com*
WISC-TV (CBS, Madison, Wisconsin). *wisctv@macc.wisc.edu*
WISH-TV (CBS, Indianapolis, Indiana). *wish08b@prodigy.com*
WJBC-AM (Bloomington, Illinois). *radiobn@heartland.bradley.edu*
WKRN-TV (Nashville, Tennessee). *wkrntv@edge.ercnet.com*
WMBR-FM (Cambridge, Massachusetts). Listener mail: *wmbr@athena.mit.edu;* News/Political Releases: *wmbr-press@media.mit.edu*
WNWV-FM (Elyria, Ohio). *maweol@freenet.lorain.oberlin.edu*
WNYC. "On the Line," (New York). *76020.560@compuserve.com*
WREV-FM (Minneapolis). *See* KREV-FM
WRKO-AM (Boston). *wrko@aol.com*
WRVO-FM (Oswego, New York). *wrvo@oswego.edu*
WSPA-TV (Spartanburg, South Carolina). *wspa@aol.com*
WSRN-AM (Cedarville, Ohio). *wsrn@cedarnet.cedarville.edu*
WSYR-AM (Syracuse, New York). *wsyrradio@aol.com*
WTVF-TV (Nashville, Tennessee). *sysop@newschannel5.com*
WVII-TV (ABC, Bangor, Maine). *wviitv@aol.com*
WVIT-TV (New Britain, Connecticut). *wvit30a@prodigy.Com*
WWWE-AM (Cleveland, Ohio). *talk11a@prodigy.com*

WXKS-FM (Boston). *kissfm@aol.com*
WXYZ-TV (ABC, Detroit). *wxyztv@aol.com*
WYDE-AM (Birmingham, Alabama). "Tony Giles Show": *tony.giles@the-matrix.com*
WYFF-TV (Greenville, South Carolina). *wyff@aol.com*
WYYY-FM (Syracuse, New York). *y94fm@aol.com*
WZLX-FM (Boston). *wzlx.com*

Computer Publications

AI Expert. *76702.705@compuserve.com*
Amazing Computing. Editorial/Content: *76174.2404@compuserve.com*; Bug Bytes: *john_steiner@cup.portal.com*; Online Column: *rhays@delphi.com*
Amiga Computing. *amigacomputing@cix.compulink.co.uk*
Amiga Report. Letters to the Editor: miles@hebron.connected.com; News and Sightings: *dtiberio@libserv1.ic.sunysb.edu*; Emulation Column: *jcompton@bbs.xnet.com*; European Market: *norjj@stud.hum.aau.dk*; Skid Marks Review: *blakader@csos.orst.edu*
Amiga World. General Comments: *amigaworld@portal.com*; Prime-Time PD: *twalsh@bix.com*
Axcess. General info, rants and raves: *editor@axcess.com*; Internet Kliff Notes: *kliff@axcess.com*; Submissions: *submit@axcess.com*
Best of Mac News (Belgium). *best.of@applelink.apple.com*
BBS Magazine. *publisher@bbscd.com*

Boardwatch (Colorado Springs, Colorado). *letters@boardwatch.com*
CIO Magazine. *ciomag@mcimail.com*
Communications Networks (United Kingdom). *75300.243@compuserve.com*
Communications News. *489-8359@mcimail.com*
Communications Week. *440-7485@mcimail.com*
Computer Currents. *73554.3010@compuserve.com*
Computer Life. *ceditors.notes@mailzd.ziff.com*
The Computer Paper (Vancouver, BC). *72627.1732@compuserve.com*
Computer Player Magazine. *compplayer@aol.com*
Computer Shopper (United Kingdom only). *100034.1056@compuserve.com*
Computer Weekly (United Kingdom). *comp_weekly@cix.compulink.co.uk*
ComputerWorld. *letters@cw.com*
Computing (United Kingdom). *computed@cix.compulink.co.uk*
Connect Magazine. *connect@aol.com*
Corporate Computing. *439-3854@mcimail.com*
Data Communications. *416-2157@mcimail.com*

Datateknik (Sweden). *datateknik@dt.etforlag.se*
DBMS. *73647.2767@compuserve.com*
EE Times. *70212.14@compuserve.com*
Electronic Entertainment. *elecent@aol.com*
Electronic Marketplace Report. *simba02@aol.com*
Electronic Information Report. *simba02@aol.com*
Enterprise Systems Journal. *543-3256@mcimail.com*
Federal Computer Week. *letters@fcw.com*
Government Computer News. *editor@gcn.com*
Home Office Computing. *hoc@aol.com*
Home PC Magazine. *homepc@aol.com*
IBM Internet Journal (Dallas, Texas). *76130.221@aol.com*
InfoLinja (Finland). *jlahi@infocrea.fi*
Infoworld. *letters@infoworld.com*
Internet Business Advantage (Lancaster, Pennsyvania). *edit@wentworth.com*
The Internet Business Journal. *mstrange@fonorola.net*
InterFace Magazine (Victoria, BC). *interface@dataflux.bc.ca*
The Internet Letter. *netwook@access.digex.net*
The Internet Novice. *tates@access.digex.net*
iX (Germany). *post@ix.de*
Journal of C Language Translation. *ljclt@iecc.com*
LAN Times. *538-6488@mcimail.com*
MACLine (Philadelphia). *macline1@aol.com*
MacUser. *letters@macuser.ziff.com*
MacWeek. *letters@macweek.ziff.com*
Macworld. *macworld@aol.com*
MacTech Magazine (formerly MacTutor). Press Releases: *pressreleases@xplain.com*; Orders, Circulation, Customer Service: *custservice@xplain.com*; Editorial: *editorial@xplain.com*; Publisher: *publisher@xplain.com*; Ad Sales: *adsales@xplain.com*; Programmers Challenge: *progchallenge@xplain.com*; Accounting: *accounting@xplain.com*; Marketing: *marketing@xplain.com*; General: *info@xplain.com*
MicroAge RealTime (Tempe, Arizona). *avidean@microage.com*
MicroTimes. *microx@well.com*
MikroPC (Finland). *mpcmagas@mikropc.fi*
Multimedia World Magazine. *75300.2503@compuserve.com*
Network Computing. *editor@nwc.com*
Network World. General, letters, Cyberspeak: *network@world.std.com*; Reader Advocacy Force: *nwraf@world.std.com*
Online Access. *oamag@aol.com*
OS/2 Developer (Delray Beach, Florida). *os2mag@vnet.ibm.com*
PC Computing. *72241.2451@compuserve.com*
PC Magazine (United States). *157-9301@mcimail.com*
PC Magazine (United Kingdom). *tony_westbrook@hades.zis.ziff.com*

PC Labs (United Kingdom). *steve_browne@hades.zis.ziff.com*
PC Plus (United Kingdom). *pcplus@cix.compulink.co.uk*
Personal Computer World (United Kingdom). *editorial@pcw.ccmail.compuserve.com*
San Diego Union-Tribune. Bi-weekly Internet section only: *computerlink@sduniontrib.com*
Telecommunications. *311-1693@mcimail.com*
Toronto Computes! *75570.2744@compuserve.com*
3W Magazine: The Internet with a Human Face. 3w@3w.com
UniForum Monthly. *pubs@uniforum.org*
UniNews. *pubs@uniforum.org*
UnixWorld. News Releases/Breaking News: *news@uworldcom*; European News: *euro@uworld.com*; Product Information: *products@uworld.com*; To get a product reviewed: *reviews@uworld. com*; Calendar Listings (4 months lead): *cal@uworld.com*; Letters to the Editor: *letters@uworld.com*; Writer Information: *write@uworld.com*; Tutorial Information: *rik@uworld.com*; Wiz Grabbag: *grabbag@uworld.com*; Answers to Unix Submissions: *ans2unix@ uworld.com*; Subscription Information: *circ@uworld.com*
Xephon (United Kingdom). *100325.3711@compuserve.com*
Windows Computer Shareware. *5648326@mcimail.com*
Windows Magazine. General: *winmag@aol.com*; Subscription inquiries: *5849664@mcimail.com*

Publishing Houses

Albion Books (San Francisco). *info@albion.com*
Berrett-Koehler Publishers. *bkpub@aol.com*
Golden Eagle Press. *gldneaglpr@aol.com*
Impatiens Press. *impatiens@world.std.com*
Monitor Publications (Arkansas). *74353.2767@compuserve.com*
O'Reilly & Associates. *nuts@ora.com*
Razorbooks USA (Arkansas). *74353.2767@compuserve.com*
Swedenborg Publishers International. *david@hslc.org*

Newsletters

Accountants on Line. *ayfdave@aol.com*
Africalink (Philadelphia). *sern@aol.com*
American Father Coalition. *afc@cap.gwu.edu*
American Society for Gravity & Space Biology Bulletin and Newsletter. *kcowing@clark.net*
Aviation Daily (Washington, D.C.). *grahamg@mgh.com*

Card Systems. *satnews@cix.compulink.co.uk*
China Business and Economic Update. *chinahand@aol.com*
Data Broadcasting News (United Kingdom). *satnews@cix.compulink. co.uk*
Dealmakers. *ted.kraus@property.com*
Drug Policy Report. *snowcap@aol.com*
Ecologia (Lithuania). *root@it.aiva.lt*
Global Environmental Change Report. *gecr@igc.apc.org*
Information Law Alert. *markvoor@phantom.com*
Infosecurity News. *2439796@mcimail.com*
IYF Bulletin (British Columbia). Triple-A high school basketball: *don_mah@mindlink.bc.ca*
ITASA-Tribune (Taiwanese-American students). *putaiwan@expert. cc.purdue.edu*
Jazz & Blues Review. *im4jbr@aol.com*
MEMO: to the president, American Association of State Colleges and Universities. *memo@aascu.nche.edu*
Creative Edge (Mercer Island, Washington). *midnight@halcyon.com*
Multimedia Business Report. *simba02@aol.com*
NewsInc. *simba02@aol.com*
New Business Watch (Sebastopol, Calfornia). *70307.454@compuserve. com*
Political Finance & Lobby Reporter.
RACHEL'S Hazardous Waste News (Maryland). *erf@igc.spc.org*
Satnews. *satnews@cix.compulink.co.uk*
Security Insider Report. *p00506@psilink.com*
The Small Business Gazette (New York). *jimd34@aol.com*
Smart's California Insurance Bulletin. *0005068090@mcimail.com*
Smart's California Workers' Comp Bulletin. *0005068090@mcimail.com*
Smart's National Comp & Health Bulletin. *0005068090@mcimail.com*
Society of Newspaper Design. *fairbairn@plink.geis.com*
Spec-Com Journal. *spec-com@genie.geis.com*
Surveillant (Military Intelligence Book Center, Washington, D.C.). *70346.1166@compuserve.com*
TRAX Music Guide (DJ and dance community). *traxusa@aol.com*
Ukrainian Business Journal (Cleveland). *ec525@cleveland.freenet.net*

Glossary

Internet Terms

Agent A software program that automatically executes a prescribed task, based on personal or static information.

America Online (AOL) A private online network service that is separate from the Internet, but offers users access to the Internet.

American Standard Code for Information Interchange (ASCII) A protocol for pure text.

Anonymous A user login name used to get access to most FTP sites.

Archie A UNIX program for finding files on the Internet.

ARPANET Advanced Research Project Agency's Network; the network created by the U.S. Department of Defense Advanced Research Project (DARPA); the network from which the Internet arose.

Asynchronous An event that is time-independent.

Asynchronous Transfer Mode (ATM) A cutting-edge protocol for transmitting data at very fast speeds. ATM is probably the only protocol that will enable entire movies to be transported over wires.

AVI A file format for storing compressed movies.

Bandwidth The amount of information that can be transmitted at one time through a communications channel at one time (seconds).

Baud The number of bits per second of communication over phone lines.

Browser A program that lets you access files and the content of files, and also provides for navigation between files.

Bulletin Board (BBS) An older system that allows users to call and interact with each other. Similar to the Internet, but on much smaller scale.

C, C++ A computer language to develop computer software.

Cache The act of storing a remote document locally in order to increase access speed on repeated requests.

CD-ROM An information storage medium for storing large volumes of information from 640 megabytes (MB) to 1.2 gigabytes (GB).

Central Processing Unit (CPU) The brains of a computer.

CERN The European Particle Physics Laboratory in Geneva, Switzerland. The group that invented the World Wide Web (WWW).

CERT The Computer Emergency Response Team to whom you should report security breaches.

Cgi-Bin Custom programs that may be used to extend the Web and make it interactive.

Client Sometimes used to refer to a browser and at other times a computer contacting to a server or host.

Clip Art Ready-made artwork; useful in creating Web pages.

Computer Professionals for Social Responsibility (CPSR) An organization concerned with the ethical use of computers.

Cracker Someone who breaks into computer systems.

Crawler A program that moves along the Web looking for URLs or other information; a type of intelligent agent.

Cyberpublicity The promotion of a Website address to other sites, directories, newsgroups, etc., to increase qualified traffic to the Website being cyberpublicized.

Cyberspace A term for immersible virtual reality; sometimes used to denote the Internet.

Database A collection of organized searchable data.

Decryption The act of making a secure file readable.

Digital Signature A secure mechanism to verify the identity of an individual.

Domain Name The name of a computer system on the Internet. Each computer system has a unique domain name.

Domain Name Server (DNS) A system that resolves an Internet Protocol (IP) address to a domain name.

Element A basic HTML command, such as <title>, which indicates the beginning of a title.

Electronic Frontier Foundation An organization of people concerned with the legal rights of computer users. Most current laws do not specifically apply to electronic communications.

Electronic Mail (e-mail) Personal messages sent between users of the Internet.

Encryption The method of making a readable file secure.

Eudora The most widely used e-mail program on the Internet. It is easy to use and runs on multiple platforms.

File Transfer Protocol (FTP) Software that transfers files to and from remote computers.

Finger A program that identifies a user.

Firewall A security measure that helps to limit pirate attacks.

Flaming An expression of displeasure at another user.

Frequently Asked Questions (FAQs) A list of helpful suggestions and answers to questions on various topics.

Gopher A menu oriented FTP-type program that does not allow the use of pictures, links or other advanced WWW features.

Graphic Interchange Format (GIF) A file format for images developed by CompuServe.

Graphical User Interface (GUI) A graphical system for interaction with the screen using at least the mouse and the keyboard.

Hacker Someone who is good at computers. A computer guru.

Home Page The first page of any Website on the Internet WWW.

Host A computer system that may be contacted by other computer systems.

Hot List A list of a user's favorite sites on the Web.

HyperText Markup Language (HTML) The language of the WWW which formats documents to look presentable. HTML is a subset of Standard Generalized Markup Language (SGML).

HyperText Transport Protocol (HTTP) The protocol for the WWW which allows text, image, audio, and video to be combined into a single document. HTTP also allows the linking of documents and document components.

HyperText Transfer Protocol Daemon (HTTPD) The WWW server software responsible for handling WWW requests.

Hyperlink An HTML element that, when clicked, allows people to move to other documents, images, sounds, movies, or other elements.

Hypertext The method of organizing documents, collecting documents, or components of documents for navigation.

Icon A small image representing a function or action. For example, a small picture of a stop sign to indicate the way to stop a program.

Inline Image An image appearing to be apart from the document it is with.

Integrated Services Digital Network (ISDN) A technology that offers six times the performance of the fastest modems, and beyond. ISDN can be used by both individuals and corporations.

Intelligent Agent A program that performs intelligent functions automatically without manual user input. It can search for information, deliver information or respond to information.

Interactive A method of allowing users to change the course of events based on their own decisions with regard to the rules of whatever they are interacting with.

Internet The term for the worldwide network of computers and users.

Internet Network Information Center (InterNIC) The organization, which through a National Science Foundation (NSF) award, is responsible for providing information to the public about the Internet.

Internet Protocol (IP) A method for handling the actual transmission of data over the Internet.

Internet Protocol Address (IP Address) A numerical address composed of four elements that uniquely identify a computer on the network.

Internet Relay Chat (IRC) A real-time talk forum.

Internet Society (ISOC) An organization that seeks to encourage the use and evolution of the Internet, and provides educational materials and a forum for discussion on the Internet.

JPEG A file format for compressed images.

Lag The amount of time in between actions.

Listserver A program that automatically dispatches outgoing e-mail based on incoming e- mail.

Local Area Network (LAN) Local networks consisting of a few computers networked together.

Login The act of accessing a remote computer

Login Name A word or series of characters users need along with a password to enter into a computer system.

Multipurpose Internet Mail Extensions (MIME) An Internet standard for transmitting audio, video, or still images by e-mail.

MILNET The original part of the ARPANET currently used by the military. It was renamed when ARPANET split.

Modem Refers to modulator-demodulator. A piece of hardware that connects to a computer which enables digital communication to a computer network.

Mosaic The name of the original browser from the National Center for Supercomputing Applications (NCSA) for accessing the Web. The first browser software for the WWW.

Mouse An input device used by one hand with choice entered by pushing buttons.

MPEG A file format used for compressed movies.

Multiple Platforms Refers to the variety of computers platforms such as PC, Macintosh, workstations, etc. A software program that runs on multiple platforms is preferred to one that runs just on one type of computer.

National Center for Supercomputing Applications (NCSA) The developers of the Mosaic software.

NetComplete An integrated software program that offers a WWW browser, FTP, e-mail, IRC, and connection to the Internet.

Netiquette The unwritten rules of etiquette on the Internet.

NetNews A forum for Internet news groups where all messages written by users are displayed as threaded list of messages.

Netscape The popular WWW browser that currently offers many cutting edge HTML features.

Password A secret word or series of characters used to enter a computer system or software program.

Phrack Someone who breaks into phone and computer systems.

Phreak Someone who breaks into just phone systems.

Pirate A software pirate; someone who steals computer programs and usually sells or gives them away.

Proxy A method for hiding databases by rerouting requests.

Public Domain Software that is free.

Robot An automatic program that will search for and retrieve information for the user.

Serial Line Interface Protocol or Point to Point Protocol (SLIP/PPP) Currently the quickest and most powerful method to access the Internet with a modem.

Server A software program or hardware that serves data.

Shareware Software that is openly available but is not free.

Snail Mail A term being used to refer to traditional mail systems, such as the postal system, Federal Express, UPS, etc. Federal Express cannot, for example, guarantee delivery in less than sixty seconds.

Standard Generalized Markup Language (SGML) The original markup language defined by the U.S. government for organizing documents in hypertext format.

Subscription Services A Website that requires users to log in.

Surf To use the Internet and WWW.

System Operator (SYSOP) The system operator of a computer system responsible for the day-to-day operations.

T1 A physical connection that provides high-speed Internet connection that is more than a hundred times more powerful than a 14.4K modem connection.

T3 A physical connection that provides even more powerful connection than a T1. A T3 connection is twenty-eight T1 lines.

Telnet A software program that lets you log into remote computers.

Throughput The amount of data transmitted through the Internet for a given request.

Transmission Control Protocol/ Internet Protocol (TCP/IP) The protocol for peer-to-peer communications and packet switching on the Internet.

Universal Resource Locator (URL) The means of identifying a home page on the Web

Viewer An adjunct program that handles nonstandard data.

Virtual Something that exists only in the electronic medium, such as a computer.

Virus A program that infects other programs and computers resulting in some sort of malfunctions.

Wide Area Information Server (WAIS) A distributed information retrieval system.

Warez Stolen software.

Warez Site A place on a computer where stolen software can be found. Quite often placed surreptitiously on legitimate computer systems by pirates.

WAV Popular file format use for audio files.

World Wide Web (WWW) An organization of files on the Internet.

Wrapper A program that helps improve security by watching user access systems.

▼

About the Author

V. A. Shiva Ayyadurai is a designer, writer, scientist, entrepreneur, and educator. He comes from the worlds of art and technology. He is currently completing his doctoral work at the Massachusetts Institute of Technology (MIT) in Information Theory and Cybernetics. His experience spans the fields of visual studies, computer graphics, neuroscience, information retrieval, mechanical engineering, computer science, electrical engineering, business, and traditional as well as interactive marketing.

His graduate and undergraduate academic education reflects his training in both the arts and technology. He holds a master's degree in visual studies from the world-renowned MIT Media Laboratory. In addition, he holds another master's degree in mechanical engineering from the MIT School of Engineering. His undergraduate degree, also from MIT, is in electrical engineering and computer science. He has taught both graduate and undergraduate courses in the MIT engineering school, as well as the Sloan School of Management.

His scientific research has been in pattern recognition and

classification of signals. He has used computer graphics and animation techniques for the scientific visualization of data. In addition, Shiva has developed a new theory of information cybernetics, which seeks to unify a variety of diverse pattern recognition problems. He is recognized as a world authority on interactive marketing and has given lectures throughout the United States, Europe, and Asia. At the age of twelve, he developed one of the world's first electronic mail systems for which he was recognized by the Westinghouse Science Talent Search.

Shiva is also the founder, president, and chief executive officer of Information Cybernetics, Inc. (ICI). ICI is dedicated to building advanced technologies and solutions for interactive media and works with Millennium Productions and Arts-Online.Com., which are subsidiaries of ICI. Millennium Productions is an art and technology company that combines visual design and technology to develop interactive productions on both Internet and CD-ROM. Arts-Online.Com, at *http://www.arts-online.com/*, is the premier multi-arts cybervenue on the Internet, offering resources, search engines, and advanced indexes for music, dance, theater, fashion, writing, photography, and visual arts.

Before starting ICI, Shiva worked for more than fifteen years at such corporations as Hewlett-Packard, Lotus Development, Information Resources, Number Nine. Through his work at these major corporations, he has consulted for such clients as Procter and Gamble, Dunn and Bradstreet, and many other multinational corporations.

Shiva has a unique ability to communicate technology to both arts and nonarts audiences in a motivating and inspiring manner. He has spoken at major international and national conferences.

▼

Index

J

K

L

M

Books from Allworth Press

Arts and the Internet: A Guide to the Revolution by V. A. Shiva (softcover, 6 × 9, 208 pages, $18.95)

The Writer's Internet Handbook by Timothy K. Maloy (softcover, 6 × 9, 208 pages, $18.95)

The Internet Research Guide by Timothy K. Maloy (softcover, 6 × 9, $18.95)

The Photographer's Internet Handbook by Joe Farace (softcover, 6 × 9, 224 pages, $18.95)

The Digital Imaging Dictionary by Joe Farace (softcover, 6 × 9, 256 pages, $19.95)

The Business of Multimedia by Nina Schuyler (softcover, 6 × 9, 240 pages, $19.95)

The Photographer's Guide to Marketing and Self-Promotion, Second Edition by Maria Piscopo (softcover, $6^{3}/_{4}$ × 10, 176 pages, $18.95)

The Fine Artist's Guide to Marketing and Self-Promotion by Julius Vitali (softcover, 6 × 9, 224 pages, $18.95)

Fine Art Publicity by Susan Abbott and Barbara Webb (softcover, $8^{1}/_{2}$ × 11, 190 pages, $22.95)

The Copyright Guide by Lee Wilson (softcover, 6 × 9, 192 pages, $18.95)

Please write to request our free catalog. If you wish to order a book, send your check or money order to Allworth Press, 10 East 23rd Street, Suite 210, New York, NY 10010. Include $5 for shipping and handling for the first book ordered and $1 for each additional book. Ten dollars plus $1 for each additional book if ordering from Canada. New York State residents must add sales tax.

If you wish to see our catalog on the World Wide Web, you can find us at Millennium Production's Art and Technology Web site:
http://www.arts-online.com/allworth/home.html
or at **allworth.com**